Faith in Reading

Recent titles in
RELIGION IN AMERICA SERIES
Harry S. Stout, General Editor

Faith in Reading

Religious Publishing and the Birth of Mass Media in America

DAVID PAUL NORD

OXFORD
UNIVERSITY PRESS
2004

OXFORD
UNIVERSITY PRESS

Oxford   New York
Auckland   Bangkok   Buenos Aires   Cape Town   Chennai
Dar es Salaam   Delhi   Hong Kong   Istanbul   Karachi   Kolkata
Kuala Lumpur   Madrid   Melbourne   Mexico City   Mumbai   Nairobi
São Paulo   Shanghai   Taipei   Tokyo   Toronto

Published by Oxford University Press, Inc.
198 Madison Avenue, New York, New York 10016

www.oup.com

Oxford is a registered trademark of Oxford University Press

Library of Congress Cataloging-in-Publication Data
Nord, David Paul.
Faith in reading : religious publishing and the birth of mass media in America / David Paul Nord.
    p.   cm.—(Religion in America series)
Includes bibliographical references and index.
ISBN 978-0-19-533578-1
1. Religious literature—Publishing—United States—History—19th century.   2. Tract societies—
United States—History—19th century.   3. Bible—Publication and distribution—Societies, etc.—
United States—History—19th century.   4. American Tract Society—History—19th century.
5. American Bible Society—History—19th century.   6. Christians—Books and reading—United
States—History—19th century.   7. Books and reading—United States—History—19th century.
I. Title.   II. Religion in America series (Oxford University Press)
Z480.R4 N67 2004
070.5'0973'09034—dc22   2003020144
Rev.

9 8 7 6 5 4 3 2 1

Printed in the United States of America
on acid-free paper

For the AAS

The varied mechanical arts necessary to the speed and perfection of printing have advanced, until a single newspaper press will issue a thousand times as many words in a minute as a speaker will utter in an hour. Whatever may have been the might of this agency while in its infancy, as employed in the great Reformation under Luther—however potent in its youth in bringing religion down from the palace to the cottage, as wielded by the Puritans of the seventeenth century, or as employed by British Christians in antagonism to infidelity at the close of the eighteenth century, it remained for associated systematic Christian enterprise in the noon of the nineteenth century, to develope the full power of this amazing instrument of light in its ripened manhood.

—*American Messenger*, June 1851

The world has gone to reading, and read they will, for weal or woe.

—*American Messenger*, May 1849

Acknowledgments

This is a book about books and readers, and to write it I depended almost entirely upon those generous institutions that take books and readers most seriously: libraries. I warmly thank the librarians, curators, and reader services staffs of the American Antiquarian Society, Library Company of Philadelphia, Newberry Library, Presbyterian Historical Society, New-York Historical Society, United Methodist Archives and History Center at Drew University, and the libraries of the University of Chicago, University of Pennsylvania, Princeton Theological Seminary, and Indiana University. Of these, the most important by far was the American Antiquarian Society at Worcester, Massachusetts. For me, the AAS has been much more than a library; it has been a benefactor, a publisher, a community, and a gateway into the history of the book. I am deeply grateful to Nancy Burkett, Joanne Chaison, Ellen Dunlap, John Hench, Marcus McCorison, Caroline Sloat, and many other friends at the AAS, my favorite library on Earth. To them all, this book is dedicated.

My understanding of the history of books and reading was stimulated and encouraged by my involvement with a group of splendid scholars (now friends) assembled by the American Antiquarian Society as the editorial board of the *History of the Book in America* project. I thank them all: Hugh Amory, James Green, Robert Gross, Philip Gura, David Hall, Carl Kaestle, Mary Kelley, Steven Nissenbaum, Janice Radway, Joan Shelley Rubin, Michael Schudson, and Michael Winship. My work in the history of popular religion was enthusiastically supported by Mark Noll, Harry S. Stout, and Leonard Sweet. I thank them as well. In both the history of books and the history of religion, my chief mentor has been David D. Hall, whose kindness, intellectual support, and scholarly example have inspired me for many years.

The libraries and archives of two religious institutions were indispensable to the research for this book: the American Bible Society of New York City and the American Tract Society of Garland, Texas. I am especially grateful to Stephen Slocum and the late Martha Kohler of the ATS.

Second only to books, scholars need dollars to get the job done. For fellowships and other financial support, I thank the American Antiquarian Society, the Lilly Endowment, the Louisville Institute at Louisville Presbyterian Seminary, the Institute for the Study of American Evangelicals at Wheaton College, the American Tract Society, and the Office of Research and the School of Journalism at Indiana University. My dean at the School of Journalism, Trevor Brown, supported this project for many years with money and good-humored encouragement. I appreciate both, especially the latter.

Portions of this book have appeared in different form over the years as articles and book chapters. I thank the editors and publishers of those journals and books for permission to use this material:

"The Evangelical Origins of Mass Media in America, 1815–1835." *Journalism Monographs* 88 (May 1984).

"Systematic Benevolence: Religious Publishing and the Marketplace in Early Nineteenth-Century America." In *Communication and Change in American Religious History*. Edited by Leonard I. Sweet. Grand Rapids, Mich.: Eerdmans, 1993.

"Religious Reading and Readers in Antebellum America." *Journal of the Early Republic* 5 (Summer 1995).

"Free Grace, Free Books, Free Riders: The Economics of Religious Publishing in Early Nineteenth-Century America." *Proceedings of the American Antiquarian Society* 106 (October 1996).

"Benevolent Capital: Financing Evangelical Book Publishing in Early Nineteenth-Century America." In *God and Mammon: Protestants, Money, and the Market, 1790–1860*. Edited by Mark A. Noll. New York: Oxford University Press, 2002.

Finally, I thank my family, including my parents, Harry and Paula Nord, who taught me more about reading and religion than they ever thought they did.

Contents

Introduction

The Finger of Providence, 1815

"The finger of Providence seems to be pointing this way," the young missionary Samuel Mills wrote in a letter from New Orleans in the spring of 1815. "Recent events in this quarter at once arrest our attention and elevate our hopes. We refer to the late wonderful deliverance of this country from an invading foe; and to the subsequent distribution of a number of English Bibles and French Testaments. Perhaps there was, in the wisdom of divine Providence, a more intimate connexion between these events, than is obvious to the world."[1]

In 1815, it was easy to believe, and many Americans did believe, that the defeat of the British expeditionary force by the ragtag army of General Andrew Jackson was an event of world historical importance. Though fought after the peace treaty had been signed, the battle of New Orleans marked for Americans a glorious end to a difficult era of international conflict and an auspicious beginning to an era of economic prosperity, national consolidation, and westward expansion. The smoke of battle had barely cleared before the politicians and ministers of the young republic began to orate the meaning of New Orleans. In speeches, sermons, and patriotic poems, they proclaimed that the battle had revealed a divine plan for America, enacted by the wit and will of Andrew Jackson and his band of backwoods sharpshooters. Victory was simultaneously the teleological outcome of God's providence and the historical handiwork of human agency. In this mythic account of New Orleans, America stood at the dawn of a new age, its destiny to be fashioned by the grace of God through the work of man.[2]

For Samuel Mills, the arrival of several hundred Bibles and New Testaments in New Orleans was an event as momentous for America as the arrival of Andrew Jackson. Mills had just come down from Natchez at the end of a long missionary tour through the Ohio and Mississippi river valleys. This was Mills's second extended tour of the West in the years 1812 to 1815, and both times he was struck by the hardscrabble lives of the new inhabitants of the American frontier. Poor, rude, and widely scattered settlements meant few schools, few churches, few organized institutions of any kind. Yet, like the western people themselves, Mills breathed the air of optimism and progress. "In these places we behold the germs of future cities," he wrote to his eastern patrons in January 1815. "The village, that now contains nothing but log cabins, will soon become the dwelling place of thousands. And those thousands may all be favourably affected by the early establishment of religious institutions there."[3]

Religious institutions, Mills believed, would save American civilization as well as American souls. The institutions he envisioned included churches and schools, of course, but his special concern was the printed word, in the form of Bibles and religious tracts. The letters sent east by Mills and his missionary companions all bemoaned the decline of literacy in the West and "the dreadful famine of the *written*, as well as the *preached* word of God." Yet amid the worry and warning lay a millennial optimism, a steady faith in the power of the printed word and a clear-eyed confidence in the ability of benevolent men and women to bring that word to those who needed it. On several occasions, Mills used the metaphor of the rising sun to associate the East-to-West flow of religious publications with the second coming of Christ. "This mode of doing good [distributing Bibles and religious tracts] operates, in the first instance, upon ministers and men of information," he said. "Some of them appear like men awaking at dawn of day. Lately all was dark around them, and their eyes were shut. But now they are eagerly looking toward the *East;* and catching the first dawning rays of the Sun of righteousness, soon to arise and bless the nations."[4]

One of those eastward-looking ministers was William Dickey of Salem, Kentucky. In the early spring of 1815, Rev. Dickey made his way down to the wharf at the confluence of the Ohio and Cumberland rivers to pick up a bundle of religious tracts sent by Mills. They were the first religious tracts Dickey had ever seen, and he quickly sent off a letter to Mills describing his reaction:

I read them eagerly, and was glad to have it in my power, to give away a present, so suitable, and so acceptable, to many a destitute family. I directed those who received them, to read them over and over, and then hand them to their neighbours. Be assured, Sir, they have excited considerable interest among all classes. Religious Tracts have been much desired by us, ever since we heard of Societies of this kind. That so many numbers, and 6,000 of each, should be printed for gratuitous distribution, astonishes our people. They say, *It is the Lord's doing, and marvellous in our eyes.*[5]

Mills, too, believed that distributing Bibles and tracts was the Lord's doing, but he knew more than Dickey knew. He knew that it was also the work of people, of human effort and organization. In this case, it was the work of the New England Tract Society, which had provided Mills with 15,000 tracts before he had left Boston for the West in July 1814. Moreover, the Massachusetts Bible Society had supplied him with 600 English Bibles, and the Bible Society of Philadelphia and the New York Bible Society had contributed 5,000 French New Testaments for Louisiana. The Connecticut Bible Society had helped as well.[6] The names of these and other organizations dot the pages of Mills's report. Indeed, Mills's letters and reports were primarily pleas for assistance from dozens of missionary associations and publication societies scattered across the settled areas of the eastern seaboard. If Mills's spiritual mission was to save souls, his chief practical work was to marshal the organizational strength of Christian America and to bring it to bear on the production and distribution of the printed word.

Rev. Dickey's parishioners were astonished by all this, and rightly so, for they were witnessing, there in the wilderness of western Kentucky, the first stirrings of something new in America: mass media. Hundreds of missionary, Bible, and religious tract societies had sprung up in the United States in the years after 1800, and by 1815 their leaders had begun to dream the dream of mass communication—that is, they imagined placing the same printed message into the hands of everyone in America. To make their dream into reality, they prayed; but they also organized. In the first half of the nineteenth century, the scattered local societies coalesced into several large national organizations, which led America into the modern era of mass publication and systematic distribution of printed material. They did not bring on the millennium of Christ, nor did they reach everyone with their publications. But they came close, at least to their second goal. In the early nineteenth century, they produced the first mass medium in America. This book tells that story.

Historians of early nineteenth-century America are fond of the phrase *the market revolution*. This was a time, they say, when commercial markets expanded enormously and market relations came to dominate economic and social life in America.[7] Printing and publishing are properly part of that story. Like other goods, printed materials gradually came to be commodified, mass produced, and sold in increasingly distant locations. During this period, commercial publishing expanded enormously in every form and genre of the printed word, from schoolbooks to novels to newspapers. Small printing offices popped up everywhere, while the leading book-publishing houses and metropolitan newspapers grew from artisan shops into major manufacturing concerns. Meanwhile, the circulation and readership of printed materials surged so rapidly that "market revolution" has sometimes been associated with a parallel "reading revolution."[8]

Religion also plunged into the market world of the early nineteenth century. The terminology of commerce and marketing is now commonplace in the history of American religion. R. Laurence Moore writes of the "commodification" of religion and the competition of religious groups and movements in "the marketplace of culture." Roger Finke and Rodney Stark frame their sweeping overview of American religious history as a story of breakneck competition in "a free market religious economy." John H. Wigger's account of the rise of American Methodism is a story of the "replacement of state-sponsored churches with a religious free market." Wigger and Nathan Hatch speak of "religious organizations taking on market form." In the early nineteenth century, religious organizations clearly were awash in a sea of commerce as well as a sea of faith.[9]

This linking of publishing and religion to the market revolution reveals much about both, but it does not tell the whole story about either. And for religious publishing, the market revolution paradigm may obscure more than it reveals. To say that religious publishers entered the commercial marketplace is to say too little and too much.[10] On the one hand, the leaders of the Bible and tract movements were utterly exhilarated by the possibilities of the commercial culture. The expansion of business and the extension of market relations, along with improvements in transportation, printing technology, and access to capital, allowed the Bible and tract entrepreneurs to imagine and to build truly national institutions (modern business firms, really) with national reach. By the late 1820s, the evangelical publishers had become leading innovators of printing technology and national business organization, and the

millennial dream of reaching everyone with books and tracts seemed imminent. On the other hand, they viewed the market as their most wily and dangerous foe. In the religious free market, heresy and infidelity were thriving,
while the traditional authority of the standing-order churches was fading. In
the secular free market, private enterprise was poisoning the nation with the
cheap trash of print culture, the literature of wickedness, sensation, dissipation,
and error. Private enterprise, obedient to the law of supply and demand, was
the great problem of America. As charity publishers, the Bible and tract societies pursued a goal that was the opposite of the private enterprise. They proposed to turn the market on its head, to deliver a product to everyone, regardless of ability or even desire to buy.

In other words, the managers of the religious publishing societies
launched their products into the currents of commerce, but against the flow.
The managers of the noncommercial Bible and tract societies made themselves
practical businessmen, savvy marketers, large-scale manufacturers, and capi-
talists in order to save the country from the market revolution.

In this enterprise, organization was the key. If the "invisible hand" of the
market could not be trusted to guide the distribution of religious books and
tracts to everyone, regardless of ability to pay, then the "visible hand" of organization must be employed instead. Long before the appearance of long-
distance railroads and other national business firms, the religious publishing
societies had worked out the essential features of a modern, large-scale business enterprise—that is, an operation that substitutes "administrative coordination" for "market coordination."[11] The religious publishers were not only
pioneers of print; they were pioneers of business, in the form of the modern,
not-for-profit corporation. The story of religious publishing in the early nineteenth century, then, is a story of the origins of the noncommercial sector of
the American economy and the contribution of that sector to the birth, not
only of mass media, but of business organization as well.[12]

Finally, it is a story of readers and reading during an important transitional
period in the history of print culture. The religious publishers of antebellum
America, like Samuel Mills in 1815, proposed to make books abundant in places
where books were scarce. Fearing the rise of cheap and seductive secular
publications, the religious publishers resolved to challenge Satan head-on. To
this end, the societies produced for free distribution countless tracts, often
written in the same sentimental and sensational style as the new secular literature. But they also produced millions of volumes of old-fashioned devotional
books, often the classic works of English Puritanism. The religious publishers
also dispatched colporteurs (traveling book distributors) to carry tracts and
books to people on the frontier of American settlement. This geographical

frontier was also a frontier of publication, a borderland where old styles of reading came into contact with the new cheap literature of the new media age. The religious publishers aimed to use modern mass media to encourage traditional reading values and habits. Reading, however, is never a simple corollary to publishing. Reading—or "reader response," in the jargon of literary criticism—has its own history.[13] And how readers, such as Rev. Dickey's Kentucky parishioners, actually responded to this mixture of the new and the old is another important chapter in the history of America's coming of age with mass media.

The organization of this book is both thematic and chronological. Chapter 1, "Religion and Reading in Early America," sketches the historical context that produced an entrepreneur of religion and reading such as Samuel Mills. My subject is the theological and organizational origins of a culture of evangelical literacy. The millennial dream of supplying *everyone* with religious reading material was a post-1800 development, but its roots ran deep into the religious and cultural soil of colonial America, especially New England. In this brief background chapter, I describe how the interplay of Protestant doctrine and New England family and social organization nurtured a special penchant for print. Though early Puritans did not believe that God's grace could be summoned by human agency, they did believe that reading the word was the means through which God's grace came to humankind.

Chapter 2, "Millennial Print," examines the beginnings of missionary publishing societies in the years after the American Revolution. In this chapter, my subject is how ideology—the will to print—begat organizational practice. I describe how a new millennial spirit in the early republic encouraged a rising faith among religious leaders, especially in New England, in human agency and human institutions. More specifically, I tell the stories of the first American missionary societies and their ventures into publishing. The chapter begins with the founding of the Society for Propagating the Gospel among the Indians and Others in North-America, which was chartered by the Massachusetts General Assembly in 1787. I also describe the early work of the first true tract and book society in America, the Massachusetts Society for Promoting Christian Knowledge (1803). The chapter ends with the creation of the New England Tract Society (1814), a new kind of society designed to serve as a noncommercial wholesale publisher with genuine national reach.

Chapter 3, "The New Mass Media: Economic Foundations," explores the interplay of economics and religion in the publishing work of the early Bible and tract societies. In this chapter, I describe how religious publishers worked out ways to deal with their central economic problem: how to run a successful marketing and manufacturing business whose goal was not to sell the product but to give it away, a business whose most needy customers were least likely to desire the product. I explore the economic nature of the new mass media as well as the special economic nature of religion itself. The chapter concentrates on the pioneering work of the New England Tract Society, 1814–1825, and the Bible Society of Philadelphia, 1808–1815. I tell the story of how these societies built substantial not-for-profit publishing, wholesaling, and marketing operations based on the principles of centralization in printing and localism in fundraising and charitable distribution. By 1815, the characteristic patterns of nineteenth-century noncommercial religious publishing—in technology, manufacturing, and distribution—were all in place. The chapter ends with a critique of "rational choice" theory in the sociology and economics of religion and with a discussion of how nineteenth-century religious publishers understood the relationship between free grace and free books and tracts.

Chapter 4, "The New Mass Media: National Institutions," describes the flowering of the great national, not-for-profit religious publishing societies in the second and third decades of the nineteenth century. The focus is on the American Bible Society, the American Tract Society, and the American Sunday School Union. Founded in 1816, the American Bible Society grew into a major American book publisher in the 1820s, just the sort of large-scale, national publishing operation that Samuel Mills had envisioned in 1815. The American Sunday School Union arrived on the scene in 1824 and the American Tract Society in 1825, both also growing into major publishing houses. These societies were innovators in modern printing technologies and distribution strategies, yet they remained essentially true to the overriding goal of charity publishing. They drew on the earlier models of the New England Tract Society and the Bible Society of Philadelphia to establish national manufacturing enterprises supported by far-flung networks of local auxiliaries. The American Bible Society, the American Tract Society, and the American Sunday School Union produced what might be called the first genuine mass media in America. In the late 1820s, they launched "general supplies," remarkably ambitious—though ultimately disappointing—efforts to place religious tracts and books into the hands of every man, woman, and child in America.

Chapter 5, "The New Mass Media: Systematic Distribution," moves from printing technology and manufacturing to business organization. Though the American Bible Society, the American Tract Society, and the American Sunday School Union had developed the technological capacity for nearly universal mass media by 1830, none of the societies' general supplies were successful. The societies could produce the books, but they lacked the organizational ability to deliver those books to all the people who needed them. As charity publishers, the ABS, the ATS, and the ASSU sought to place books with readers regardless of their ability to pay. In other words, they sought to divorce supply from demand and to move their products against the flow of commerce. The failed general supplies taught the society managers that their distribution systems were still too tied to the logic of the marketplace. Focusing mainly on the work of the American Tract Society and the American Bible Society in the 1830s and 1840s, this chapter shows how the religious publishers created new structures and strategies of business organization to do through the visible hand of administration what could not be done by the invisible hand of the market.

Chapter 6, "How Readers Should Read," is the first of two chapters on the readership of religious tracts and books in the first half of the nineteenth century. This chapter explores the publishers' understanding of readers and reading. At the American Bible Society, the American Tract Society, the American Sunday School Union, and the denominational publishing houses, the managers imagined that they lived in the midst of a dangerous reading revolution. They viewed much of the burgeoning output of the commercial press as the Devil's fare, and they vowed to beat the Devil at his own game. To do this, they needed not only to produce tracts and books as cheaply as possible; they needed to teach readers how to read them properly. Proper reading was serious, thoughtful, and intensive—the opposite of the frivolous reading-for-entertainment that they abhorred. To win their battle with secular print culture, the religious publishers sought to reproduce the traditional texts of English nonconforming Protestantism and the traditional reading habits of the New England Puritan family.

Chapter 7, "How Readers Did Read," turns from the publishers' ideologies of reading to the actual practices of ordinary readers. Drawing on statistical and descriptive information collected by colporteurs of the American Tract Society and the Presbyterian Board of Publication, I describe how readers around the country responded to the flood of Bibles, tracts, and books from the national religious publishing societies in the 1840s and 1850s. These colporteur reports do not quite take us inside the heads of readers, but they are a rich resource for exploring how readers received, owned, shared, read, and talked about religious books and tracts in antebellum America, especially in the new frontier communities of the trans-Appalachian West. This chapter tells a story of change from scarcity to abundance in the realm of cheap religious publications and of the manifold ways readers responded to that change.

In a brief epilogue titled "Fragmentation and Denomination," I describe the transition of mainstream religious publishing from the millennial high of general supplies conducted by great ecumenical societies to the more steady, though fragmented, world of the denominational publisher. By the early 1860s, the largest religious publisher in America was no longer the American Bible Society or the American Tract Society but the Methodist Book Concern. Both the ABS and the ATS lived on; indeed, they continue to live on today, in an age of multimedia CD-ROMs and e-tracts. But after 1860 they learned to live within an enormously diverse constellation of denominations and religious publishing enterprises. Today, the American Tract Society operates out of a modest warehouse print shop in Garland, Texas, a sprawling commercial suburb of Dallas. The building's sign—American Tract Society, Est. 1825—must surprise many passersby who have never heard of the American Tract Society nor seen an ATS tract. But though its nineteenth-century glory has dimmed, the legacy of the American Tract Society and its fellow societies lives on in every not-for-profit organization in America that still strives, often with remarkable success, to distribute the printed word—whether on paper, on CD-ROM, or on a dot.org Website—against the flow of the commercial marketplace.

In late April 1815, Samuel Mills embarked from New Orleans by sea, sailing home to tell his story. At each port along the way—Baltimore, Philadelphia, New York, Boston—he met with the leaders of local Bible societies and described to them innumerable scenes of spiritual darkness and "destitution," a term he used to mean a lack of reading material as well as a lack of money. Tens of thousands of families, from Lake Erie to the Gulf of Mexico, had no Bibles, no tracts, no religious publications of any kind. All the Bibles that had been sent west by all the societies in the United States, he said, had not even equaled the yearly increase in the number of the destitute. He believed that a half million Bibles would be needed to supply all of the spiritually destitute people of America.[14]

Could this be done? The fact that it needed to be done was "a foul blot on our national character," Mills declared. "Christian America must arise and wipe it away.—The existing Societies are not able to do it. They want union;—they want co-operation;—they want resources."[15] "A National Institution" was required to do the job, he said. Could such an institution be organized in such a vast and thinly populated country as the United States, a country with a localized, handicraft printing industry, a primitive transportation network, and almost no experience with national organization? In the millennial spring of 1815, many Americans were ready to join Mills in believing that it could be done and in setting out to do it.

I

Religion and Reading
in Early America

Though fueled by a new millennial optimism in the early nineteenth
century, Samuel Mills's dream in 1815 of supplying a Bible to everyone had roots sunk deep into the history of Protestant Christianity.
Christians had always been a "people of the book." From the earliest
days, long before the Bible was canonized, Christians had collected,
copied, and circulated the letters of Paul and the Christian Gospels,
as well as the ancient Hebrew Scriptures. The Protestant reformers
of the sixteenth century not only reaffirmed the textual basis of
Christianity; they preached the virtue of Bible reading by ordinary
people in their own vernacular languages, and they idealized a powerful new technology for reproducing texts: the printing press. Martin Luther, the most prolific patron of the early German press, proclaimed printing to be "God's highest and extremest act of grace,
whereby the business of the Gospel is driven forward." No one put
the matter more forcefully than the English reformer John Foxe in
his classic Reformation spellbinder, the *Book of Martyrs*: "The Lord
began to work for his Church, not with sword and target to subdue
His exalted adversary, but with printing, writing and reading. . . .
How many printing presses there be in the world, so many block-
houses there be against the high castle of St. Angelo, so that either
the pope must abolish knowledge and printing or printing at length
will root him out."[1]

Samuel Mills's dream was nourished as well in the soil of his
native New England. New Englanders, of course, were not the only

people in the New World or the Old who revered books and reading. In the Chesapeake in the seventeenth century, for example, educated Anglican and Catholic colonists often brought books, especially Bibles, with them to their new frontier plantations, and many taught their children to read.[2] But New England was the most serious nurturer of religious reading in America. There, the religious, social, and institutional environment lavishly favored the growth of a culture of literacy and print. Early nineteenth-century New Englanders, such as Mills, carried this culture into the age of modern publishing, but the roots of it go back to the founding. Early New Englanders were Calvinists who believed in a sovereign God, judgmental yet merciful, and a fallen humanity, entirely dependent upon God's unconditional, irresistible grace. Yet theirs was a curiously active and self-reliant Calvinism. In the first century of settlement, their theology, their church and civil polity, and their organization of family and social life all combined to make New England perhaps the most literate place on earth.

At bottom, New Englanders' commitment to evangelical literacy rested on Reformation doctrines of *sola scriptura*, the priesthood of believers, preparation for grace, and sanctification. *Sola scriptura* declared that religious truth lay in the word of God, in the Bible alone. The priesthood of believers took that idea a step further and asserted that the word could—and must—be grasped directly by the individual believer, unmediated by priests or clerical authority. Preparation for grace affirmed that, while faith and salvation were free gifts of a gracious God, human beings could prepare their hearts and minds to receive grace if it were poured out upon them. Sanctification meant spiritual discipline, practical piety, and the regenerate believer's growth in grace throughout life. Taken together, these doctrines inspired people to read the word and to reach out with the word to others. But none of these doctrines were simple or uncontested, and the tensions and ambiguities embedded in them helped to shape New England's special penchant for print.

 Sola scriptura and the priesthood of believers would seem to have left little need for either a professional ministry or a religious literature beyond the vernacular Bible. The individual soul in communion with Scripture would seem to have fulfilled the spirit and letter of the Reformation. But that was not how it worked. As Protestant reformers stripped the priesthood of its special powers of mediation between God and man, priests did not disappear but rather transformed themselves into something new: preachers, teachers, and writers. The Bible was imagined to be a plain text, its meaning transparent and open to the direct perception of ordinary readers. But this belief simply drove the leaders of reform, the religious elites, to step up their efforts to explain to ordinary people what the Bible so plainly meant. Despite the doctrines of *sola scriptura* and the priesthood of believers—or perhaps because of those doctrines—the Protestant Reformation produced a proliferation of ministers and a flood of print that has never subsided even into our own day. The giants of English Puritanism—John Bunyan, Richard Baxter, Joseph Alleine, and others—were foremost writers and publicists. The era of the Puritan Reformation in England and America was a golden age of preaching and publishing, encouraged by, not obviated by, the widespread distribution of the English Bible.[3]

The doctrines of *sola scriptura* and the priesthood of believers, however, could not be coopted completely by the reign of scribbling ministers. In old England and new, Puritan ministers asserted authority by virtue of learning, of their facility with languages and words, including the word of God; and ordinary people usually deferred to the authority of this learned ministry. But not always. If the meaning of God's word were plain and directly accessible, then men and women might retain for themselves the right to judge for themselves and to read for themselves. And they did. Puritanism was a movement that inspired and empowered *both* leaders and laity in a culture of literacy. As David D. Hall put it, "The interplay of clergy, printers, and readers worked in complex ways both to heighten clerical authority and to make it vulnerable to challenge from beneath."[4]

The doctrine of preparation for grace also fostered the culture of literacy and evangelical print. On its face, Calvinism would seem to have had little need for human effort. The Puritans' God was an eternal, omniscient, omnipotent majesty, who had ordained before time began the salvation of some, the damnation of others, and the inability of anyone to change the course of destiny. Divine grace would come—or not come—unconditionally and irresistibly. And yet few supposed that simply waiting on God was all that could be done. True, the elect (if they really were the elect) could do nothing to save themselves, but at least they could learn, as the Puritan minister Thomas Shepard put it, to "lie like wax" beneath the seal. For most of the founders of the New England way, preparation was possible, and a key element of it must be hearing and reading the word. "It is your power to doe more than you doe," wrote Thomas Hooker, a leading advocate of preparationism among the first generation of New England Puritans. "Your legs may as well carry you to the word, as to an Ale-house; . . . you may read good books, as well as Play-books."[5]

In a famous chapter titled "The Expanding Limits of Natural Ability," Perry Miller, the formidable scholar of American Puritanism, argued that New England Puritans pushed the doctrine of preparation to the brink of Arminianism, the very un-Calvinist belief that humans possessed the free will and agency to seize or to reject the grace of God. In Miller's account, the Puritans' God was a rational god who employed and responded to reasonable argumentation. "The history of the notion of preparation," Miller declared, "has carried us from the medieval universe of Protestant scholasticism to the very threshold of the Age of Reason."[6] More recent historians have dismissed Miller's story of the early decline of orthodoxy in New England. The doctrines of election and irresistible grace lived on, they say; Puritans were not Arminian hypocrites. But arguments for the continuing vitality of doctrines of human depravity, free grace, and predestination need not exclude an emphasis on preparationism as well. They merely underscore the complexity and ambivalence inherent in a living religious tradition. One recent historian, Janice Knight, wrote that the Puritan mind had two hemispheres: one rational and preparationist; the other more emotional, more mystical, more fully absorbed in the unconditional love of God. David Hall described the struggle of one minister to comprehend the mysterious mixture of activity and passivity that marked New England's religious sensibility. It "may seem a paradox," wrote Samuel Willard, yet "it is an evangelical truth that a Christian must acknowledge that he can do nothing, and yet resolve, and bind himself to do all."[7] Preparation for grace was not an easy thing to understand or to do, and its very difficulty as a doctrine and a practice drove New Englanders to search their souls and to search the Scriptures. Whatever preparation was or was not, it was surely a spur to religious reading.

Calvinism would also seem to have had little need for a doctrine of sanctification. In its strictest form, Calvinism asserted not only that the elect were predestined to salvation, but that the elect would necessarily persevere in grace after they had first received it. They could not fall away. In practice, however, uncertainty over the assurance of election and doubts about the validity of their own conversion experience encouraged the faithful (and the merely hopeful) to persist in piety, to make the seeking of assurance a never-ending preoccupation. In a sense, preparation did not stop at conversion; it shaded into sanctification, into a lifelong process of spiritual study, meditation, and discipline.[8] For many Puritan seekers, the stages of preparation, justification (conversion), and sanctification blurred and merged in the actual living of life, far removed from the niceties of formal theology. Even preparationist theologians recognized the difference between an act of God and a human being's fuzzy perception of it. "Justification is a slow sunrise," wrote Andrew Delbanco, describing the theology of William Ames, a leading English Puritan theorist. "There may be a moment when, in some absolute sense, the sun has risen, but men

do not have the epistemological equipment to say, 'the moment is now. . . . '
God may dispense his gift of renovation in an instant, but that flash is always
diffused and scattered for the human recipient into a lifetime of tantalizing
subtleties."[9]

Not all Puritan ministers stressed the subtleties and uncertainties of the
conversion experience. Some urged believers to rest assured in the unconditional, overwhelming love of God. But the assurance of grace also inspired a
preoccupation with sanctification, for the supreme goodness of God flowed
into, through, and out of the human heart. "Grace not only sanctifies what the
saint sees and feels," writes Janice Knight, "it dictates all that she or he says
and does. To be true, sanctification must be turned outward, converted to labors
of love." Thus doubt and lack of doubt had the same outcome: a commitment
to a lifelong process of piety, spiritual discipline, and right living—"the action
of sanctification."[10]

No Puritan believed that sanctification came easily. Nor did anyone suppose that sanctification banished sin from human life. Only in the millennial
optimism of the nineteenth century could the idea of sanctification evolve into
a doctrine of human efficacy, even perfectionism, the belief that the Christian
could achieve perfect holiness here on earth. For New England Puritans of all
stripes, sanctification was a spiritual state brought about entirely by the grace
of God, not by human effort. But divine grace inspired human effort. "Repen-
tance flowed seamlessly into an ethical activism," writes David Hall. "Practical
divinity was saturated with the language of duty, whether understood as sanctification or as a disciplining first step toward the work of grace."[11] Puritans
were called by God to action, to vocation, to duty. And one duty that always
loomed was to read the Bible.

The interplay of these four doctrines—*sola scriptura*, the priesthood of believers, preparation for grace, and sanctification—inspired a passion for preaching,
writing, and reading in colonial New England. But though these doctrines
involved the individual soul, the culture of evangelical literacy was nurtured in
corporate institutions, including the family, the church, the town, and the colony, all of which blended public and private in a special New England way.
New Englanders understood social life through the concept of covenant, a
contract of mutuality and reciprocity. The idea of covenant harked back to God's
tribal relationship with Abraham in the Old Testament, and the Puritan founders sometimes imagined their own relationship with God in similar terms.[12]

Just as important, they imagined their relationships with each other in terms of covenant. The way New Englanders organized their families, communities, and institutional lives would have a profound impact on the growth of the culture of evangelical literacy.

More than other American colonies, the first settlements in New England were peopled by families, and the family served as the chief institution for the acquisition and use of literacy.[13] Especially in the early decades, the home was the school, and the mother was the reading teacher. With hornbooks, primers, psalm books, and Bibles in their laps, children learned to read through oral recitation, sounding out letters, syllables, and words. Throughout the colonial period, reading and writing were taught separately. Writing was an occupational skill, useful in commerce, government, and the ministry, and thus was reserved for boys. Reading, on the other hand, was a vital religious skill, a means of grace, taught to everyone, girls and boys alike.[14] Though historical literacy rates are difficult to estimate, especially for women, who were less likely than men to be able to write, it seems probable that by the second half of the eighteenth century, reading literacy for both men and women in New England approached 90 percent, highest in the American colonies and substantially higher than nearly all of the countries of Europe.[15]

Families, however, were not left on their own as incubators of literacy. The larger community took notice. In 1642, the Massachusetts Bay colony passed legislation requiring that all children be taught to read. If parents neglected to perform this essential public duty, their children were liable to be apprenticed to someone who would perform it. In 1647, Massachusetts passed its first public schooling law, which required towns of more than fifty families to employ a schoolmaster, though for most of the colonial period children were expected to have mastered elementary reading before they entered the town school. Formal schooling, in other words, was for boys to learn writing and perhaps Latin. Meanwhile, many towns organized informal "dame schools" for both boys and girls, taught by local women—a modest extension of ordinary home schooling. Only gradually did public schools emerge as substitutes for family-based instruction. But as the movement to community public schools gained momentum, New England led the way.[16]

The New England approach to schooling and literacy reflected a more general corporate style that blended public and private action. Before the American Revolution, corporations and formal voluntary associations were rare in New England, but they flourished abundantly in the late eighteenth and early nineteenth centuries. That is largely because they grew in a soil long enriched by religious notions of calling and covenant and by communal experience in the government of church, town, and colony. From John Winthrop's call to

Christian charity to Cotton Mather's essays on benevolence to Jonathan Edwards's explication of true virtue, New Englanders understood themselves obligated to live right and to do good in the community. In practice these obligations—for example, aid to the poor—were usually worked out through local private action, but private action was instigated and supported by public law and public money.[17] Harvard College, the oldest eleemosynary corporation in America (founded 1636), is perhaps the best example of an institution that developed as a private corporation but was controlled largely by public officials, supported by public revenue, and fully clothed in public purpose. The idea of organizing private institutions to do the public's business became, by the late eighteenth century, an important facet of the New England way and, indeed, the American way.[18]

In the history of the institutionalization of religious literacy in New England, one enterprise associated with Harvard College offers an especially revealing and important example of the mixing of private organization with public purpose. This is the Cambridge Press, the first, and for many years the only, print shop in British America.

The Cambridge Press supplied few of the books that New Englanders read. As in other American colonies, most books were imported from England. While it held a monopoly on printing in the seventeenth century, the little shop at Harvard turned out a handful of important steady-selling titles, notably the *Bay Psalm Book* (first edition, 1640) and Michael Wigglesworth's *Day of Doom* (first edition, 1662), but even these famous fruits of New England piety were soon reprinted in London and exported back to America. In most ways, the Cambridge Press operated as a quasi-official agency of government and college. The early printers dabbled in private projects, trying hard to make a little money on the side, but throughout its life the Cambridge Press depended on subsidy, not on commercial enterprise. Only when printing and publishing moved to Boston in 1674 did New England begin to supply a considerable proportion of its own reading material—and then only very gradually.[19]

Though its actual output was small, the Cambridge Press launched one particular publishing enterprise that nicely illustrates both the New England commitment to evangelical literacy and the form of corporate organization that helped to turn that commitment into practical reality. This was the Indian-language publishing project. This enterprise, which arose from John Eliot's mission to Massachusett Indians, became the major patron of the Cambridge

Press in the mid-seventeenth century. Catholics and Anglicans mounted more ambitious Indian missionary efforts in the New World, but the New England mission more vividly reveals how religious doctrine and organizational style flowed together into a culture of religious reading and publishing. Though the early New England mission was a modest affair, its publishing work presaged the more dramatic efforts that came out of New England much later.

The centrality of literacy and the printed word was the most striking characteristic of the Indian mission in New England. Given New Englanders' almost tribal sense of themselves as a chosen people, it is not surprising that many ignored or even resisted evangelism among the Indians. But those who did believe that the Indians should be Christianized agreed that literacy education must be part of the process. Some favored teaching English literacy; others, such as John Eliot, the minister at Roxbury, Massachusetts, favored publishing (as well as preaching and teaching) in the Indians' own languages. Like the heroes of the Reformation who had proclaimed the doctrines of *sola scriptura* and the priesthood of believers, Eliot set about to translate the Bible into the vernacular of the Massachusett Indian people. This was an extraordinarily difficult project of translation, for it required first inventing a written version of an oral language marked by many variant dialects. It was also a difficult and immense project for the little Cambridge Press. Eliot's Indian Bible was by far the largest printing job in seventeenth-century America, and it was done in a written language that was new to all of the compositors and printers, even the Indians who assisted. But, given the imperatives of Puritan belief, there was little choice: Christians must be readers.[20]

The Indian Bible (published between 1661 and 1663) was the inspiration of Eliot but the collective work of many collaborators, in both New England and old. Eliot was a savvy organizational entrepreneur who knew how to operate in the quasi-public environment of Massachusetts and how to raise money in England. In Massachusetts, Eliot persuaded the colony government to support the mission with land grants, while friends in England raised funds to support a second press and printer at Cambridge. For this purpose, the English Parliament in 1649 chartered the Society for the Propagation of the Gospel in New England, commonly known as the New England Company. (This organization preceded by decades the better-known Anglican Society for the Propagation of the Gospel in Foreign Parts, which was chartered in England in 1701.) The New England Company sent a skilled English printer, Marmaduke Johnson, to work on the Indian Bible, and Eliot recruited several Indian converts to assist in the translation and printing.[21] The scope and speed of the project required organization and capital as much as technological skill. This was, in effect, the first great corporate philanthropic enterprise of colonial New

England. The fact that the goal was to manufacture a printed book testifies to the vital centrality of evangelical literacy in New England culture.

Despite the doctrines of *sola scriptura* and the priesthood of believers, however, the Bible was not enough. Eliot and his collaborators labored to produce other Indian-language works as well, including a catechism (issued in 1654), several tracts and devotional books, and an Indian primer. Though he held the Bible to be fundamental, Eliot also believed, in typical Puritan fashion, that reading should permeate all aspects of a Christian's life. In the summer of 1663, Eliot sent a letter to Richard Baxter, the leading Puritan publicist in England, to ask his permission to publish a translation of one of his books as the second major work of the Cambridge Press in the Massachusett language. "My work about the Indian Bible being (by the good hand of the Lord, though not without difficulties) finished," he wrote, "I am meditating what to do next for these Sons of this our Morning; they having no Books for their private use, of ministerial composing."[22] The book Eliot chose was Baxter's *A Call to the Unconverted*, which had been first published in London in 1658.

Baxter's *Call*, as it came to be known, was the ideal choice, the perfect text for evangelical literacy. Though Baxter claimed that he was no Arminian, the *Call* brushed aside strict Calvinist doctrines of election and limited atonement and preached an unlimited, universal atonement available to all believers. The sacrifice of Christ's death was given for all, Baxter declared, not just for a special elect. God offered "salvation, certain salvation; a speedy, glorious, everlasting salvation, to everyone of you." The *Call* also unabashedly affirmed the free will and free agency of men and women to choose either sin or salvation. In the cadence of a revival preacher of an age yet to come, Baxter urged his readers to turn, to turn, to turn. Again and again, he told them: "turn, or die," "turn, and live." And turn immediately, this day. It is "now or never," another phrase Baxter hammered, through repetition, into the hearts of readers and into the vernacular of evangelical literature. In the *Call*, Baxter described the horrors of hell, but only to awaken the soul, for God wished all to be saved. "There is mercy in God," he proclaimed, "there is sufficiency in the satisfaction of Christ, the promise is free, and full, and universal; you may have life, if you will but turn."[23]

A Call to the Unconverted was itself a plea for reading. Firmly in the Puritan intellectual tradition, Baxter declared that God's word was sufficient for instruction and sufficiently plain for all to understand, yet he was not too modest to resist adding thousands of words of his own. One of the most prolific English-language religious writers of all time—"scribbling Dick," his detractors called him—Baxter believed that "education is God's ordinary way for the conveyance of his Grace" and that reading books was the way to education, better than hearing the spoken word. In the *Call* and elsewhere, he described how serious reading should be done, whether of the Bible or his own books: "I pray you read this leaf again, and mark it," he admonished his reader. Like the Protestant reformers of the past and the Indian missionaries of the present, Baxter idealized the printing press and the culture of evangelical literacy that the press had made possible in Europe and America. "In short," writes Baxter's biographer, "he had a vision of a community in which all were literate, all had an ample supply of books, and all were in the habit of reading. Such could not but be a society of saints."[24]

Few Indians ever read the Massachusett edition of *A Call to the Unconverted*, but hundreds of thousands of others read it in English over the next two hundred years. Baxter's *Call* became one of the classic works of evangelical Protestantism on both sides of the Atlantic. In the early eighteenth century, Baxter's *Call* was part of the arsenal of publications shared by a thriving network of evangelical English and American Protestants. During the revival tours of the great English preacher George Whitefield in the 1740s, newspapers and magazines were increasingly important for propagating the latest revival news, but the traditional library of English Puritanism, including Baxter, remained in print and in circulation in both Britain and America.[25] In the early nineteenth century, when large-scale religious publishing came of age in America, Baxter's *Call*, along with the Bible, was often the book pressed into the hands of potential converts.[26] Baxter's *Call* lived on because it so well exemplified the optimistic, self-reliant, evangelical strain of the Anglo-American Puritan tradition. Yes, God was sovereign and his grace was free and irresistible, but ordinary people could act to receive it. They could read. They could repent. And they could turn. In the soteriological scheme of Baxter—and of John Eliot and many others—reading was the way.

In the end, the Indian mission in New England was largely a failure; few Indians learned to read in the Massachusett language and few were converted to Christianity. But the model of the Indian mission—with its corporate organization, its commitment to literacy and evangelical publishing, and even its devotion to particular books—lived on.

In *A Call to the Unconverted*, Richard Baxter supposed that the Bible texts he opened were plain, unambiguous, transparent. And because he believed in the transparency of the Bible, he believed the same about his own devotional and theological work. In other words, Baxter's commitment to publishing was based upon what we today might call a theory of reading. For him, meaning flowed directly from text to reader; ordinary laypeople could get it. In a sense, this was the doctrine of the priesthood of believers as literary theory. "We do not as the Papist priests, teach our people to see with our eyes, and no matter for their own," he wrote, "but we help to clear their own eye-sight." For Baxter, reading was not only a means of grace; it was like grace. The meaning of a text would automatically infuse and fill up the well-prepared mind and heart. The American Puritans shared this sense of how reading worked.[27]

But, of course, reading does not work this way. Today, reader-response literary critics, such as Stanley Fish and Norman Holland, are fond of reminding us that literature is in the reader, not in the text. The author (and the text) may propose a meaning, but readers will respond in their own ways, drawing on their own experiences. "In my model," says Fish, "meanings are not extracted but made and made not by encoded forms but by interpretive strategies that call forms into being." Authors and readers may share interpretive strategies; indeed, they must share some, or communication would be impossible. In stressing the idea of interpretive strategies in reading, Fish insists that meaning is necessarily communal and cultural. Texts are open to a broad range of interpretations, ultimately controlled by the reader, not by the author or the language of the text itself.[28] Similarly, historians of reading, such as Roger Chartier, have argued that readers read in specific contexts, "that reading is always a practice embodied in acts, spaces, and habits."[29] These notions, now truisms of literary theory and the history of reading, suggest the dangers to religious orthodoxy of the doctrine of the priesthood of believers in the realm of reading. In Protestant England and America, ordinary people zealously guarded their right to read and judge for themselves. And despite the sanguine expectations of Baxter and other Puritan publicists, this was a recipe for heterodoxy and heresy.

Puritan leaders naturally viewed the rise of heterodoxy and heresy as declension, a falling away from truth. An older historiography of colonial American religion followed their lead and made the decline of religiosity the theme of the story. But that has changed. Recent historians, more attuned to social and cultural history, to the lives and thought of ordinary people, have traced in eighteenth-century America a rising tide of Christianity, but a Christianity of immense variety. Drawing on the work of Jon Butler, Patricia Bonomi, David Hall, and other recent historians, Charles Cohen has written that the operative *p* word in the historiography of colonial religion, so long "Puritanism," has become "pluralism."[30]

To a large extent, the rise of religious pluralism is a story of reader response. Encouraged to see truth through their own eyes, ordinary people necessarily brought to the experience of reading the experiences of their own lives. As David Hall has shown in his study of popular religion, folk culture provided the rich interpretive context for ordinary people to make sense of what they read. This is not to say that their reading was idiosyncratic; people brought to their reading the shared codes and conventions of their culture. But culture is always multifaceted and multilayered. In colonial New England and most of Christian America, even nonliterates were fluent in the language of the Bible, but they were fluent as well in folk traditions of ritual and wonder, conventional wisdom, and common sense. Hall's story is the intermingling of the texts of Christianity with the ebbs and flows of ordinary daily life.[31] Even an apparently unifying cultural experience, such as George Whitefield's highly orchestrated and media-savvy intercolonial revival tours in the 1740s, produced enormously varied responses, as people judged for themselves what they heard and read. As Frank Lambert put it, "By preaching outside parish boundaries in the marketplaces and communicating to a mass, public audience through newspapers, Whitefield expanded the range of possible meanings men and women could construct concerning spiritual matters. The result was a new sense of individualism by which laypeople challenged not only their parish ministers but often Whitefield himself."[32]

Fashioning meaning from the Christian word, whether printed or preached, was an especially strange and disorienting experience for the new Christians gathered together by John Eliot: the so-called praying Indians. Coming from a completely different religious culture, Christian Indians not surprisingly mingled the language of Scripture with their own native spirituality to produce an unorthodox Christianity that was often wonderfully syncretistic and, to the Puritan ministers, wonderfully appalling. For the few Indians who learned to read, literacy was far from the simple, straightforward path to true Christianity and civilization that the Puritans supposed it would be.[33]

Jill Lepore tells the tragic story of perhaps the most literate Indian in seventeenth-century New England, John Sassamon, who was skilled in English and Massachusett, both spoken and written. The son of Christianized Indians, Sassamon grew up to serve as an assistant to John Eliot in the translation and production of the Indian Bible. He also employed his bilingual literacy in service to Metacom (King Philip), the Pokanoket sachem who later made war on the English, destroying Eliot's hopes of Indian Christianization and destroying most copies of the Indian Bible as well. Because of his literacy, Sassamon lived a perilous life caught between two cultures. His murder in December 1674 was the event that precipitated the genocidal King Philip's War. Why Sassamon was killed remains a mystery, but it certainly had to do with his cultural inbetweenness and his suspect double-identity—too English to be Indian, too

Indian to be English. "Sassamon's is a small, highly allegorical tale," writes Lepore, "but it suggests that the acquisition of literacy acting in tandem with conversion to Christianity can be a dangerous, even fatal combination."[34]

That literacy could be dangerous, even fatal, was a fact well known from the Protestant Reformation, when many martyrs went to the fire unwilling to budge from their heretical readings of their precious vernacular Bibles. In America, variations in reader response prompted a few executions but mainly produced schism, denominationalism, and, in the early years, the settlement of Rhode Island by heretical Puritan exiles. But orthodox Protestant leaders, especially in New England, never lost the will to print. From settlement onward, they remained faithful to a theory of evangelical literacy that flowed logically and forcefully from the doctrines of *sola scriptura*, the priesthood of believers, preparation for grace, and sanctification of the Christian life. How the will to print was transformed into practical enterprise is a separate but related story, a story of technology, organization, and money as well as religious commitment. And how printed texts were actually read is still another story, more complicated and more interesting, for it is in the slippage, the disjuncture, the tension between publishing and reading that the cultural history of religious literacy truly lies. These are the stories told in the chapters to come.

2

Millennial Print

In 1762, "a number of gentlemen" in Boston planned a new mission to the Indians. They organized a society, sought a charter from the colony of Massachusetts, and "began warmly and zealously to prosecute their pious and benevolent work." But when they sent their charter to England for approval, the archbishop of the Church of England persuaded the king to veto it, presumably to preserve the prerogative of the English Society for the Propagation of the Gospel in Foreign Parts and to protect the episcopacy of the Anglican church.[1] In the 1760s, English authorities had reason to fear the independence of a voluntary association run entirely by religious dissenters 3,000 miles from Canterbury. A few years later, the American Revolution would sever this umbilical cord and inspire Americans to reimagine their world and to organize it in their own way.

In 1787, the Boston gentlemen revived the plan of 1762 and launched the Society for Propagating the Gospel among the Indians and Others in North-America, the first missionary society to be organized in the newly independent United States. In its early years, the Society for Propagating the Gospel had little success among the Indians of North America and only a little more success among the "others," who turned out to be mostly the new settlers in the hardscrabble communities of inland Maine.[2] But the SPGNA, as I will call it, had influence of another sort. In several important ways, it served as a model for the more ambitious and successful evangelical associations that followed its lead. Some of the contributions of the SPGNA were structural: the society pioneered legal, administrative, and organizational arrangements that would become commonplace in the voluntary associational milieu of the new republic. But, more important, the founders of the Society for Propagating the Gospel nurtured a new millennial vision of evangelical work. Theirs was a sober, New England-style millennium, built upon a foundation of traditional Calvinist doctrine. Central to their vision was a firm faith in knowledge, learning, and the efficacy of print. This chapter tells the story of how the commitment to millennial print, made flesh in the founding of the SPGNA, energized a broad movement of missionary and publication work in New England in the first decades of the nineteenth century.

The American Revolution, which touched many things, dramatically changed how Americans imagined the Christian millennium. The term *millennium* refers to the end times, to the thousand-year reign of Christ on earth, prophesied in the Book of Revelation. Traditionally, most Christians had believed that the millennial era of peace and happiness would come after Christ's literal return to earth and after an extended period of chaos and catastrophe (the apocalypse). The stunning success of the American Revolution inspired a more optimistic vision of the end times, with more emphasis on millennium and less on apocalypse. Indeed, to many writers in the 1770s and 1780s, and no doubt to many ordinary people as well, the days of glory and happiness were already at hand, with America now in the role of God's vanguard and beacon to the world. Some millennial rhetoric, such as Tom Paine's effusive proclamations of a new age dawning, was purely secular, though often couched in religious metaphor. But even many devout Christians came to believe that the millennium would come *before* the physical reappearance of Christ and the destruction of the world.[3] Though still fluid in the era of the Revolution, millennial thought would in the nineteenth century gradually congeal into two broad categories: *premillennialism*, the belief that Christ's second coming would be sudden and would precede the millennium; and *postmillennialism*, the belief that the millennium would come gradually, with Christ appearing in physical form only at the end, to conduct the last judgment. In the nineteenth century, postmillennialism often faded into an optimistic faith in human progress, which was as useful to political creeds, such as manifest destiny, capitalist prosperity, and American civic righteousness, as to religious eschatology.[4]

Postmillennialism suited the Calvinist world view of the postrevolutionary

New England clergy. The New Divinity theologian Samuel Hopkins, for example, building upon the eschatological thought of his mentor, Jonathan Edwards, stressed the figurative quality of the prophecies of Revelation. Christ would come in spirit to the church and to the hearts of men and women. It was "contrary to all reason," he wrote, to expect Christ to appear in human form to rule a kingdom on earth when he already sits upon the throne of the universe, ruling both heaven and earth. Hopkins, however, did not share the sunny optimism or the faith in human agency of a political millennialist like Paine. Nor by the 1790s could he believe that the millennium was imminent; he expected the world to pass through a long period of tribulation and darkness (perhaps another 200 years) before the eventual but gradual dawn. In accordance with traditional Calvinist doctrines of the sovereignty of God and the depravity of man, Hopkins believed that the millennium would come "by the power and sovereign grace of Christ, . . . not by human might or power."[5]

Moderate Calvinists who wrote about the latter days tended to share Hopkins's postmillennial faith. One such writer, who would become a key player in the Society for Propagating the Gospel and in other religious publishing ventures, was Jedidiah Morse, Yale graduate and after 1789 pastor of the Congregational church at Charlestown, Massachusetts. In the 1780s, Morse was typically optimistic about the American prospect. In a 1789 book on American geography, which quickly became the standard work in the field, Morse envisioned a continental American empire, moving ever westward and poised to play a providential role in world history. But *The American Geography* was no *Common Sense*, and Morse was no Tom Paine. Though Morse could see glory days ahead, especially for the new United States, he never doubted that the work of providence was always God's work, not man's.[6] And in the 1790s, as the French Revolution turned to terror and atheism, Morse's vision of the near future darkened. He saw in French Jacobinism the evil power of the Antichrist. Though he remained secure in his millennial faith, and though he expected the millennium to come sooner than Hopkins did, Morse did not suppose that it would come painlessly. Writing in the style of the classic Puritan jeremiad, Morse beheld in current upheavals and disasters the "hand of Providence" and the punishment of sin. "There is reason to fear," he wrote in 1799, "we shall be obliged to drink deeper than we have yet done of that cup of calamities, mingled by a just God, of which many of the European nations are now drinking even to the very dregs."[7]

But Morse saw hope as well. The modern age was "a period of great sufferings," and its "darkest part is doubtless yet to come," he wrote, yet the millennium may be near. While much of the earth still groaned under the weight of sin and judgment, righteousness was growing. "The events of the present day seem to be adapted and designed, by the Providence of God, to prepare the world to receive the Gospel." Indeed, Morse explicitly described the "signs of the times" as "mixed": wickedness and righteousness, darkness and light, alarm and hope.[8]

Under such a dispensation of judgment and grace, what could human beings do? On that question, New Divinity men such as Hopkins and moderate Calvinists such as Morse diverged somewhat, though the ideas of both flowed from orthodox doctrines of preparation, sanctification, and *sola scriptura*. Both doubted not at all that the millennium would be inaugurated by a sovereign God, not by the agency of sinful man. Hopkins recommended little more than traditional preparation for grace—"prayer, and promoting the interest of religion, and the conversion of sinners"—with the usual emphasis on knowledge of the holy Scriptures. Morse agreed, but he laid more emphasis than Hopkins did on the spread of knowledge, on missions, on evangelical action. Though he trusted God's providence and downplayed human ability, terms such as "zeal," "vigorous exertions," and "wonderful means" crept into his vocabulary. "While the Lord shall be thus executing his strange work," Morse said, "in punishing the nations for their wickedness, he will, at the same time, by new and uncommon means, be spreading his word, and the light of his Gospel, and increasing every species of useful knowledge; and will, by the instrumentality of his knowledge and these judgments, purify multitudes of people." What were these "new and uncommon means"? "Institutions," Morse declared, such as the Society for Propagating the Gospel among the Indians and Others in North-America. If this was a calamitous age, it was also an age "unparalleled for diffusing the knowledge of [the Gospel] to every creature under heaven."[9]

In the decades after its founding, the SPGNA sent missionaries to preach and teach, but from the beginning the society was also committed to evangelism through the printed word. Religious tracts and books were not new to America; an organized system for distributing them freely was the "new and uncommon means" that Morse had in mind.

For the organizers of the SPGNA, as for John Eliot more than a century before, literacy was crucial to missionary work. In Indian missions especially, they believed that "to civilize these people is one great and necessary step towards christianizing them." To this end, the society provided Indians with two kinds of implements of civilization: plows and hoes, and Bibles and spelling books.[10]

The Calvinist founders believed that religious conversion could come only through knowledge and learning; the sacred word was the only means. Though the times were full of signs and wonders, there would be no miracles. "The connexion between knowledge and faith, is such, that the latter cannot exist without the former," the Reverend John Lathrop reminded the society's members in an 1804 sermon. "The deplorable condition of such of the human race, as are still in the darkness of heathenism, cannot be changed for the better, without the use of means. . . . Before they could exercise faith, they must have the knowledge of the truth." Preachers and teachers, schools and churches were needed, but nothing was more important than books.[11]

Though its nominal goal was to Christianize the Indians of North America (meaning, mainly, those of New England), the society almost immediately after 1787 turned its attention to the "others" mentioned in its name. From the start, it was clear to the learned founders that the need for Christian knowledge was nearly as pressing among frontier whites as among the Indians. The problem in the rural reaches of northern New England, especially Massachusetts's own province of Maine, was simply (and frequently) expressed in SPGNA reports: ignorance. With few schools, churches, or other institutions of civilization, the people of Maine lived in a "state of barbarism" and in "almost a total ignorance of God and religion," according to the society's first account of the work. "Few of them are taught to read, and those who have been taught, cannot now procure books," the society's secretary lamented:

> Many families have not had a bible or a testament in their houses
> for years past, and such is their poverty as to forbid their purchasing
> them. Many of them have lost their reverence for the Lord's day, and
> are strangers to religious institutions. Their children are educated
> not only in an ignorance of religion, but also without human learn-
> ing, or even the arts of civilization.[12]

Revealingly, this lament did not mean that religious instruction was entirely absent from the spiritual wilderness of Maine. The society's first missionary, Daniel Little, did find preachers and teachers there, but they were, he said, "illiterate men, chiefly of the Baptist persuasion," and their "bigotry and enthusiasm . . . and pretense of superior divine teaching, have lessened the credit of literature and a learned ministry."[13] For the Congregationalists of the SPGNA, an unlearned, illiterate religion was no religion at all.

Given its commitment to learning, it is not surprising that the distribution of books quickly became the chief work of the society. By 1795, the SPGNA had distributed 6,299 books in Maine, plus several hundred books to the Indians of Martha's Vineyard and mainland Massachusetts. By the end of the first decade of work, the total number stood at 8,987, including 310 Bibles, 768 New Testaments, 969 spelling books, 634 Psalters, 1,566 primers, and sundry other treatises, devotional books, and pamphlets.[14] The society did not print books itself. The managers procured them through donations, purchases from booksellers, and direct publishing contracts with printers. And the society did not sell books. It gave them away.

Giving away books required organization and money. Perhaps the most important organizational aspect of the society was formal incorporation. One of the first charitable corporations chartered in Massachusetts after the Revolution, the SPGNA provided the model for a new kind of institution: the voluntary association as corporation. Alms giving, even organized alms giving, had always been part of the culture of Christianity, and the corporate form was not unknown in colonial America. In New England especially, legislatures had long drawn on English models to charter a variety of corporations to manage towns, districts, schools, societies, and other public institutions. The SPGNA was modeled upon the Society for the Propagation of the Gospel in Foreign Parts, chartered in England in 1701. But after the Revolution, the formal, chartered corporation flowered lavishly in the new United States, again especially in New England. In the nineteenth century, America would lead the world in adapting the corporation to private business enterprise. In the early years of the republic, however, state legislatures chartered corporations mainly for governmental, charitable, and other not-for-profit purposes.[15] The most common purpose turned out to be religious evangelism. In the thirty years after 1787, New Englanders established at least 933 Bible, tract, missionary, and Sunday school societies, many of them granted corporate charters.[16] The first of these was the Society for Propagating the Gospel.

The chief virtue of the corporate form was the power to accumulate, manage, and perpetuate capital. The trustees of the SPGNA sought to build a permanent endowment through bequests, special church collections, donations, and membership subscriptions. In the early 1790s, the society also received a multiyear grant from the Massachusetts General Assembly for missionary work in Maine. By 1810, the society's income derived in part from member subscriptions and private donations, but the bulk of it flowed from the endowment, which was invested in stocks, bonds, and mortgages.[17]

To manage these funds and to do the business of the corporation, the society needed effective administration. This required the usual array of officers—president, vice president, treasurer, secretary, and so on—and the requisite committees, membership lists, and annual reports. But charity book work imposed a special kind of administrative burden. Books were manufactured goods, expensive, somewhat delicate, and shipped from a central depot,

Boston. Because the books were not sold but were given away freely (gratuitously, as the society put it), distribution could not be based on price or commission, as in commercial bookselling. The books had to be entrusted to someone accountable to the society, who had to assess the needs of a mission district and to evaluate the worthiness of book recipients. With no price system to allocate books, the society was forced to rely on administration to make sure the books were delivered "to those least able to purchase, and best disposed to use them." To do this, the society endeavored to engage "persons of integrity and virtue only" as missionaries and as local volunteer agents in distant places. The society required its missionary-agents to gather information and to keep "a daily journal," including "an exact account of the manner in which you distribute the books entrusted to your care."[18] Such tools of accounting and management of employees in the field would become common in religious publishing societies in the nineteenth century.

The Society for Propagating the Gospel never grew much beyond its modest beginnings, and in the nineteenth century it was eclipsed by other, more aggressive missionary and publishing societies. But the SPGNA had a permanent impact, nonetheless. The model of organization pioneered by the SPGNA in the 1790s—the corporate form, organized upon a base of members, administered by a board of trustees or managers, and funded by a combination of membership subscriptions, special donations, and legacies—flourished in the world of religious associations and publishing societies in nineteenth-century America. More important, the Society for Propagating the Gospel provided an inspirational model of evangelical action that would gradually grow into genuine human agency. As the Reverend Thomas Barnard told the society's annual meeting in 1806, "Christianity entered our world, and began to be propagated; not by the mere action of the Almighty power from whence it was derived; but by it, in cooperation with human beings, illuminated and qualified for the sacred purpose."[19]

The first missionary societies to draw on the model of the SPGNA were the Missionary Society of Connecticut (founded 1798) and the Massachusetts Missionary Society (founded 1799). Drawing on Calvinist notions of knowledge, reason, and faith, the founders of both of these societies stressed the sovereignty of God and the depravity of man—and yet the ability of human beings to do something. "Since men are rational beings and capable of exercising themselves, in moral matters," Cyprian Strong told members of the Connecticut society in 1800, "and, particularly, in the great affair of their salvation, although salvation itself be the effect of Divine power, it is reasonable, that some exercises should be prescribed for men." One of the chief promoters of the Massachusetts Missionary Society delivered a similar message to that society. Nathaniel Emmons, a New Divinity man who insisted on the moral inability of sinners to repent and who saw much darkness and wickedness in the world of 1800, nevertheless prodded his society to evangelical action. "We . . . believe Satan will shortly lose his malignant influence, and that all nations will embrace the Lord Jesus," Emmons declared:

> Remembering then, that Zion's God directs all the revolutions of kingdoms and empires; that the hearts of all men are in his hand, we cannot but thankfully notice the christian charity and zeal which have lately originated and endowed so many Missionary Societies, both in Europe and America. . . . While, therefore, we expect the rapid wheels of providence will soon introduce the joyful days of Zion, shall not the followers of the lamb gird up their loins and double their diligence?[20]

For these societies, as for the Society for Propagating the Gospel, neither divine providence nor evangelical ardor was enough. Information and practical organization were crucial as well. The Massachusetts Missionary Society frequently badgered its missionaries for hard information from their fields (market research, we might say) and for careful accounts, including "particular abstracts and summaries for publication." Diligence and system were preferred to enthusiasm. Though the goal—the salvation of souls—was sublime, the method was mundane. According to the managers, a good missionary report should be detailed and factual, reading something like this: "During my absence, I rode eleven hundred and thirty-three miles, preached sixty-three sermons, baptized fifteen persons, attended thirty-four conferences, gathered two churches and assisted in gathering another. I received, in contributions for the use of the Massachusetts Missionary Society, 21 dols. 78 cents, and was in their employ sixteen sabbaths."[21]

The new missionary societies valued books and used them in their work, but books were not their main business. The first American organization devoted solely to religious books and tracts was the Massachusetts Society for Promoting Christian Knowledge (MSPCK), organized in 1803, largely through the efforts of Jedidiah Morse. Like the SPGNA, this new society was patterned on a British model, the century-old Society for Promoting Christian Knowledge. The Massachusetts society also drew inspiration (as well as books and tracts) from the Religious Tract Society, founded in London in 1799, and its predecessor, the Cheap Repository for Moral and Religious Tracts, founded by the prolific evangelical writer Hannah More in 1795.[22] After 1811, the MSPCK supported missionaries, but before then the work was strictly books and tracts. The society conducted its first "general distribution" in 1804, giving away 6,253 tracts and books. In a second major effort in 1806, the society distributed 9,174. Most of these were scattered through the rural reaches of Massachusetts, including Maine; some went to Rhode Island, Virginia, South Carolina, and Georgia. By 1815, the society had distributed 30,350 tracts and 8,224 bound volumes.[23]

In organization and fundraising, the Massachusetts Society for Promoting Christian Knowledge followed the model of the SPGNA, though with some important changes. Like its predecessor, the MSPCK struggled to accumulate a permanent capital fund. The society launched its work with an endowment of $1,165 contributed by the twelve original founders. Other donations plus reinvested interest brought this fund to $2,983 by 1815. By 1815, however, most of the society's new money went directly into its "distributing fund" for current expenditures. Over its first twelve years of operations, the MSPCK's expenditures totaled $7,673, its income $7,741, only $1,200 of which derived from endowment interest. The rest came from annual assessments of members, annual subscriptions by individuals, and special donations raised by small missionary societies, which were sprouting up throughout New England. This gradual move to income derived from other societies and from expanded membership subscriptions, rather than from a permanent endowment, would become increasingly common among tract and book societies in the nineteenth century.[24]

The Massachusetts Society for Promoting Christian Knowledge also followed its predecessor in its administrative arrangements for the acquisition and distribution of books and tracts. It contracted with a printer, William Hilliard of Cambridge (later Hilliard and Metcalf), for print work and for handling its inventories. It arranged with ministers and pious gentlemen in distant places to gather information on the state of religious practices in their areas and to conduct distributions of books and tracts. To ensure that the publications were given only to deserving indigents, the society provided printed instructions to volunteers and required them to sign formal agreements, to keep daily journals, and to submit detailed written reports. The society's annual reports and financial accounts were considerably more detailed than the reports of the SPGNA; they included lists of all titles in print, tables of county-by-county figures on distributions, reports on income and expenditures, and printed forms for subscriptions and bequests. In its annual reports, the society also greatly expanded a feature that would become a commonplace in organizational reports in the nineteenth century: the publication of excerpts from the reports of workers in the field on how the tracts and books were received.[25]

What the agents found in the mission fields was just what the society's founders feared: appalling ignorance. The inhabitants of these "desolate, benighted" places, these "dreary, deadly" lands, were wicked, vulgar, poverty stricken, and illiterate. They profaned religion, denounced learning, and ridiculed missionaries. One agent wrote of a group of young men setting up a Bible as a target and pelting it with stones. Another told of a town that had "no minister, except a negro, who could not read a word . . . and often boasted, 'I did not know B from a bull's foot.' " Where were these strange, foreign places, and who were these exotic folk? These were the mission fields of nearby New Hampshire and Rhode Island, and the people were not totally irreligious. According to the agents, they were Methodists, Baptists, Smithites, Christyans, and assorted Arminians, Socinians, and Freewillers.[26] But for the Congregationalist agents and managers of the MSPCK, that was irreligious enough. For them, genuine religion was not about miracles, enthusiasm, direct revelation, human will, or even uninformed faith; it was about knowledge, learning, and reading the word. The Massachusetts Society for Promoting Christian Knowledge was thoroughly committed, not just to Christianity, but to Christianity in print.

Illiteracy, however, was not the only problem. The society's managers could see that the United States in the years after 1800 was fast becoming saturated with printed material, and people were reading it. But, unfortunately, in the view of the society, much of this material promoted infidelity and irreligion. This was an evil print culture in the making, borne up by a rising tide of French atheism abroad and Jeffersonian infidelity at home. Bad books, not just the lack of books, were now a serious problem in America, just as they were abroad.[27] Jedidiah Morse was horrified by this poisonous new literature of infidelity, deism, and sectarian error, and he believed that evangelical religious tracts and books were the correct and sufficient antidote to it. Morse's colleague Eliphalet Pearson, one of the society's early presidents, agreed. "What was to be done?" he asked. "An antidote was necessary to counteract this moral poison. By books of almost every description had this poison, variously prepared, been circulated through the community. Books therefore appeared the proper vehicle for conveying the only remedy, *the truth, as it is in Jesus.*" Pearson explicitly renounced censorship. The proper course, as the society's British mentors had put it, was "to foil the enemy at his own weapons."[28]

The founders of the MSPCK imagined orthodox Christianity under siege from two opposite flanks. On the one flank was atheism, deism, and sundry religious liberalisms, ranging from unitarian Congregationalism to Methodism to Universalism. To moderate Calvinists such as Jedidiah Morse, these movements, even though nominally Christian, were radically irreligious, for they rejected fundamental tenets of Reformed Christianity, including the sovereignty of God and the depravity of man. They seemed to teach instead that man possessed the moral ability to seize God's grace and to effect his own salvation. On the other flank were the fierce Calvinists who preached the doctrines of unconditional election, limited atonement, and the inability of man either to choose or to reject the irresistible grace of God. One MSPCK agent lamented that many people he met in Rhode Island had been so disgusted by some severe Congregational missionaries' emphasis on predestination and damnation that they vowed never to converse with a missionary again. Supporters of the MSPCK denounced missionaries of that stripe as vigorously as they blasted deists and liberals.[29] Falling between these extremes was a middle way, a moderate, evangelical Calvinism that reserved for God the power of grace but allotted to men and women the ability to learn and to teach the knowledge that opens the heart to grace. For these moderate Calvinists, evangelism was preeminently about knowledge, not about the flash of religious enthusiasm or the selective gathering of the elect into covenanted churches.[30] And for them the quintessentially modern vessels of religious knowledge were cheap books and tracts.

What kinds of publications did the society distribute? The society's first choice was the Bible, of course. After that, the managers aimed to stick with simple "evangelical truth and piety," to avoid sectarian controversy, and yet to maintain "the essential and distinguishing doctrines of the gospel, as professed by our pious ancestors, the first settlers of New England." Their publication lists included recent works borrowed from English sources, such as the tracts of George Burder, Richard Cecil, and William Newman. Many publications were older classics of English Puritanism, including the devotional works of Philip Doddridge, the hymns of Isaac Watts, and Richard Baxter's *A Call to the Unconverted*, which John Eliot had worked so hard to publish in the Massachusett Indian language more than a century before. From the outset, the founders of the MSPCK promised orthodoxy: "No atheistical, deistical, skeptical, heretical, nor immoral book or tract; nor any book or tract that is tinctured by any such principle or sentiment, shall ever be purchased, printed, published, or distributed by this Society."[31]

Jedidiah Morse, founder of the MSPCK and key promoter of the SPGNA, was an ideal entrepreneur of print-driven evangelism. Morse styled himself an orthodox Calvinist, and he made his reputation within Congregational denominationalism as the scourge of Unitarians and the negotiator of rapprochement between the moderate Old Calvinists, who dominated the MSPCK, and the more strict New Divinity men, who were influential in the new missionary societies that had sprung up in Massachusetts and Connecticut. Morse cared about theology, but he cared more about pragmatic, organizational success. He was part of a generation of New England Federalists who, when displaced from political life by the Jeffersonian revolution of 1800, turned increasingly to voluntary associations and institutions.[32] In the first decade of the nineteenth century, Morse launched a new seminary (Andover) and a new religious magazine (the *Panoplist*), as well as the MSPCK. Meanwhile, he nurtured yet another career as the author of popular works on American geography and history, which placed him squarely into the practical business world of book publishing.[33]

In the years after 1810, Morse and his colleagues began to work out a plan for evangelical publishing that was much more grand than that of either the Society for Propagating the Gospel or the Society for Promoting Christian Knowledge. As small missionary and tract societies modeled on the MSPCK proliferated, the need for a larger, umbrella society grew as well, a society that could actually publish tracts and books in large numbers and sell them at cost to smaller societies for free distribution. The MSPCK began to play this role in a minor way, but very minor. In its annual report for 1815, the society listed a total income of $7,741 for the period 1803–1815. Tucked away among the figures appeared a modest but portentous entry of $191.65: "Receipts for books and pamphlets sold."[34]

For Morse, as always, the signs of the times were mixed. The current outlook was dark, but dawn loomed just over the horizon. In "To the Friends of Religion in New England," published in 1814, Morse wrote:

> The period is portentous. While war with its dire calamities rages
> over Christendom; while the worst passions of men are let loose
> from restraint; while the world is overturned and the earth rent in
> pieces; it becomes the friends of Zion to adore the righteous Provi-
> dence that is thus smiting the nations. But it becomes them not to
> sit down in sloth. God has made every man responsible for the use
> or abuse of his personal influence. . . . Multitudes throng the road to
> death. These immortal creatures cannot be brought to consideration,
> till they are first brought to read. They cannot read without books;
> and a great proportion of them will never have books, unless they
> are furnished by the hand of charity. Here then is an urgent call for
> the exercise of Christian benevolence on a large scale.[35]

Morse's audacious plan for Christian benevolence on a large scale took institutional form in the New England Tract Society (founded 1814). And Morse was not alone. Other entrepreneurs of religious publishing were hatching similar grand schemes about the same time. Their stories are the subject of chapters 3 and 4.

For five decades after the Revolution, visions of the Christian millennium inspired religious missionary and publication societies. But the relationship between the millennium and religious publishing changed, gradually but dramatically. In 1793, Samuel Hopkins imagined the millennium as an era of what we today would call mass media and globalization. He believed that in the millennium all people would again speak and read one universal language, as they had before Babel, and that this language would be used to communicate all knowledge to everyone. At times sounding more like a media economist than a theologian, Hopkins wrote that a universal language coupled with new printing technologies would "render books very cheap, and easy to be obtained by all. . . . Many hundreds of thousands of copies may be cast off by one impression, and spread over all the earth. And the Bible, one of which, at least, every person will have, by printing such a vast number of them at one impression, may be afforded much cheaper than it can be now."[36] For Hopkins, one of the chief glories of the millennium would be cheap books for everyone. But, significantly, Hopkins expected these revolutions in printing, publishing, and reading to come *in* the millennium, not *before* it. By 1814, some entrepreneurs of religious publishing, such as Jedidiah Morse, had pushed the idea further and could imagine something like mass media even during the premillennial era of tribulation. Filled with energy and ambition as well as foreboding, and schooled in both popular publishing and philanthropic organization, Morse knew that great things could be done, events could be made to happen. Yet neither Hopkins nor Morse granted full agency to man. God alone could make his kingdom come.

By the 1830s, this kind of sober, Calvinist postmillennialism had eased into something not Calvinist at all, though knowledge, printing, and literacy remained at the heart of it. In 1833, a Boston publisher brought out a book titled *The Harbinger of the Millennium*, by William Cogswell. Except for its fascination with mass media and new printing technology, this book was utterly unlike Hopkins's book on the millennium forty years before. It was neither a biblical exegesis nor a treatise on eschatology. It was, essentially, a recent history of missions and evangelical reform societies, especially religious publishers. It was about organization, not theology. Looking back on the early nineteenth century, a period that Hopkins could only imagine, Cogswell believed that religious mass media had already arrived, and, through the "systematic effort" of publication societies, these new media were the potent means that were actually bringing on the millennium. "Let us rejoice in the different religious enterprizes," Cogswell declared. "They all help to usher in the latter-day glory of Zion. The day-star has already risen. The twilight has appeared. Signs burst forth on every side and indicate that the world's redemption is drawing nigh. This age of benevolent effort and of pouring out of the Holy Spirit, is the Harbinger of the Millennial day."[37]

3

The New Mass Media

Economic Foundations

Jedidiah Morse's 1814 plan for the New England Tract Society called not just for a larger organization with regional or even national reach, but for a different kind of organization: an umbrella society that would supply tracts to smaller societies by selling them at cost. This was the first such plan for religious tract work in the United States, but it was similar to another form of charity book work that had made its appearance in America in 1808–1809: the Bible society. The purpose of a Bible society was simple: to circulate the Christian Scriptures as widely as possible. Organizationally, a Bible society was no different from a religious tract or book society, such as the Massachusetts Society for Promoting Christian Knowledge—except that the Bible was a very big book (a thousand pages or more). The production and distribution of Bibles was a costly enterprise. It is not surprising that the economic foundations of not-for-profit religious publishing were laid by early Bible society entrepreneurs who sought technologies and business strategies, both beneficent and efficient, for placing a Bible into the hands of everyone who needed one.

In the beginning, it was taken for granted that Bible societies in America, like other charitable associations, would give their alms—Bibles—freely. The goal of their founders was not profit but universal circulation of the Scriptures. Their favorite Bible passages emphasized the word *free*: "freely ye have received, freely give," and "the word of the Lord may have free course, and be glorified."[1] Their business was benevolence, not bookselling. But though the word of God itself was free, the vessels that carried the word were the costly works of man. Like God's grace, the word was abundant, but the books were, to use an economist's term, scarce. They had to be manufactured, purchased, and delivered. All of the early American Bible societies, especially the larger ones, struggled to work out a practical mix of religion and economics, of abundance and scarcity, of benevolence and business. For the Bible society managers, the pressures were great to give freely; the pressures were great to sell as well. In the end, it turned out that the best strategy was to do both. And the best way to do both, in charity Bible work and in charity tract work, seemed to be through centralized production and locally organized distribution.

A wave of enthusiasm for charity Bible work swept the United States in 1808 and 1809, and that enthusiasm was matched by organizational effort. Within a span of a few months, Bible societies were launched in Pennsylvania, Connecticut, Massachusetts, New Jersey, and New York. The founders of these societies, many in communication with each other and with evangelical Christians in England and Europe, shared a sense of the "remarkable signs of the times." War and chaos abroad portended a time of tribulation, and yet the nations of Europe were forming Bible societies to spread the knowledge of salvation. The American founders were struck by the opportunities as well as the calamities of the age. "A *universal* circulation of the Holy Scriptures" was now possible, the Connecticut Bible Society declared in its 1808 address to the public. "We believe it . . . to be unquestionable, that the christian world has never had opportunities of distributing the bible, equally favorable to those which present themselves to the present generation." In a burst of millennial confidence, the organizers of the Bible Society of Philadelphia proclaimed in 1809 that "before the present generation shall have passed away, the holy Scriptures will be read by all the principal nations under heaven: And thus the way be opened for the fulfillment of the prediction of the prophet, '*The earth shall be full of the knowledge of the Lord as the waters cover the sea.*' "[2]

Though Bible societies had recently been organized in Denmark, Germany, and other European countries, the chief inspiration for the American Bible movement was the British and Foreign Bible Society (BFBS), founded in London in 1804. American evangelicals were enormously impressed by what the British had done in just five years. In their initial addresses to the public, all the new American Bible societies praised the work of the BFBS in Bible translation and distribution. The first reports of the new Philadelphia society and the new Connecticut society both noted that the British and Foreign Bible Society had spent £12,000 sterling (some $54,000) on Bible production in just one year, an astonishing sum to the Americans. The leading light of the New-Jersey Bible Society, Elias Boudinot, pronounced the early work of the BFBS nearly miraculous. But the British society did more than lead by example. Through reports, letters, personal connections, and even financial aid, the officers of the BFBS directly encouraged their American cousins to organize societies and to join the worldwide Bible movement.[3]

In most ways, but not every way, the American societies followed the model of the British and Foreign Bible Society. Most important, the Americans, like the British, sought to avoid sectarian controversy by distributing the Bible "without note or comment"—no prefaces, no interpretations, no explanatory apparatus. And the Bible would be provided in vernacular translations, in the languages that ordinary people could read. This was the practical application of the Reformation doctrines of *sola scriptura* and the priesthood of believers. The founders of the Bible society movement in both England and America hoped to unite Protestant Christians—from Anglicans and High-Church Episcopalians to Calvinist Congregationalists to Arminian Methodists—on the one evangelical doctrine they shared: Bible literacy. The BFBS even drew in a few Roman Catholics, though the Americans could not tolerate quite that much ecumenism. Like their British mentors, the American founders understood a Bible society to be not so much a religious organization itself as an organization that provided the *means* of religion.[4]

In two keys ways, however, the Bible society movement in America differed from the British model. One difference lay in local versus national organization. The British were keen to see established in the United States a society that would encompass the entire country. They pressed their American colleagues to create a truly American Bible society in the largest and most centrally located city, Philadelphia. They even offered financial aid to make that happen. The managers of the new Bible Society of Philadelphia were eager to get the money, but they were at pains to convince the British that a national society was impractical in a country as large and diverse as the United States. In "the American confederacy," localism in an organization was necessary to maintain vigor and enthusiasm, the Philadelphians argued in their early reports; the state level was the highest level at which an efficient organization could be maintained.[5] Only a few years later, a national Bible society was organized in the United States, but localism would remain a major factor in the American way of charity Bible work.

Another difference between the British and the Americans involved a crucial economic question: should Bibles be sold or given away for free? From the beginning, the British and Foreign Bible Society had a policy of selling, not giving—at least for common English-language Bibles distributed in the British Isles. Bibles should be cheap, very cheap. But not free. The chief reason for selling Bibles at home in Britain was to finance foreign translations and distributions abroad, but there was another reason as well. The BFBS managers believed that recipients would value their Bibles more if they paid for them. If they got them for free, they might discard them or, perhaps even worse, pawn them. Even the poorest recipient should be put on a time-payment plan of a penny a week until the book was paid for. The British understood the "Bible transaction," as they called it, to be a commercial one; it was about reciprocity, not gratuity. The shiftless poor were to be taught lessons in thrift and financial planning as well as religion. To do this, wrote one BFBS staff member, the "evil of gratuitous distribution" must be avoided.[6]

The Americans thought otherwise, especially in the early years. For them, gratuitous distribution was what a Bible society was all about. At heart, these were traditional local charitable societies, whose alms just happened to be books. The constitutions of the new societies affirmed that their purpose was to supply Bibles to the "destitute," a term they used to mean lack of Scripture as well as lack of money. The Bible Society of Philadelphia was the first American society to get under way (December 1808), and the opening sentence of its constitution made its charitable mission clear. That mission was "the distribution of [the Bible] among persons who are unable or not disposed to purchase it." In an address to the public in 1809, the organizers of the Philadelphia society declared that "it is the intention of the Society to offer the Bibles which they disperse, as the sacred treasure which they contain is offered, 'without money and without price.' "[7] This phrase, which comes from the Book of Isaiah (55:1), is one of the many passages in the Bible that use metaphors of money and price to suggest pricelessness. It became a favorite of the American Bible movement. It reads in full: "Ho, every one that thirsteth, come ye to the waters, and he that hath no money; come ye, buy, and eat; yea, come, buy wine and milk without money and without price."

The Americans were aware of what we today would call the "free rider problem," but they were much less concerned about it than the British were. (*Free riders* are people who get more benefits from an organization than they pay for or deserve. They take from a collective effort more than they give.) The managers of the BFBS worried that the unscrupulous poor would abuse a system of gratuitous distribution. The only way to make a man value a Bible, they believed, was to make him pay for it. The Americans disagreed. The Philadelphians, for example, declared their concern for people *unwilling* as well as *unable* to buy. The New England founders agreed. It should come as no surprise, the Connecticut Bible Society managers wrote, that people often were careless of the Bible, that even people who could afford to buy a Bible often would not do so. Their resistance was due to sin. Should they, therefore, be excluded? Not at all. "They are surely to be pitied the more," the Connecticut managers declared in their initial public address. "They are under a more pressing necessity of aid." Sin is the fault of the sinner; these conservative Congregationalists had no doubt of that. "But is the sinner not therefore the object of charity? . . . Is it not the fault, the sin, of mankind that renders charity, in *temporal* things, necessary?" The managers of the Philadelphia society even professed to be unconcerned that a recipient of their charity might sell or pawn a free Bible. "It is scarcely possible to traffic it away," they said. "Wherever it shall be found, it will be a Bible still, and it may teach the knave to be honest, the drunkard to be sober, and the prophane to be pious."[8]

Selling versus giving, national versus local organization, exclusion versus inclusion of free riders—these were practical business issues, but they were fundamental religious issues as well. The founders of the first American Bible societies were necessarily prudent businessmen, but their goal was extravagant and non-economic. It was to carry the word to everyone.

Though a half dozen state-level Bible societies were founded in the United States in 1808–1809, the Bible Society of Philadelphia quickly emerged as something more than the first among equals. Despite encouragement from England, the Philadelphia managers had declined to launch a national Bible society in America. For organizational and economic reasons, they chose to turn inward and to keep their charitable work close to home. But economic forces pulled them outward as well, and the Philadelphia story nicely illustrates how religion and economics, charity and business, would eventually be reconciled in not-for-profit religious publishing in nineteenth-century America.

At first, beginning in 1809, the efforts of the Bible Society of Philadelphia to carry out its charitable mission were simple and unsystematic. It raised money through local membership subscriptions, bought Bibles and New Testaments (mainly from Mathew Carey of Philadelphia, the leading publisher of Bibles in the United States at that time), and then gave them to the poor folk of Philadelphia and vicinity. It also sent copies off to more distant lands with missionaries, travelers, and pious sea captains. This was standard charity. But in their first door-to-door canvasses, the managers of the society were stunned by the magnitude of the problem they faced:

> The deficiency of Bibles has been found to be much greater than was expected; and it is believed to be as great in many other places. The number of families and individuals, who are destitute of a copy of the Scriptures is so great, that the whole of the funds in the possession of the Society, could be profitably expended in supplying the wants of this city alone; and the opportunities of distributing them in other places are so numerous, that if their funds were tenfold as great as they are, they would still be inadequate to satisfy the demand.[9]

With this grim scene looming before them, the managers of the Bible Society of Philadelphia made a fateful decision. They would become *publishers* as well as *distributors* of the Bible. And they would become capitalist manufacturers, sinking their meager resources not into an interest-bearing endowment, as the old Society for Propagating the Gospel had done, but into a new and capital-intensive printing technology: stereotype plates.

In Philadelphia in 1809 this was a daring and visionary plan. Stereotype printing was still a new process even in England, where Cambridge University Press had just begun a few years before to adapt it to Bible printing. In stereotypography, a plaster-of-paris mold was made of a page form of movable type, and in that mold a thin metal plate was cast. After each mold was made, the types could be redistributed and used again. In this way, a set of printing plates for an entire book could be made and then used, stored, and used again without the expense of keeping moveable type "standing" or of resetting type for each new edition. Stereotype plates were not the economical choice for all types of printing, but they were well suited to the printing of steady-selling books in many editions over time—books such as the Bible.[10]

But stereotype plates were expensive. The single set of plates that the Philadelphia society ordered from England cost about $3,500, an enormous sum for these fledgling publishers. The managers of the society were wary but resolute:

> When they considered that the possession of a set of such plates would enable them to multiply copies of the Bible at the lowest expense, and thus render their funds more extensively useful; and still more when they reflected that it would put it in their power to give greater effect to the operations of other Bible Societies, which are

springing up daily in every part of the country, the Managers did not hesitate to order the plates to be procured and forwarded from London as soon as possible. The expense is indeed great, when compared with the fund at their disposal; but they were willing to believe, that the obvious and high importance of the measure could not fail to draw from the public liberality a sum sufficient to counterbalance the heavy draught.[11]

This statement suggests the economic implications of stereotype printing. Even though the society would continue to contract out its printing, it would henceforth be a publisher of Bibles as well as a buyer and distributor of them. And to derive the full benefits of the economies of scale from its capital investment in plates, the society would have to become a large publisher, serving other societies' needs as well as its own.[12]

In other words, the Philadelphia society would have to *sell* Bibles. This was a problem, however, because the constitution of the society seemed to contemplate only gratuitous distribution. One way of solving the problem was to deny that it existed, at least at the wholesale level. The managers took for granted that they could sell at cost to other Bible societies, especially the large societies that had loaned them money to help buy the plates. They were less certain that they could sell to ordinary people or sell at a profit. As late as 1813 the managers turned down a request from a Virginia minister for Bibles to be sold to raise a fund to buy tracts for gratuitous distribution. Even this scheme for selling Bibles in a way that would raise money for free tracts was deemed "inconsistent with the avowed object of this Society." Instead, the society sent him twenty-four Bibles to be given to the destitute in his neighborhood—for free.[13]

After some creative soul searching, however, the managers decided that they could sell Bibles, so long as the income was plowed back into the charitable enterprise. Their reasoning was ingenious and is worth quoting at length, for it nicely reveals the seductive power of economies of scale in stereotype printing:

> The copies of the sacred Scriptures, from your press, it is expected, from the excellence and beauty of the type, will be much superior to those which are generally in our market; and the managers have, at several meetings, deliberated on the question, Whether it be their duty to use the means which Providence has put in their hands for increasing your funds (all of which must be expended in a gratuitous distribution of the sacred volume) by selling, at a moderate gain, to other persons, as well as to Bible societies, who may prefer

their copies, and send orders. After mature consideration of this question, they have resolved, that . . . it is both their duty and their interest, to supply any orders that may be sent to them for Bibles.

After the introduction of stereotype printing, then, economic logic prevailed over constitutional scruple. Indeed, of the very first stereotype edition of the Bible (1812), 250 copies of 1,250 "were on finer paper and for sale."[14] Happily, duty and interest could be made to coincide.

Still, most of the new stereotyped Bibles were intended for free distribution. But here, too, the economies of scale in stereotype printing encouraged (even forced) the managers to expand their own work dramatically. How they planned to do this was outlined in *An Address of the Bible Society of Philadelphia to the Friends of Revealed Truth in the State of Pennsylvania*, a pamphlet widely circulated in 1810, shortly after the society had decided to invest in stereotype plates. To raise money to pay for the plates and to set up a delivery system for the flood of Bibles that would soon flow from them, the society announced a plan to establish "a little Bible Society in every congregation of Pennsylvania." These congregational groups would collect donations and seek members for the parent society in Philadelphia. In return, they would "be allowed to demand Bibles from the managers of the Society, at first cost, and to the full amount of the contributions made;—the Bibles to be distributed as a free gift, by the congregations, or by their agents, to the poor of their own neighbourhood, or to whomsoever else they may choose." Though the Philadelphia society would become a publisher and wholesale bookseller, the auxiliary societies must remain purely charitable, the managers declared. "Let it be remembered that the sole object to which this money is to be applied—the sole object to which by our charter we can apply it—is the purchase and printing of the Bible, to be ultimately bestowed as a free gift."[15]

Thus, as the production side of Bible work became more centralized, the distribution side became more localized. The central society increasingly needed local auxiliaries for two reasons. First, its large capital requirements now forced it to seek funds far beyond the city of Philadelphia, where it was beginning to tap out local largess. As the managers admitted, "Those individuals among ourselves who could reasonably be expected to make donations of important sums, have mostly made them; and the contribution of five dollars, paid by each individual who becomes a regular member of the Society, and which can be demanded but once, has likewise been received." They needed new money and therefore new people and new organizations to get it. Second, the society needed local help with distribution. It needed volunteers to go out into the neighborhoods and give Bibles away—to "seek out the individuals who ought to receive the invaluable present of a Bible."[16]

The local auxiliaries would also play a role in handling free riders. Despite their initial sanguine approach to the free-rider problem, the managers in Philadelphia gradually became more concerned as expenses mounted and distribution moved beyond their own participation and control. Bibles were costly, and without the invisible hand of a price system to allocate them, a conscious human choice—to give or not to give—had to be made. Only local people knew the local scene well enough to distinguish between the pious poor and the "impostor." Accordingly, the managers directed the little Bible societies to make "the most particular inquiries . . . into the character of those who should apply for bibles. . . . The best endeavours should be used, before a book was bestowed, to ascertain that it was likely to be applied to its proper use. . . . All proper means should certainly be devised and employed, to prevent impositions and to detect impostors." At minimum, this meant careful, house-by-house investigations and interviews. At the same time, the Philadelphia managers insisted that Bible distributors not exclude worthy free riders (the pious poor) and instructed them not to worry too much about seemingly unworthy free riders (impostors), for even they might benefit mightily in the end. In their third annual report, the managers even quoted their own early statement that a Bible was a Bible, no matter how a person obtained it:

> Care, indeed, must be taken not to discourage, but rather to invite
> applications, from those who need, and who will duly prize the gift
> of a bible; . . . though the guilt of the frauds contemplated admits of
> no palliation, yet the favourers of this charity ought to be less influ-
> enced by the apprehension of them, than perhaps in any other con-
> cern; for though a bible may be improperly obtained, yet "wherever
> it shall be found, it will be a bible still; and it may teach the knave to
> be honest, the drunkard to be sober, and the profane to be pious."[17]

By 1816, then, on the eve of the founding of the American Bible Society in New York City, the economic arrangements of charity Bible work were largely in place in Philadelphia. In less than a decade, the Philadelphia society had evolved from a local charity, passing out a few free books, to a substantial publisher and high-tech printer. In its first three years of stereotype printing, the society had published 55,000 volumes. At the same time, it had become the parent society of a far-flung network of local societies. These two developments were inseparable. The Philadelphia society required a multitude of local organizations precisely because it had become centralized and highly capitalized. The mission remained unchanged: "Our Society has for its chief object the free gift of the holy Scriptures to all the poor of the state of Pennsylvania."[18] But after 1812, when it launched its stereotype-printing enterprise, the society needed to *sell* Bibles as well as *give* them; indeed, it needed to sell them in order to give them. Large revenues were needed to achieve the economies of scale required to lower the costs sufficiently to give Bibles away. And that was the ultimate goal. The stereotype plates and the little societies made it possible.

As the Bible Society of Philadelphia experimented with ways to achieve both economy in production and efficiency in charity distribution, the managers discovered, without fully realizing it, that giving and selling need not be dichotomous. They chanced upon the rudiments of what economists call *price discrimination* or, as I like to call it, *differential pricing*. Differential pricing means simply selling at a variable price, charging each buyer the price he or she is able or willing to pay, *all the way down to zero*. That last phrase is crucial, because setting a price at any level above zero would exclude some buyers: those who would pay less or those who would receive the product for free. And any number excluded is too many, if the goal is *universal* circulation. On the other hand, setting the price at zero, though splendid for universal circulation, is unnecessarily inefficient, because it subsidizes those buyers who can pay and who are willing to pay. For a commercial business to produce and sell at a price of zero or at any price below the marginal cost (the cost of the last unit produced and sold) would be irrational. But for a religious publisher whose goal is not profit but universal circulation, selling at a price that falls to zero is not irrational at all; it is simply charity.

The Philadelphians did not follow the logic of differential pricing this far; they did not attempt to set a price for each individual recipient. The society worked out, essentially, four prices: (1) a premium price for trade Bibles on fine paper; (2) a price modestly above cost for regular Bibles sold to outsiders; (3) a "first cost" price for Bibles sold to other societies and auxiliaries; and (4) a zero price for Bibles given to destitute persons through the Philadelphia headquarters directly or through the little societies. Though economic pressures to sell were great, the Bible Society of Philadelphia in its early years tried to remain true to the traditional American belief that charity meant giving, not selling. Most Bible grants must be free, they believed. This fundamental principle, however, was gradually eroding. It would erode still further in the era of the great national societies that emerged after 1816. Those societies grasped, better than the early Philadelphia managers ever did, the logic of differential pricing for universal mass media.

The Bible Society of Philadelphia played a unique role in the Bible movement in America before 1816. Because of its early adoption of stereotype printing, it became a national supplier of Bibles even to other large state societies, though it was not a national society in any other sense. At the same time that the Philadelphians plunged into the risky venture of stereotype printing, the New-York Bible Society held back. In 1809, the New York managers considered importing stereotype plates but decided against it because of the "delay, expense, and uncertainty." Instead, they purchased 2,000 Bibles from Hudson and Goodwin, printers of Hartford, Connecticut. In 1812, they were drawn into the supply system that the Philadelphia society had launched. In their 1813 report, the New York managers described their dealings with Philadelphia. Because of the "heavy cost" of the stereotype plates, the Philadelphia society had solicited business from all of its fellow institutions. The New Yorkers voted to loan Philadelphia £100 sterling (appropriated from a BFBS grant), to be repaid in stereotyped Bibles at the rate of 65 cents per copy. The New Yorkers were delighted with the deal, "which, considering the beauty of the type, and the superior quality of the paper on which it is printed, is a cheaper rate than any edition of the Bible could be procured at in this country." The Bible Society of Philadelphia was soon able to lower the price, selling to New York and other societies at a price of 60 cents per Bible, leather bound, and 22 cents per New Testament.[19]

These first stereotyped Bibles were no cheaper than the cheapest editions that could be obtained from leading American Bible printers, such as Mathew Carey of Philadelphia or Hudson and Goodwin of Hartford, though they may have been of higher quality for the low price. Carey, in particular, had made himself a major publisher of Bibles in part by holding costs down through high-volume production. By the time the Bible societies arrived on the scene, Carey had two Bibles set in type that he kept "standing," which allowed him to avoid typesetting and proofreading costs for each new edition. Though this required a very heavy capital investment sunk into type, it allowed Carey to keep these Bibles in print over time with no composition costs and, thereby, to undersell all other American publishers and importers.[20] But Carey and other publishers made the most money from more fancy and expensive Bibles for the commercial trade, and they gradually abandoned plain, cheap Bibles to the Bible societies and their stereotype plates. The New-York Bible Society acquired its own plates in 1815; the Bible Society of Baltimore had a set by

1816. After 1816, the stereotype process would become standard in Bible society publishing in America; it would take a few more decades to become commonplace in all book publishing.[21]

By 1816, the year the American Bible Society was founded, more than one hundred Bible societies were operating in the United States. The oldest and largest of these had evolved into suppliers for many smaller societies. The defining characteristic of the system was increasing concentration in publishing and printing alongside continued decentralization in organization and distribution. After eight years, the Bible movement in America had distributed altogether about 150,000 Bibles, according to calculations of the Connecticut Bible Society. Though impressed by this number, the Connecticut managers noted that it paled in comparison with the British and Foreign Bible Society's output, which had reached 1.3 million copies by 1816. Yet the end was nowhere in sight. Supply seemed to increase the demand, and the more the societies accomplished, the more remained to be done. Echoing their colleagues in the Bible movement across America, the Connecticut managers pronounced the work arduous but the times propitious: "It is the general opinion, that the promised glory of the Church on earth is to be realized not by miraculous interposition, but through the agency of man."[22]

Compared to a Bible, a religious tract is a very inexpensive vessel for carrying the word. While a complete Bible may run to a thousand pages or more, the typical tract in 1800 was just four or eight pages. Though its Gospel message may have been a pearl of great price, the tract itself was a species of literary ephemera—simple, free, something light to catch the attention of the busy sinner in an unguarded moment. Because tracts differed from Bibles, tract societies differed from Bible societies, and the entire tract movement differed as well. Selling versus giving, for instance, was less of an issue, for tracts were always designed to be given away freely (though payment might be accepted). Sectarian controversy, on the other hand, was more of an issue. Tracts were not simply Bible excerpts "without note or comment"; they were little narratives or homilies written by religious individuals situated in some doctrinal tradition. Because tracts were so small in size, the need to stereotype them was less pressing, though tract societies eventually did move into stereotypography because tracts, like Bibles, were steady sellers, routinely published in many editions over time. Finally, tracts involved a style of reading different from Bible reading. They were designed to be popular literature—edifying, of course, but entertaining as well.[23]

Still, tract societies and Bible societies shared the same goal—not profit, but the universal circulation of the word—and to achieve that goal they adopted similar business strategies. In both Bible work and tract work, the message was abundant and free, but the medium was necessarily a manufactured product. The economics of not-for-profit tract publishing and distribution required a style of organization similar to a Bible society, a similar blend of business and benevolence. Like the Bible movement, the religious tract movement tended toward centralization in production and localization in distribution. As in Bible work, the economic imperatives of tract work encouraged the system of a large parent society affiliated with numerous local auxiliaries.

The first American tract society to move beyond the model of simple alms-giving charity was Jedidiah Morse's New England Tract Society, founded in 1814, a time of rising enthusiasm for home missions, religious magazines, and the organized distribution of Bibles and tracts. The New England Tract Society was something new. While the Bible Society of Philadelphia had reluctantly backed into the role of national wholesaler of Bibles because of its investment in stereotype plates, the New England society was designed from the beginning to be a wholesaler, though not a stereotype printer.[24] Only after ten years of operation did the society decide to invest in plates. Eventually, tract publishers, like Bible publishers, adopted the new technology, but not as quickly.

The founders of the New England Tract Society declared explicitly that their job was sales, not charity: "This establishment, considered by itself, is not, at present, to act as a Charitable Society in the *gratuitous* distribution of Tracts; but to furnish to Tract Societies, on the easiest terms, the most abundant means of accomplishing their designs." In a burst of enthusiasm, the founders ordered the printing of 300,000 copies of fifty different tracts even before the society's formal organization in May 1814. Within a year of that date, the society had published 141,000 more tracts and had established formal relationships with several printers, mainly Flagg and Gould of Andover, Massachusetts. Meanwhile, it had begun to link up with existing local tract societies and to form new ones around the country.[25]

To supply these far-flung societies, the New England Tract Society developed a depository system. The General Depository was located first in Boston and after 1816 in Andover at the offices of Flagg and Gould. By 1817, thirty-three regional depositories had been established, most in New England, but several as far south as Charleston and as far west as Natchez. Operated by volunteer agents out of their houses, offices, or churches, these depositories by 1817 held stocks of tracts worth $6,406, ranging from $1,072 (Boston) to $19.65 (Concord, N.H.). The tracts remained the property of the national society. That is, the depositories held them on consignment, with full right of return, and the agents received a 10 percent commission on sales to societies.[26]

A national distribution system built upon scattered regional depositories required considerable capital, but not capital vested in a permanent endowment, in the tradition of the Society for Propagating the Gospel, nor in manufacturing equipment (stereotype plates), in the tradition of the Bible Society of Philadelphia. The managers of the New England Tract Society, now operating as wholesale merchants, needed working capital in the form of tracts. And they never had enough. In report after report, the managers laid out their needs, hopes, and desires: "A larger capital is needed to enable the Committee to prosecute the business to the best advantage. It must be evident to every Member and Friend of the Society, that a large quantity of Tracts must constantly be kept on hand, in order to meet the wishes and expectations of those who would purchase."[27]

By 1821, the society had seventy-one depositories, and the managers estimated that they needed capital sufficient to supply each with an average of $100 worth of tracts (100,000 pages, approximately). To support these regional depositories, the General Depository required an equivalent stock on hand. Thus, the society needed capital of at least $14,000 just to maintain efficiently its current operations. But it had less than half that amount. The managers dreamed of a day when they could support a hundred depositories, with stocks sufficient to circulate 6 million tracts a year. (The actual number circulated in 1821 was 468,000.) Because these tracts would be sold to auxiliary societies, the stocks could be replenished without reducing the capital. This was the "principle of permanency," as the managers explained it to members and friends: "The funds which are given to this Society are never expended. They remain as in a bank, to be employed forever in furnishing Tracts. And not only is the interest employed, as with permanent stock in other Societies, but the principal. And yet no part of it is ever expended."[28]

This was working capital, and the managers of the New England Tract Society relentlessly sought ways to get it. Memberships provided some income, though the society retained only one-fourth of each member's subscription; three-fourths was returned in the form of tracts. Auxiliary societies were also supposed to transmit one-fourth of their income to the national society, but few did. Miscellaneous donations and legacies raised some money, though never enough. In the rough economic year of 1819 (a financial panic swept the nation that year), donations amounted to a paltry $22.13. By 1820, the society's finances were in "a state of much embarrassment," and "the publication of

Tracts was much retarded, and almost suspended for a time." In desperation the managers hired an itinerant agent, Louis Dwight, to solicit donations throughout New England. Remarkably, he was able to raise nearly $4,000, though about half of that came in the form of loans.[29] By 1821, the society had incurred a debt of $2,500, all sunk into tracts, with few prospects for repayment. One money-making scheme that paid off for the society was the launch of the *Christian Almanack*, an annual publication that became a popular steady seller and major source of income after 1821. Finally, the society started up the *American Tract Magazine* in 1824, a chief purpose of which was fundraising.[30]

The managers of the New England Tract Society imagined that if they just had enough working capital the strategy of selling at cost would produce "permanency," a favorite word in annual reports. "The sum is never expended, or even diminished," they said again and again, "but, should Providence so order, it may continue in operation to the end of the world." Throughout its first decade of operations, however, the New England Tract Society never achieved that goal. The managers struggled with slow remittances, overdue payments to printers, meager donations, and nagging debts. They regularly begged supporters for unencumbered donations. "The constitution provides that each donor may receive three fourths of his donation in Tracts," they wrote in 1820. "Let this right be relinquished, at least, till the society is able to pay its debts, and borrow no more money."[31] In the end, the society never accumulated the capital it thought it needed to achieve the "delightful feature of permanency."[32]

Finally, in 1824, despite its financial troubles or perhaps because of them, the New England Tract Society decided to follow the path taken by the Bible Society of Philadelphia twelve years before. The annual report for 1824 announced that "the Committee have begun to use *stereotype plates*. This mode of printing will promote correctness, and at the same time add to the neatness of the impression, and a large advance of capital, will be required, yet your Committee are assured, that the pecuniary interests of the Society, will, in the progress of a few years, be essentially promoted by the measure."[33]

Though always struggling financially, the New England Tract Society churned out several hundred thousand tracts each year, with production peaking in 1824 at 770,000 tracts. Altogether the society published 4.2 million tracts and served more than 500 local societies during its ten years of independent operations.[34]

In this era, many tract societies were established in the United States, including large societies in New York (1812), Boston (1813), Philadelphia (1815), Baltimore (1816), and Hartford (1816). Two of these (New York and Philadelphia) published more than a million tracts each before 1824.[35] The New-York Religious Tract Society was the largest, though considerably smaller than the

New England Tract Society. Like the New Englanders, the New York managers imagined themselves in a battle of words with the Devil. "The press is a weapon," they wrote in their first report, "which the great adversary of the Church has learned to employ, in the cause of error and licentiousness. . . . Shall not the friends of righteousness on the earth, employ equal diligence and skill, in diffusing the light of the knowledge of the Lord?" Though able to print nearly a quarter of a million tracts per year by 1824, the New York society, like the New England society, was perpetually overextended, with the managers regularly bemoaning "the great embarrassment of their finances." But they knew they had two things going for them: the great power of the printed word to save souls and the splendid location of New York City for the future of religious tract work in America.[36]

For the tract movement, the year 1825 was analogous to the year 1816 for the Bible movement. It was the year a truly national tract society was organized, the American Tract Society of New York City. But already by 1824 the economic foundations of religious tract work had been laid. Like the Bible Society of Philadelphia, the New England Tract Society had pioneered a system of tract work that depended upon centralized printing (including stereotypography) and distribution through local auxiliaries. Like the Philadelphians, the New Englanders sold tracts so that others could give them away. Like the Bible movement, the tract movement worked out a practical amalgamation of business and benevolence and was now set on a course toward large-scale manufacturing and national organization. That is the story of chapters 4 and 5.

Many of the economic terms that I have slipped into this chapter—economies of scale, differential pricing, free rider, universal circulation, even supply and demand and mass media—are anachronistic jargon. The managers of the early Bible and tract societies did not describe their work in those terms; they preferred the language of Protestant Christianity and the King James Bible. And yet, beneath the surface and between the lines, their writings suggest an intuitive understanding of the economics of both mass media and evangelism. In our day, nearly the opposite is true, at least among scholars who practice the sociology of religion. Today, there is more jargon, but less understanding. Recently, the sociology of religion has been infused with the ideas and language of rational-choice economic theory. Sociological studies of religion—on both contemporary and historical topics—now brim with discussions of religious markets, religious capital, religious commodities, supply-side analysis, terms of exchange, consumer preference, maximizing behavior, costs and rewards, externalities, free riders, firms, competition, and deregulation.[37] Some of this scholarly work has dealt directly with religious movements in early nineteenth-century America, and it has been quite useful in suggesting why some religious organizations grew and some declined.[38] Yet my sense is that the early Bible and tract society managers had a better grasp than some of our own sociologists and economists of the economics of media and evangelism.

Current sociologists of religion often speak of a "new paradigm" in their field. The chief aim of this new paradigm has been to overthrown the "secularization thesis," the idea—going back to Weber, Durkheim, Marx, and even Smith and Hume—that modernization inevitably leads to the decline of religiosity and religious institutions. The new sociologists of religion instead see sustained and even growing religious belief and practice in modern societies, especially in the United States, and they attribute this growth to disestablishment of state churches and the rise of religious pluralism and competition. The new paradigm is a theory of religious markets that emphasizes the supply side: the more religious supply, the more religious practice. In short, when people have choices, they choose; and the more choices, the more religion. Finally, the new paradigm stresses *rational* choice. Though religious commodities are obviously more elusive and ethereal than, say, corn or refrigerators, rational-choice theorists such as Laurence Iannaccone insist that "individuals act rationally, weighing the costs and benefits of potential actions, and choosing those actions that maximize their net benefits."[39] If the social scientific study of religion was once a branch of abnormal psychology, today it is a branch of neoclassical economics.

But the rational-choice theory of religion is challenged by an interesting historical anomaly: strict conservative churches have tended to do better than lax liberal churches, even though the former require their adherents to pay higher "costs" for presumably similar "benefits." To explain this apparent anomaly, the rational-choice theorists turn their attention to the economic nature of organizations and to the free-rider problem. The free rider has long been a central concern in the sociology of organizations. Voluntary associations, including churches, produce "collective goods" that benefit individuals. Laurence Iannaccone describes what can and often does go wrong:

> The problem arises whenever the members of a group receive benefits in proportion to their collective, rather than individual, efforts. Because each member benefits whether or not he contributes to the

common cause, each has a strong incentive to minimize his own efforts and "free ride" off those of others. If enough members yield to
this temptation, the collective activity will surely fail.[40]

In their provocative study *The Churching of America*, Roger Finke and Rodney Stark make much of the free-rider problem in churches and sects, including those of early nineteenth-century America. Like Iannaccone, they argue
that "religion is a *collectively produced* commodity," that is, that individuals gain
religious rewards within a shared, communal experience. Free riders consume
the group's resources—both material and psychic—without contributing their
fair share. This saps the vitality of the group. Since the early nineteenth century,
strict churches in America have been more successful than lax churches because they have devised ways to exclude these organizational free riders. By
requiring more sacrifice of their members, strict churches raise the cost of
membership, which screens out free riders and thereby raises the average level
of participation and commitment. Paradoxically, in an organization, an increase
in the cost of participation can produce *more* participation and therefore more
individual satisfaction.[41] In short, more cost means more benefit.

This turn to organizational sociology may be helpful in studies of free
ridership in organizations, including religious organizations, but the managers
of the early American Bible and tract societies had a completely different understanding of the free rider in religion more generally. Their understanding
was closer to the model of the free rider as a consumer of media than as a
member of an organization. They understood a fundamental economic fact
about media: the message (the word) and the medium (the book or tract) are
different things with different cost structures. To put it in economic terms, the
message has no marginal cost, that is, it is not used up when consumed (read).
If there is no cost at the margin, if the product is never used up, there may be
no reason to exclude free riders. The managers routinely spoke of "the word"
in the same language they used to speak of the grace of God. It was, as St.
Paul put it, abundant, free, sufficient for all. Even the strictest Calvinist in the
early nineteenth century did not suppose that God's grace was a scarce commodity in the economic sense. But, of course, the *medium* was another kind
of product altogether. Books and tracts did carry a cost, and for Bibles that cost
was substantial. For commercial publishers, the cost of the medium was the
key, and free riders were excluded by price. But in Bible and tract societies, the
focus of the managers was always on the message, which was—and must
remain—abundant and free. Their whole purpose was to make the medium
as free as the message.

In short, evangelical religious publishers *sought* free riders. The distributors of religious media reckoned the utility of their products (their use to the consumer) to be valuable beyond price. That utility was nothing less than eternal life. Yet consumers did not easily recognize that value. They often scorned it. Such a striking difference in the valuation of utility meant that many consumers would buy far less of a product than the publishers thought was good for them. This was a recipe for subsidy. And subsidy, in this sense, was what religious publishing—indeed, all religious evangelism—was all about.

In the language of religious media and religious evangelism, whether in the past or today, the targets of charity are not savvy consumers seeking religious utility. They are not seekers at all. They are sinners, resisting the word. They are lost sheep, whom the things of this world have led astray; rational choice will not bring them into the fold. These sinners are the free riders sought by evangelism. Though the founders of the early Bible and tract societies did not speak in the jargon of economics, they did understand this principle. They sought those who were *unwilling* as well as *unable* to buy. They would have agreed with the current supply-side portrayal of the religious economy. The more the word is circulated, the more the demand for it—but only if sinners (free riders) have the word pressed into their hands. "The more the Bible is distributed," the Connecticut managers wrote in 1816, "the greater is the desire of possessing it among those who before felt themselves in no calamity from a destitution of that book. By giving to one we awaken the anxiety of others. . . . Thus diffusive and reciprocal is the spirit of the Gospel. Thus charity is repaid; and she gains by giving."[42]

Religious evangelism and religious publishing merge easily because their economic natures are the same. The word is free. The media message, like its subject—the grace of God—has no cost at the margin. These are "public goods," an economist would say, goods that are not used up when consumed. The mission of the evangelist and the religious publisher in early nineteenth-century America was to deliver the free word as freely as possible. The free rider could be carried at little cost (indeed, in a latter age, the age of broadcasting, he could be carried at no cost at all). In organizations—including churches and even little Bible societies—the exclusion of free riders through strictness, discipline, and sacrifice may well be needed for cohesiveness and strength. That is important, and it is part of the story of chapter 5. But evangelism and mass media move in another economic realm, a realm of infinite abundance. The Bible has passages aplenty to vindicate the proponents (and the economists) of religious strictness and discipline. But the religious publishers sang a different economic song: "Freely ye have received, freely give," "The Word of the Lord has free course, and is glorified," and "Yea, come, buy wine and milk without money and without price."

4

The New Mass Media

National Institutions

In the summer of 1813, Samuel Mills, a young graduate of Andover Seminary full of evangelical zeal, had just returned from the first of his two missionary tours to the Ohio and Mississippi river valleys. He was appalled by how many people in the West lacked Bibles; he was cheered by how eager they were to receive them; and he was frustrated by how difficult it was to collect Bibles in the East for distribution in the West. By 1812, Bible societies were flourishing in most of the older states, but this very proliferation of societies had made the work difficult for Mills and his traveling companion, John Schermerhorn. "At the present time, to accomplish our object," he wrote in a letter to Jedidiah Morse's religious magazine, the *Panoplist,* "we have to go or send to the several Bible Societies from Maine to Georgia; and to wait until we receive information from the directing Committee. Four, five, or six months must elapse, perhaps a year, before we are able to make a report. And by this time the most favorable opportunity for distributing the Bible may have passed by." And they may not have received the Bibles they needed anyway. "After all our efforts, we may have to send to the Directors of the British and Foreign Bible Society, requesting that *they* would make a donation of Bibles for the supply of the destitute within the limits of the United States." Given that the United States was at war with Great Britain at the time, this struck Mills as a rather embarrassing circumstance. What was needed, he wrote, was "some general bond of union" in the American Bible movement—specifically, "a *General Bible Society*."[1]

Samuel Mills's plea for national union in Bible work was slightly premature in 1813. This was an inauspicious moment for American nationalism and American enterprise. A war was on; battles raged on the northern and western frontiers; international trade was dead; and sectional animosities ran so high that some New Englanders were agitating for secession. Two years later, however, the national climate had improved dramatically. At the end of his second missionary tour of the West in 1814–1815, after the Treaty of Ghent and after the battle of New Orleans, Mills returned to a country flush with optimism.[2] Business entrepreneurs everywhere sensed that the time was now ripe for large-scale commercial enterprise. Religious entrepreneurs, adding their own millennial gloss to the optimism of the day, agreed. A year later in New York City, a group of enterprising men from a half dozen religious denominations made Mills's dream a reality by founding the American Bible Society, the first of three great national, multidenominational religious publishing houses. Over the next several decades, the American Bible Society (1816), the American Tract Society (1825), and the American Sunday School Union (1824) created something new in America: the national not-for-profit business enterprise devoted to universal mass media.

These societies were launched into what historians have come to call the "market revolution," which swept America after 1815.[3] Like commercial entrepreneurs, the entrepreneurs of religious publishing were energetic national businessmen. They envisioned the entire country (even the world) as a field for their enterprises. Though many had roots in New England, they proposed to concentrate capital and manufacturing in the nation's largest cities, mainly New York, and to organize efficient distribution systems that would extend to every corner of the land. They were wedded to commerce and infatuated by new technology.

But unlike their fellow marketers, these society managers were not profiteers. Their work was *in* the market but not *of* it. They proposed to make supply drive demand. Their goal was to achieve universal circulation of their product in the most efficient way possible, not because it would generate profit but because it would save souls. Universal circulation, however, did not necessarily mean free circulation. Building upon economic foundations laid by the Bible Society of Philadelphia and the New England Tract Society, these national institutions blended centralization of production with localization of distribution. To manufacture good-quality books cheaply, they needed modern technology and centralized printing facilities. To deliver books widely, they needed networks of local auxiliaries. To do these things efficiently and on a grand scale, they needed capital. And so they stretched the idea of charity to include retail sales as well as free distribution. In order to give books freely to the indigent and indifferent, they needed revenues gained from sales to those who could and would pay. By 1830, all three national institutions—the American Bible Society, the American Tract Society, and the American Sunday School Union— would launch "general supplies," national efforts to place religious publications into the hands of *everyone* in the United States. These general supplies—the first mass media in America—were remarkable efforts, but in the end they failed, undone by the very market forces the societies had hoped to subvert.

In retrospect, the founding of the American Bible Society in 1816 seemed almost inevitable, the logical culmination of the Bible movement that had begun in 1808 and the beginning of a new era of national voluntary organizations, the so-called Age of Reform. At the time, however, it seemed a risky venture, championed by a handful of individuals linked to Andover Seminary. When Samuel Mills first began to promote the idea of a national association in 1813, few existing Bible societies were interested. Indeed, when Mills wrote to the Bible Society of Philadelphia to report on his 1812–1813 tour of the West, he did not even mention the plan for a national society that he had sent to Jedidiah Morse. Mills knew that the Philadelphians had opposed the formation of a national Bible society in 1808–1809 and had not changed their minds. He understood that "the funds of the Philadelphia Bible Society were nearly exhausted, by the purchase of their stereotype press," and thus he could make "no promises to the Bible Societies of the west of any immediate or particular assistance." So, Mills simply thanked his Philadelphia patrons for their past support and registered his hope that as their means increased, their support of the West would increase as well. Meanwhile, back in Andover, he plotted with Morse and other evangelical entrepreneurs to ignore the naysayers and to press forward with plans for a genuine national Bible society.[4]

One state leader outside New England who responded favorably to Mill's entreaties was Elias Boudinot, president of the New-Jersey Bible Society. Boudinot was an old Federalist, a friend of George Washington, former president of the Continental Congress, leader of the Alexander Hamilton forces in the House of Representatives in the 1790s, and a prominent Presbyterian layman. In 1801, out of power and out of sympathy with the Jeffersonian temper of the times, the sixty-year-old founding father published his first book, *The Age of Revelation*, a Bible-based denunciation of Thomas Paine's *Age of Reason* and the secular spirit of the French Enlightenment. In the preface to his book, Boudinot wrote how shocked he had been to learn "that thousands of copies of the *Age of Reason* had been sold at public auction, in this city [Philadelphia], at a cent and a half each, whereby children, servants, and the lowest people, had been tempted to purchase, for the novelty of buying a book at so low a rate; my attention was excited to find out what fund could afford so heavy an expense, for so unworthy an object." Boudinot resolved to dedicate much of his remaining life and fortune to building a counterfund and counterorganization for what he considered a more worthy object. His labors led to the formation of the New-Jersey Bible Society in 1809 and the American Bible Society in 1816.[5]

Boudinot was much impressed by the missionary work of Mills and Schermerhorn, and in August 1814 he persuaded the New-Jersey Bible Society to issue a call to existing Bible societies to send delegates to a meeting in Philadelphia the next May for the purpose of forming a "General Association of the Bible Societies in the United States." Almost immediately several key societies objected, including most prominently the Bible Society of Philadelphia. The Philadelphia response was thoroughly negative and was widely circulated. The Philadelphia managers, led by Episcopalian bishop William White, president of the society, published a long list of objections to the New Jersey plan. It was unseasonable during time of war and economic travail; it was unprecedented, as no similar institution existed in America; it was unnecessary, given the number of Bible societies already in operation; it was likely to be injurious to the work of existing societies, sapping their vitality and their funding; and, finally, it was impracticable.[6]

In a reply published in January 1815, Boudinot rebutted these arguments point by point and in minute detail, though the gist of his reply was simple: he urged the Philadelphians (and other critics) to have faith in God and to take the risk, just as they had risked their own funds and future by investing in stereotype plates. Boudinot believed that Christ's second coming was near, that time was short, and that a national society would surely succeed if people simply believed it could. He was especially puzzled, even annoyed, by Bishop White's claim that the project was "impracticable." "I confess this objection surprized me . . . ," he wrote. "If we never meet together on the subject, it certainly will be impracticable. But as we can do it if we will, and if we should do it and agree on some useful plan and carry it into execution, it will be practicable."[7]

A year later, in early 1816, the prospects for a national Bible society, like those for the country, appeared considerably brighter. Mills had returned from his second missionary tour in the spring of 1815 and had plumped for the national union idea all along the Atlantic seaboard on his way home by ship from New Orleans to Boston. Boudinot had kept up the agitation as well. Meanwhile, the Connecticut Bible Society voted its support for the idea in May 1815, and the New-York Bible Society came on board in late fall. The Philadelphians remained intransigent, but the tide seemed to be turning. In January 1816, Boudinot issued another call to state and local societies to send delegates to an organizational meeting set for May 1816. There was one major change from the year before, however. This time, the meeting would held be in New York, not Philadelphia.[8]

The move to New York was championed by another evangelical Federalist who had lately joined Mills's and Boudinot's crusade: William Jay, son of John Jay and a leader of the Westchester (New York) Bible Society. Shortly before the May gathering, Jay published a model constitution for a national society, which served as the basis for the constitution actually adopted. Jay's society would be a completely new and independent organization, not a mere confederation of delegates of existing societies; it would have its own individual members and auxiliary societies. It would be an efficient business enterprise capable of gathering and publishing information from the field, as well as printing Bibles. It would be conducted by a board of managers, the majority of whom must be laymen "because laymen are generally more conversant with the details of business, and better qualified to superintend the concerns of an extensive establishment." And it would be headquartered in New York City. "New York," he wrote, "is fast becoming the London of America, and already possesses facilities for correspondence with and transportation to all parts of our own and other countries, which are enjoyed in an equal degree by no other city on the continent."[9] A noncommercial, charitable business was a business nonetheless, Jay believed, and the future of American business lay in New York. In 1816, that seemed to be true.

When the news of the Treaty of Ghent ending the War of 1812 arrived in February 1815, "tumultuous joy and gladness" swept through the streets of New York. Within twenty minutes, most of the windows on lower Broadway were illuminated. Soon, skyrockets were flying. When the news hit the markets the next day, commodity prices dropped precipitously. Public officials, merchants, ordinary people, even newspaper editors were ecstatic. "It is really wonderful to see the change produced in a few hours in the city of New-York," the *Evening Post* declared. "In no place has the war been more felt nor proved more disastrous; putting us back in our growth at least ten years; and no place in the U. States will more experience the reviving blessings of a peace." As if to confirm the city's new role as the communications nexus of America, the news had arrived first in New York and from there was dispatched by special express to Albany, Boston, Providence, and New York's new satellite city, Philadelphia.[10]

New York was the ideal location for a national Bible society. Already the nation's largest city by 1810, New York would lead the United States into its historic economic takeoff after 1815. No other American city could match New York's access to foreign sources of supply (such as paper) and to the burgeoning settlements of the trans-Appalachian West, where Bibles were most needed. By 1821, some 23 percent of the nation's imports came through New York. By 1831, the proportion was 50 percent, and no longer was there any doubt that New York was the commercial metropolis of the New World. In 1825, the year the Erie Canal was completed, 500 new mercantile businesses opened their doors in the city.[11] New York also became a leading center for manufactures and technology, including technological innovations in the art of printing. The founders of the American Bible Society believed that "concentrated action is powerful action," and they proposed to concentrate everything—administration, capital, and technology—in New York.[12]

For the concentration of capital, New York was the obvious choice. Though New Yorkers were probably less religious than Bostonians, those who were religious tended to have more money. Many, in fact, were themselves New Englanders by birth and faith, though nouveau New Yorkers by business. And at least some of these evangelical New York businessmen were in a position by the 1810s and 1820s to endow Christian benevolence with financial clout. In the early 1820s, for example, the American Bible Society was able easily and quickly to raise $22,500 for a new building. Perhaps the most important of these rich, benevolent New York businessmen was Arthur Tappan, a native of Northampton, Massachusetts, who made a fortune in New York in the import trade. Tappan, always a great friend to the American Bible Society, supported dozens of philanthropic and reform causes, ranging from pure missionary crusades to radical antislavery organizations. In the 1820s, New York was a place where men could afford to be benevolent.[13]

The concentration of printing in New York also worked out well for the American Bible Society. This was an era of rapid technological innovation in printing, and the ABS was an early adopter of stereotypography, steam-powered printing, and machine-made paper. In the 1820s, these innovations inspired the society's managers to believe that the concentration of all Bible manufacturing in New York was more than efficient; it was providential. By the end of the 1820s, the society's New York operation was one of the largest and most highly capitalized publishing houses in the country, virtually monopolizing the production of inexpensive Bibles in the United States. As early as 1827, the managers of the society reported, matter-of-factly, that the "printing of Bibles and Testaments in this country has fallen, in good measure, into the hands of the American Bible Society." This claim was exaggerated; other publishers continued to print and sell Bibles. But it is true that commercial publishers in the 1820s and 1830s gradually turned to more expensive, illustrated, annotated, and specialized Bibles, while conceding to the ABS virtually the entire market for cheap Bibles "without note or comment."[14]

In 1816, it already seemed obvious that stereotype printing was the key to low-cost, high-volume Bible production, and immediately after the founding of the society the new Board of Managers resolved that their "first exertions ought to be directed toward the procurement of well-executed stereotype plates." Almost immediately, the three stereotypers then operating in New York began to compete for the business of the American Bible Society. In August, the board sought bids from all three, and awarded its first contract for three sets of plates costing $4,000 to D. & G. Bruce. Meanwhile, the New-York Bible Society voted to turn over its plates to the new national society.[15] By the end of its first year, the society had printed about 10,000 Bibles—the first imprint of the American Bible Society. By the end of its third year, the society owned eight sets of plates for the whole Bible and two for the New Testament and was printing more than 70,000 volumes annually on eight hand presses, which were in constant use. Within eight years, the ABS owned twelve sets of plates and had struck off 265,000 copies at a cost of $250,000.[16] The acquisition of stereotype plates would remain a major item in Bible society budgets, and the ABS would remain a major supporter of the handful of firms that comprised the stereotype founding industry in New York.[17]

Even the most zealous centralizers in the American Bible Society did not at first propose to concentrate all of its stereotype plates in New York. They feared the country was too large for that. Instead, they imagined a network of several regional printing centers. In late 1816, the managers voted to send plates to Lexington, Kentucky, to serve the trans-Appalachian West. By 1819, the Kentucky Bible Society was printing Bibles for the ABS.[18] Very quickly, however, the Kentucky experiment proved to the New York board that branch printing was a mistake. The theory was fine, but the practical results were not. Western paper was expensive and poorly made; press work was sloppy; bindings were inferior. An ABS committee reported that suitable materials and skilled workers were not available in Lexington, and, in any case, the society there had neither the funds nor the demand to keep the plates efficiently employed. "The Committee," they wrote in 1819, ". . . feel confident that the Auxiliary Societies in the Western Country would be more satisfactorily supplied with Bibles from the Depository in New York, notwithstanding the expenses of freight and transportation." The New York board decided to keep the Kentucky plant going for a few more years, because of the currency crisis that followed the Panic of 1819. (For several years, western money was virtually worthless in New York, and western Bible societies begged to be allowed to spend their bouncing banknotes in Lexington.) But, except for currency exchange, regional printing had few advantages, and the first branch was the last.[19]

Stereotyping was the most important but not the only technological innovation in printing that the American Bible Society helped to bring into practical service in America. The society was also one of the earliest publishing houses to install steam-powered presses. Of course, power presses were not necessary for mass printing; many hand presses could do the job. And the Bible Society had at least twenty hand presses at work constantly by the mid-1820s. But the faster a single press could work, the more efficiently it could employ the capital tied up in stereotype plates. Moreover, cheaper unskilled labor could be hired to operate power presses, a kind of efficiency not always greeted with sanguinity by the skilled artisans of the printing trade. But for the owners of capital, efficiency is efficiency, and from the beginning, the managers of the American Bible Society actively encouraged innovations and improvements in the printing press itself.[20]

Most significantly, the Bible Society was an early adopter of Daniel Treadwell's steam-powered bed-and-platen press, the first generally successful powered printing press to be built in the United States. Treadwell, a Bostonian, had studied steam-powered printing in England during a visit in 1820. The most famous English power press at that time was the cylinder press developed by Friedrich Koenig and first put into service on the *Times* of London in 1814. The Koenig press was extremely fast, but it was expensive to install, was hard on type, and was not suited to fine-quality work. In America, where newspapers were highly localized and individual newspaper circulations were small, it was not newspapermen but book printers who first experimented with power printing. And for them, in the 1820s, the cylinder press was unsuitable. What Treadwell did was design and build in 1822 a press that stood, technologically, between the traditional hand press and the new cylinder steam press, which would soon be adopted in America for large-circulation newspapers and periodicals. In Treadwell's design, much of the work was still done by hand, and the pressure was applied downward by a platen. But there was no bar to pull. The platen was moved by steam, water, or horsepower, and the speed of the work was much faster than on a hand press. The Treadwell press, later improved by Isaac and Seth Adams, remained the standard machine in much of the publishing industry for more than fifty years.[21]

The managers of the American Bible Society learned of Treadwell's experiments as early as 1822 or 1823 and were immediately interested. They contacted him in 1823 and began negotiations that would eventually lead to the installation of sixteen Treadwell presses by 1829. These presses were probably built by Robert Hoe of New York, under a franchise arrangement with Treadwell. The firm R. Hoe & Company, then in its infancy, grew to be the leading manufacturer of printing presses in nineteenth-century America.[22] Commercial book publishers, by contrast, embraced steam-powered printing much more slowly, in part because they believed the early power presses could not produce the kind of fine work they desired. Harper and Brothers was the largest commercial book publisher in New York and in the United States at that time, and it installed its first steam-powered press, an improved Adams, in 1833. Harper had only one horse-powered Treadwell press and no more than seven hand-powered presses in 1829, the year the American Bible Society had sixteen steam presses and twenty hand presses in service.[23]

The introduction of mechanical power at the American Bible Society was managed by Daniel Fanshaw, chief printer to the society for many years. Fanshaw was the leading entrepreneur of the steam-powered bed-and-platen press in New York City. He held exclusive rights to use the Treadwell press in New York, and he was an enthusiast of power printing. In the late 1820s, he was constantly seeking loans and mortgaging his property to finance more steam presses, and he was constantly nagging manufacturers such as Hoe for faster delivery. Fanshaw was also an expert in the use of stereotype plates, having worked for D. & G. Bruce before signing on with the ABS about 1817. Fanshaw seems to have been more of a developer than an inventor, though he is sometimes listed as a claimant to the title of the first steam-powered printer in America.[24]

In addition to its early promotion of stereotyping and power printing, the American Bible Society was also a pioneer patron of machine papermaking in the United States. Before 1800, papermaking was a slow, costly handicraft. A skilled worker made each sheet of paper individually on a screen frame dipped by hand through a vat of water and macerated cloth fibers. The first successful papermaking machine was developed by Nicholas-Louis Robert in France in the late 1790s. Robert's machine, which was later taken over by the Fourdrinier brothers of London, used an "endless wire cloth" (screen belt), in place of the hand-held frame, to produce an endless web of paper, without the need of skilled workers. And it did the work, as Robert said in his patent application, at "infinite less expense."[25] Though Robert exaggerated the cost savings of his machine, his process, under the name Fourdrinier, did transform the paper-making process, allowing for increased production and uniform quality, while gradually cutting the price of paper by about 60 percent over the first half of the nineteenth century.[26]

The first papermaking machine in America, somewhat different from a Fourdrinier, was developed by Thomas Gilpin of Delaware and put into service in 1817. Gilpin's product immediately sparked the interest of newspaper and book publishers, and the first American book to be printed on American machine-made paper appeared in 1820, published by Mathew Carey of Phila-delphia. In the late 1820s, several Fourdrinier machines (the style of machine that proved most successful) were imported from England and France. Then in 1829, George Spafford and James Phelps began to build their own improved Fourdrinier machines in South Windham, Connecticut. The buyer of the first Fourdrinier papermaking machine to be built in America was Amos H. Hub-bard, who had been operating a handmade-paper mill at Norwich, Connecti-cut.[27] Hubbard was a chief paper supplier to the American Bible Society.

In its earliest years, the ABS preferred paper imported from France and southern Europe, and tried aggressively to have Congress exempt its imports from the 30 percent duty imposed by the tariff of 1816.[28] The society also tirelessly shopped around among domestic papermakers in the 1810s and early 1820s. By the end of the 1820s, the society had developed major contracts with three or four manufacturers, including most prominently Amos Hubbard. Hubbard not only supplied paper to the American Bible Society, he enthusi-astically supported its work. He was an active member of the Norwich auxiliary, and in August 1829—just three months after the installation of his new Four-drinier machine—he became a "life member" of the national society, making his donation in reams of paper rather than money.[29]

The ABS was almost certainly Hubbard's chief customer, perhaps his only customer, in the first few years after he automated his mill. He worked closely with Daniel Fanshaw, the society's printer, to rapidly expand Bible production in 1829 and 1830. From time to time, Fanshaw complained, but in general the ABS was pleased with the quality and the price of Hubbard's machine-made paper. And Hubbard by 1830 was a true believer in the process. "I find that the Paper-makers generally do not feel very cordial towards me because I sell paper so cheap," he wrote. "One man remarked that it would oblige him to stop his Mill."[30]

By the late 1820s, the managers of the American Bible Society felt that they had developed the technical expertise—in stereotyping, printing, and pa-per manufacturing—to make the whole nation their audience. In 1829, society secretary James Milnor declared that the printing plant had the capacity to produce a Bible for every family in the land—between 500,000 and 600,000 annually. "It is apparent," he told the annual meeting, "that there can be printed and bound, and issued from this Depository, during the ensuing two years, and for every succeeding period, all the Bibles and Testaments that public exigency in its most extended requisition can call for at our hands."[31]

In sum, New York was a splendid place for a national publishing enterprise—and not just because of economies in printing. As early as 1820, the American Bible Society managers believed that New York also met the communication and transportation needs of the national institution very well:

> The constant intercourse maintained between a great metropolis,
> like New-York, with other ports, and with the interior of the country
> in every direction, supplies opportunities, at every season of the
> year, of conveying Bibles, with cheapness, security, and expedition,
> to the most distant places. And when to these propitious circum-
> stances is added the comparative difference of expense in conduct-
> ing an establishment on a large and on a contracted scale, in the
> purchase of materials, the cost of labor, and the superior execution
> of the work, the Managers feel warranted in the belief, that Bibles,
> issued from the general Depository of this Society [in New York],
> can be afforded at a much lower rate, in proportion to their quality,
> than from any other source.[32]

But not everything could be done in New York. To power its enormous, centralized publishing operation, the American Bible Society, like the Philadelphia Bible Society before it, needed a decentralized network of local societies. James Milnor put it nicely in his exhortation to the annual meeting in 1829:

> The machinery of a mill may be mechanically perfect in all its parts,
> but not a wheel will move without the impetus of water. And so
> those stereotype plates, giving so much facility to the art of printing,
> and those power-presses, multiplying with such unexampled rapidity
> impressions of the sacred pages, to produce their expected results,
> must be supplied, and for these means, the occupants of these
> plates and presses must be dependent on their Auxiliaries.[33]

The American Bible Society depended upon auxiliary societies because it was a charity publisher. Unlike a commercial publisher, the society could not use a market-price system to get the books out. Local societies were needed to raise money and to distribute Bibles in their areas. From the beginning, the ABS relied heavily on its auxiliaries, and its annual reports were filled with news and information about the auxiliary societies, especially the formation of new ones. The society added 84 new auxiliaries in its first year of operations, 157 in 1817–1818, 194 in 1818–1819, and 207 in 1819–1820. The society made most of its free grants of Bibles through the auxiliaries, and this was how the managers preferred it: "Whether the Scriptures shall come to the needy as a gratuitous gift immediately from the Parent Institution, or from its Auxiliaries, it amounts to the same thing in the end—'The Word of the Lord has free course, and is glorified.' "[34]

But, like the Philadelphia society, the American Bible Society also needed to sell books in order to give books away. Simple charitable donations were insufficient and inefficient. Eventually, the American Bible Society traveled further down the road to selling than the Philadelphia society had dared to go. The ABS managers came to believe that to achieve real efficiency in charity publishing on a grand scale, they needed to develop a full-blown system of differential pricing (selling books at a price each individual recipient was able or willing to pay, all the way down to zero).[35] And only local auxiliary societies could make that happen.

In the beginning, the plan of the American Bible Society was the standard Bible society mission of "gratuitous distribution": giving Bibles away. Like the Philadelphia society, it would sell books at cost or even below cost to its auxiliaries, and the auxiliaries would distribute them for free to the worthy poor. In 1819, however, the society began to urge auxiliaries to move away from simple giving and more into selling, but on a differential-price basis. The charitable purpose and economic implications of the new plan are nicely summarized in the society's annual report for 1821, which deserves quoting at length:

> The plan recommended by the Managers, of selling Bibles and Testaments at cost or at reduced prices, where persons are able and willing to pay, has been highly approved by all the Auxiliaries from whom accounts have been received; and has been carried into effect, in many instances, with unexpected and very pleasing success. Those who needed Bibles have usually preferred to give something for them; and the process of distribution has not been impeded, if it has not been accelerated, by the measure referred to. The Auxiliaries have found their ability enlarged by it; and they have been enabled to supply more fully the necessity of those who were not possessors of the Sacred Volume, and yet could not, or would not, purchase it.

For it should be distinctly understood, that the Managers were very far from designing, by the plan, to diminish the circulation of the Scriptures: they designed rather to add to it. They were satisfied that many persons would gladly become possessors of a Bible by paying the full, or a reduced price, whose feelings of independence revolted from receiving it as the gift of charity. On the plan which the Managers have recommended, the Scriptures are still given freely to the destitute who are without means, or without disposition to pay for them; while receiving the whole, or a part of the cost from such as are willing to pay, the funds are rendered more availing, and a degree of security is obtained, that the volume which has been purchased will be prized, preserved, and used.[36]

This policy of differential pricing was mainly a revenue enhancer, for these were difficult financial times after the Panic of 1819. But the policy also suggests a psychological insight into pricing and utility, especially with a product as ethereal as religion. It is an economic truism that people will pay more for something they value more, but the reverse is often true as well: they will value something more if they pay more for it. It is a twist on the old saying, "You get what you pay for." It may be that in religion this is automatically so. The British and Foreign Bible Society had argued this position from the beginning.[37] The Americans came to it gradually, incompletely, and somewhat reluctantly.

The society's new policy to sell Bibles struck some critics as confirmation of their own Jacksonian suspicions: that the society was a conspiracy of self-aggrandizing elitists whose aim was "wealth and power" and "political privilege," not charity, as one anonymous writer put it in an 1830 pamphlet titled *An Expose of the Rise and Proceedings of the American Bible Society*. This pamphleteer, probably a disgruntled printer or bookseller whose business had been crippled by ABS competition, ridiculed the society's use of the traditional motto of Bible work: "without money and without price." The reverse was true, he declared:

> The Managers of the Parent Institution, in their Fourth Report [1820], mention the fact of their having sent a Circular to their Auxiliaries, urging them to use their influence and endeavours to *sell*, not to *give*, the "bread of life." This they have iterated and reiterated, year after year, with a pertinacity worthy of a better cause. The effect of this has been to make almost every pulpit in our churches a stall for the sale of their books, or clerical bookstores of temples of worship; and our pious young men have become travelling pedlers and

hawkers, forcing their entrance into families which they had never
before seen, and urging them to buy, at reduced prices, the books
issued by this "National Institution." They district cities, towns, and
villages, and scour them, either singly or in squads, seeking pur-
chasers with money, not the indigent without it.

Furthermore, the writer continued, "the Managers . . . would render nugatory
all competition." By subsidizing the price of Bibles through charitable contributions (money for production and labor for distribution), the ABS was able
to undersell all commercial competitors and thereby to monopolize the Bible
market.[38]

This latter judgment is fair enough. The ABS did hope to dominate the
market, at least for cheap Bibles. In that way only could it achieve maximum
economies of scale in printing and thus maximum return on its capital investment. But this is not to say that the organization was interested only in
selling. That judgment by the writer of *An Expose* is unfair. He assumed a false
dichotomy between giving and selling: the former was charity; the latter, commerce. The ABS managers believed, on the contrary, that efficient charity required *both* selling and giving. It required differential pricing, with the price
falling to zero. And such a price system is what they tried to achieve, as they
lectured, nagged, and cajoled their auxiliaries throughout the 1820s.

Much of the time, the managers strongly urged auxiliaries to sell books,
at cost or at reduced rates. In a typical exhortation, they wrote:

> The Managers deem it expedient to renew their recommendation to
> the Auxiliaries to sell the Scriptures at cost or at reduced prices, in
> preference to distributing them gratuitously. There are some, and
> even many, cases in which it may be advisable to give a Bible or a
> Testament without receiving any amount as the price of its purchase;
> but in general this is found in our country and in other countries
> not to be the wisest course. Whatever sum may be obtained for a
> Bible or a Testament, is so much preserved to the funds whence the
> really needy are to be supplied. Men ordinarily value that which they
> have bought, far more than that which they have received for the
> asking, or which they have been pressed to accept.

Furthermore, auxiliaries should sort good free riders from the bad:

> Those who are really unable to pay any thing, should be supplied
> gratuitously without hesitation: but this is by no means the condi-
> tion of all who are not possessors of the Scriptures. And as to such
> as can pay, and will not pay any part of the price of a Bible or a Tes-

tament, there certainly is very little reason even to hope that they would use and improve the sacred Book, were it placed into their hands.[39]

From this it would seem that the ABS managers had forgotten the Philadelphia Bible Society's dictum that a Bible was a Bible, no matter how it was obtained. But while the American Bible Society certainly made sales and the scrutiny of free riders higher priorities, it had not completely abandoned traditional Bible charity. When overly parsimonious auxiliaries took the new policy to be a mandate to grant no free books at all, the managers chastised them for being too strict with free riders. "The principle of the Parent Society seems to have been misapprehended," they wrote about one such case. "It is designed that the Scriptures shall be furnished gratuitously to those who are truly poor, and will faithfully use them. We would cheerfully *give* in such cases, and trust Providence to furnish means for the future."[40]

If the auxiliaries were doing a good job, the wide circulation of books through differential pricing seems to have worked fairly well. And the ABS annual reports and *Extracts* (the society's magazine) throughout the 1820s were filled with correspondence from auxiliaries describing their efforts to follow company policy, to sell and give simultaneously. In a typical report, the officers of the Nassau-Hall Bible Society of New Jersey wrote: "To some we sold Bibles at reduced prices; and before we gave gratuitously, we were careful to ascertain the inability of the persons to purchase, and their desire to use the Bible aright." They resisted the pressures of greedy free riders who "were displeased because we did not give Bibles to them as well as to their neighbors, who, in their opinion, were not more worthy than themselves."[41] Sorting the good free riders from the bad—the sheep from the goats—was not an easy task, but the energetic auxiliaries struggled to do it.

Not all auxiliaries were energetic, however. Indeed, the most troubling free riders turned out to be neither the unworthy nor the worthy poor, but the third kind, the kind the sociologists and economists worry about, the *organizational* free rider—in this case, the lax and self-serving members of the auxiliaries themselves. Auxiliary societies often used Bibles as lures to membership, and many people, it seems, joined the local societies just to get cheap Bibles for themselves and their families. They paid little attention to the destitute. Some members were selflessly diligent for a while, but only a while. The managers back in New York constantly complained of auxiliaries "languishing." In 1824, in a typical lament, they wrote that "some of the auxiliaries were as if in a deep slumber, or slowly wasting away, or in the last feeble struggles of existence, or actually dead and existing only in name." To boost morale, the New York office sometimes gave struggling auxiliaries free books. But, as with individual grants, this could have an effect opposite of the one intended, inducing "a spirit of dependence" that seemed to further drain away their zeal.[42] Especially troubling, from a practical point of view, many auxiliaries failed to pay for the books they ordered on credit. By 1829, auxiliaries had run up some $36,000 in unpaid bills, and the exasperated managers in New York seriously considered dunning them for interest.[43] Worst of all, in many newly settled parts of the country, there were no auxiliaries of any kind, languishing or otherwise.

At the end of the 1820s, then, the American Bible Society had a system in place for conducting a charity through both selling and giving, based on centralized printing and decentralized distribution. Parts of the system were working well. Production of Bibles was prodigious—in both meanings of that term. With sixteen power presses and twenty hand presses on line at the New York Bible House by 1829, the managers were confident that they could produce enough Bibles to supply everyone in the country. Meanwhile, many state and local auxiliaries were running efficiently and were bubbling with enthusiasm. To many Bible men and women, the times seemed propitious for a great national commitment: the general supply of the entire United States within two years. Still, the New York managers were wary. They knew that many auxiliaries were neither efficient nor enthusiastic. They knew that money and Bible workers were scarce in the West. And they knew that everything would depend on the auxiliaries. Without water, the great mill in New York could not turn. But they agreed to try, and in the summer of 1829 the first general supply of Bibles to the United States was launched.[44]

In the 1820s, other national religious publishing societies were organized on the model of the American Bible Society. The two most important were the American Tract Society and the American Sunday School Union. Both of these nondenominational societies were founded (mainly, though not exclusively, by Congregationalists and Presbyterians) on the now-standard premise that knowledge was the foundation of faith. "Though men are fallen by their iniquity," the founders of the American Tract Society declared, "and are to be recovered from their apostasy and condemnation only through the redemption that is in Jesus Christ, and by the renewing of the Holy Ghost, yet does this method of mercy most distinctly recognize the use of means in the business of their salvation."[45] For these organizations, "means" meant publications. The sole mission of the American Tract Society was to distribute tracts and books;

the mission of the American Sunday School Union was to found and support Sunday schools, but to a large extent that meant supplying them with children's books and periodicals. To this end, both societies built large, modern publishing operations in the 1820s. Both centralized their printing work, and both followed the pattern of the American Bible Society in distributing their publications through ever-growing networks of local auxiliaries.[46]

The American Tract Society was organized in 1825 to capture economies of scale in printing and distribution. Like the ABS, the ATS was designed to be a genuinely national institution, headquartered in New York. Jedidiah Morse's New England Tract Society had hoped to play such a national role and had even changed its name to the American Tract Society in 1823. But by then it was clear to nearly everyone, save a few New England chauvinists, that Andover, Massachusetts, was not the communications metropole of America. In 1825, if the concentration of print work were the goal, New York City was the obvious location, as the ATS founders explained in their initial address to the public. The new society also expected to achieve distribution economies by locating in New York, "where there are greater facilities of ingress and egress, and more extended, constant, and direct intercommunications with foreign ports, and every part of our interior, than are to be found in any other locality in the nation." New York also was the place where the money was. Expatriate New Englander Arthur Tappan and three other New York merchants underwrote the founding of the ATS to the tune of $25,000, which allowed the society to build a "commodious edifice . . . in one of the most eligible portions of the city."[47] Happily, the founders declared their new city the city of destiny: "The City of New-York, eminently distinguished by its natural and local advantages, its accumulating population, and its increasing commercial prosperity and influence, seems destined, in the wisdom of Divine Providence, to become the centre of these extended operations."[48]

Like the ABS, the American Tract Society quickly became a major patron of technological innovation in printing. Its predecessor, the New England Tract Society, had begun to stereotype its tracts in 1823 (the same year it changed its name to the American Tract Society), and stereotyping became an even more urgent project for the new national society in New York. Indeed, the founders declared in their initial address to the public that the centralization of stereotype printing was "a powerful argument in favor of union." "Tracts are now exceedingly cheap," they said, "but the Committee are greatly deceived if the formation of the American Tract Society does not render them cheaper than they are now."[49] In its first year, the ATS took over the existing plates of the New England and New York tract societies and launched its own stereotype operation. At the end of the first year, it had plates for 155 tracts (some 2,000 pages). By the end of the second year, it had stereotyped 45 more and had provided for a stereotype foundry in the basement of its new building.[50]

The American Tract Society also moved quickly into steam-powered printing. Under the supervision of Daniel Fanshaw, the printer for the American Bible Society, the ATS installed ten new Treadwell presses shortly after its founding. Except for some earlier experimental presses in the city, Fanshaw's Treadwells at the American Tract Society were the first power presses in the publishing business of New York.[51]

For the ATS, modern printing technology was more than a tool; it was a gift of God, a harbinger of the millennium. In their earliest publications, the society's managers linked the events of the age to the expanding power of print. Just as God had originally handed down his word in written form to humankind, so he now provided the "mighty engine" of the press to broadcast that word to the world.[52] Throughout the first half of the century, the American Tract Society continually played its rhapsody to technology. In the 1840s, the society launched a popular monthly newspaper, the *American Messenger*, whose primary mission was to extol the millennial power of the press. "The impossibilities of a century ago are the easy achievements of the age of steam," the *American Messenger* proclaimed. "For practical purposes oceans are bridged and mountains leveled, and continents spanned. The most subtle and powerful elements of nature are tamed by science and harnessed to the car of human progress." One writer imagined the voice of God enjoining Christians to take up the new technology and to make it their own: "I the Lord have given you power and wealth, mountains of iron and valleys of gold, a boundless territory and a free government. . . . I have added the ocean steamer, and the rail-way, and the steam printing-press, and the telegraph; employ all these for my glory and for the establishment of my kingdom!"[53]

The power of the modern press inspired a similar awe among Protestant denominational publishers. The Methodists had been enthusiasts of printing from the eighteenth century onward, and the leaders of the Methodist Book Concern in the early nineteenth century wrote frequently of the "mighty engine" of the press.[54] The conductors of the Presbyterian Board of Publication never doubted "the moral power of the press," in government or religion. Indeed, God himself was a printer, delivering his law to Moses engraved in stone.[55] Baptist publishers spoke of the "resistless power of the press." The press was lightning, "the electric flame that rives the oak"; it was "a mighty throbbing heart gushing its thrilling thought-currents through all the swelling arteries of the world's life"; it was the "flying artillery" of Christ's army on earth.[56]

The men who launched the American Tract Society (and the other societies) were both appalled and fascinated by the market revolution. Like Elias
Boudinot and the founders of the American Bible Society, the ATS viewed with
growing alarm the burgeoning print culture of the American market society.
The managers were shocked by the flood tide of "vicious literature" washing
over the land—works of religious infidelity, fictions and fantasies, stories of
romance, piracy, and murder. From the founding onward, the society's
publications brimmed with denunciations of the "satanic press." The first
book-length account of the society's activities declared that "the plagues of
Egypt were tolerable, compared with this coming up into our dwellings of the
loathsome swarms of literary vermin to 'corrupt the land,' to deprave the
hearts, and ruin the souls of our citizens."[57]

To fight this foe, the American Tract Society urged competition, not censorship. "A corrupt press cannot be legislated into truth-telling and decency,
in politics or morals," the ATS managers declared. "No. The remedy lies not
at all in political action; but in that conservative power which alone exists in
'the glorious Gospel of the blessed God'—in the speedy evangelization of the
whole people." Every form of the new technology must be marshaled for the
struggle:

> Shall we content ourselves with the post-coach speed of the eigh-
> teenth century, in schemes for evangelization, while all worldly
> schemes are propelled with the locomotive speed of the nineteenth
> century? Shall we creep along the beaten path our fathers trod, and
> *because* they trod it, eschewing or neglecting all the increased facili-
> ties Providence has given us for publishing the great salvation, while
> steam, and electricity, and the printing-press are left to be the agents
> of ambition, avarice, and revolution?[58]

Again and again, from the 1820s on, the society reiterated its marketplace
mantra: if the Devil works fast, let us work faster.

Though willing, even eager, to compete in the marketplace of ideas, the
American Tract Society could not rely upon the marketplace of trade. Private
enterprise was the cause of the evil print culture of America; it could not be
the cure. This theme was emphasized routinely in society publications:

> No nation on the globe, perhaps, has so large a reading population;
> and in none is the press more active, or more influential. What the
> reading matter prepared for such a nation would be, if left solely to
> private enterprise, may be inferred from an examination of the cata-
> logues of some of the respectable and even Christian publishing

houses. Self-interest would shape the supply to the demand; and the mightiest agent God has given to the world for moulding public opinion and sanctifying the public taste, would be moulded by it, and be made to reflect its character, were there no conservative, re-deeming influences.

The *American Messenger* argued that "if the public taste be wrong, the press with its indescribable power perpetuates and extends the injury thus inflicted on vital interests. The question is, *What will sell?* and as in other shambles and markets, so here, supply responds to demand, although souls are included in the traffic."[59] The ATS proposed the reverse: make supply drive demand.

To accomplish this charitable mission—to distribute tracts and books against the current of the commercial market—the American Tract Society organized a network of local auxiliaries. By the early 1830s, the society had nearly 1,000 formal auxiliaries and had links to more than 2,000 other groups. Like the auxiliaries of the American Bible Society, these local organizations were supposed to administer a noncommercial distribution system. The goal was to "tender the message of the Gospel to *all*—high and low, rich and poor," and the auxiliaries were the key players. They bought tracts and books at cost from the parent society and raised money through donations and sales.[60]

Following the lead of the American Bible Society, the American Tract Society quickly began to urge its auxiliaries to sell, as well as give. Small tracts were designed to be given away freely, but in 1827 the ATS launched a program to publish full-length books as well as tracts. Soon the society's managers were praising the virtues of retail sales. At the same time, however, they implored their auxiliaries not to let financial considerations drive their work, but to carry tracts and books to everyone, regardless of ability to pay. "*It is no scheme of pecuniary profit*," they said. "*It is, from beginning to end, purely an effort of be-nevolence*, to tender Divine truth in these interesting and durable forms to those who would not come after it—who have but a feeble desire to obtain it; but who, without it, may perish eternally." Like the ABS, the ATS told its aux-iliaries that a system of differential pricing provided the best mixture of evan-gelism (universal circulation) and economics (permanent capital and revenue flow):

It is most clear, that the tremendous influence of the public press in our country *may not be left* solely to the operation and influence of sales for the purposes of gain. The most valuable books must be *pre-pared in an attractive style, and furnished at cost, or less than cost*, and Christian efforts must be put forth all over the land *to place them in*

the hands of people—by sale, if it can be done—gratuitously, if it cannot. . . . To every donor to the Society there is also this encouragement, that as the volumes are chiefly *sold*, the amount of each donation returns with every sale; is sent out again, and again returns;
and thus continues to revolve, and may, and probably will revolve
long after the benevolent donor shall be sleeping in dust.[61]

The third great national religious publishing society of the early nineteenth
century was the American Sunday School Union, organized in Philadelphia in
1824. The mission of the ASSU was to found Sunday schools, especially in the
West. To this end, the society appointed itinerant missionaries and agents—
twenty-seven by 1826, seventy-eight by 1832. Like the leaders of the American
Tract Society, the founders of the ASSU believed that the printed word was the
vital means of grace. The problem of America was ignorance (religious and
otherwise), and knowledge was the cure.[62] At the heart of every Sunday school,
then, must be a free library filled with books and periodicals for all. "Whenever
the American Sunday-School Union accomplishes the purpose for which it
was instituted," the managers proclaimed, "the children in all our land will
read intelligently; they will have the free use of good books, adapted to their
wants and capacities."[63]

To produce the materials they thought children needed, the managers of
the American Sunday School Union followed in the tradition of the ATS and
ABS and became a large-scale publisher. Indeed, the chief impetus to national
union was economies of scale in publishing. In 1825, its first full year of operation, the society published 224 separate editions of books, pamphlets, and
periodicals, amounting to more than 14 million pages. As with the other national societies, stereotyping was the crucial technology. The ASSU established
a stereotype foundry at its headquarters, and its annual reports happily reported
the numbers of plates added each year. By the end of four years, the society
had more than 10,000 stereotype plates on hand. By 1831, the Board of Managers claimed to be able to print 4 million pages a week.[64]

Like the American Tract Society, the ASSU proposed to compete with the
commercial press for the attention of its intended audience: the children of
America. The new print culture was polluted with bad books, "books abound-
ing with foolishness, vulgarity, and falsehood." To entice children to choose
virtue over vice, virtue must be presented in its "most attractive garb of blended
instruction and amusement." Some supporters of the Sunday school movement were skeptical of the light, popular style of many ASSU publications, and
the managers were frequently moved to explain to their critics that children

would not automatically read even the best religious literature. "It should be borne in mind," they insisted, "that there is no such thing as a *natural taste* for religious reading." The opposite is true; there is a natural distaste. To succeed, therefore, children's books must "arrest the attention and interest the feelings of the child."[65]

ASSU leaders believed that they were foiling the market, not following it. They did not seek to sell books to children; they provided them for free use through Sunday school libraries. Children could often be drawn into the school by the privilege of a free library, even if they were not interested in religious instruction. In the long run, the ASSU managers believed that the supply of Sunday school books would increase the demand for them, perhaps even drive bad books out of circulation. Their goal was the same as that of the Bible and tract societies: to subvert the literary marketplace by providing free reading material to everyone regardless of demand.[66]

To establish free libraries everywhere, the American Sunday School Union needed money, and in the 1820s it went about raising funds in the usual way. The key players were local auxiliaries. Like the Bible and tract societies, the ASSU sold books at cost to organizations that would make them available to children for free through Sunday schools. Though the usual pricing strategy of the ASSU was to sell at cost, the managers understood that a better system would be differential pricing, if they could make it work. In their 1832 report, they said they hoped to be able to provide to a school that could raise only $5 the same set of books they would supply to a school that could raise $10. To cover the cost of this kind of subsidy, the society depended on donations, and the flow of donations depended on the auxiliaries. In the end, the object of the society was universal circulation of the word. "For this purpose," the managers declared, "the instrumentality of auxiliary societies is exceedingly important."[67]

By the end of the 1820s, the American Bible Society, the American Tract Society, and the American Sunday School Union had become such large-scale publishers that their leaders could imagine something new in American print culture: mass media. From the beginning of the Bible and tract movements, evangelical publishers had hoped to produce genuine mass media, that is, *universal* circulation of the same message. Now, at last, they believed that they had the technological and economic resources to do the job—that is, to place their publications into the hands of everyone in America. Though inspired by millennial dreams, the American Bible Society gave these efforts a businesslike name: general supply.

The American Bible Society launched its first general supply at the society's annual meeting in May 1829. The assembly resolved to distribute Bibles to every family in the country that needed one and to do it within two years. With a full complement of stereotype plates and power presses on line at the New York Bible House, the managers were certain that they could supply all the Bibles needed. They were less certain that the auxiliaries could supply the "systematic organization" and the "judicious and systematic division of labor" that would be required to move the Bibles from New York into the hinterlands where they were needed.[68] Despite their practical reservations, the managers held fast to a millennial hope that the project could not fail. "Its resolution, in dependence upon Divine aid to supply all the destitute families of these United States with the sacred Scriptures within two years," they said, ". . . is one of those bold, but not presumptuous measures, to which, in quick succession, the Most High is prompting his servants, as harbingers, we believe, of the latter day glory of the church."[69]

Success in this first general supply depended upon systematic surveys and organized distributions at the level of the local auxiliary. There seemed to be evidence by 1829 that these things could be done. Ten state organizations at that time were already engaged in efforts to canvass and supply all destitute families in their areas. That is, they had, or at least thought they had, the capability to knock on virtually every door in their states. Moreover, several of the larger state societies pledged to the general effort, not only cooperation in the distribution of Bibles, but financial support as well. The New Hampshire society pledged $12,000; Vermont pledged $10,000; Connecticut also $10,000; and so on. Wealthy individuals, including the usual New Yorkers, also offered aid. Arthur Tappan, for example, pledged $5,000 for the general supply.[70] While outright donations were crucial, universal circulation required the auxiliaries to maintain the delicate balance between selling and giving. In its instructions to auxiliaries participating in the general supply, the ABS managers declared:

> Let local agencies for allotted districts be immediately established, comprising for each individual no more than a strictly practicable range of operation, within which he may ascertain with accuracy, who are destitute of the Scriptures, who are able and willing to purchase them at cost, who will receive them at a price below their value, and who require to be supplied by gratuitous donation. Let

these agents be assiduous in urging the wealthy to give liberally of
their abundance, and those of more moderate means as God may
have blessed them, to the supply of the multitudes of their distant
brethren who, through unavoidable necessity, are unable to purchase for themselves the bread of life.[71]

On the production side, the general supply was a triumph. During the
official two-year period, the society distributed nearly a half million Bibles and
New Testaments, and in the three years 1829–1831 the society's presses
churned out more than 1 million volumes. In a country of only about 3 million
households, this was an impressive and unprecedented publication performance. And the work of distribution went well in some parts of the country.
According to the managers' calculations, thirteen states and territories were
already fully supplied by 1831.[72]

But by the spring of 1833, the managers were disappointed. After more
than four years, many remote areas remained entirely unsupplied. Many had
not been canvassed at all. Even in areas that were fully canvassed, the managers
said, "the work was often imperfectly done—many families were overlooked."
Before the grand project was even under way, the auxiliaries had run up tens
of thousands of dollars of unpaid bills owed to the national society. And this
trend continued. After 1829, many auxiliaries defaulted on their special pledges
for the general supply, and the national society was plunged deeply into debt
to banks and paper suppliers. By 1830, the managers lamented that only about
a third of the $100,000 pledged by auxiliaries for the general supply had been
remitted. In 1830–1831, only 127 of 710 auxiliary societies actually donated
money to the parent society, and only 14 of these were in the West or Southeast.
The vast majority were in the Northeast. Even worse, many auxiliaries had
failed to pay for books received on credit from the General Depository. During
the general supply, to help achieve the goal of universal circulation, the society
allowed more free grants than usual, but this relaxed policy led many who
could afford to pay to demand free Bibles (free riders, again). This, of course,
drove up the cost of the enterprise.[73]

Perhaps most disappointing of all, even some of the stronger auxiliaries, which did conduct systematic surveys and careful distributions, could not
sustain the effort for long, and "apathy . . . followed the season of high excitement and great exertion." In their 1833 report, the managers complained that
"many Auxiliaries which supplied their destitute families two or three years
ago have not ordered a Bible since."[74] All in all, the managers of the American
Bible Society judged the general supply a failure and the auxiliaries largely to
blame.

The millennial vision of a general supply also inspired the leaders of the American Tract Society. In 1829, beginning in New York City, the leaders of the ATS commenced what came to be known as the Systematic Monthly Distribution plan. The goal was simple: to place in the hands of every city resident at least one tract—the same tract—each month. The idea was the ideology of modern mass media: to have everyone reading and talking about the same thing at the same time. The plan involved an intricate network of ward committees and district distributors. Under the plan, the city's fourteen wards were divided into 500 districts, with about sixty families per district. Each ward had a committee and a chairperson, and each district at least one door-to-door distributor. In March 1829, when the project began, the society counted 28,771 family units in the city and visited all of them. According to the society's report for the month, 28,383 families were willing to take a tract; only 388 declined.[75]

The whole process was meticulously organized, mainly by such evangelical businessmen as Arthur Tappan (in charge of Ward 5) and his brother Lewis (in charge of Ward 1). Each district distributor was provided with a printed card of instructions, forms for reporting back to the central committee, and, of course, the proper supply of the tract-of-the-month. The instructions were very explicit, describing precisely when and how the district canvass and distribution should be done.[76] By 1831, the New York society was delivering more than 5 million pages of tracts per year to the city's 36,000 families. In addition, some of the more aggressive distributors had begun systematic distributions at the city's wharves, markets, hospitals, and public institutions. By 1833, more than 700 distributors were regularly engaged in this "efficient effort."[77]

Other cities picked up on the New York plan. Some 200 New England towns, including Boston, had launched monthly distribution programs by 1831. Philadelphia, Baltimore, Charleston, and other large cities also had programs under way. Even some rural counties were wholly covered, including some sparsely populated areas of the West. The national office of the American Tract Society publicized the New York plan heavily and pressed it upon its auxiliaries and branches everywhere. In 1834, the national office began a broader effort in the South and West, dubbed the Volume Enterprise, the aim of which was to place at least one religious book into every household. While not disparaging what they called "miscellaneous distributions," the society's executive committee argued that only systematic, organized efforts by the auxiliaries would lead to the great goal of reaching all.[78]

Like the American Bible Society's general supply of 1829–1831, the American Tract Society's Systematic Monthly Distribution over the same period was labeled a failure. The managers admitted in 1831 that some 10 million Americans were still beyond the net of the society's legions of distributors.[79] Like the ABS, the ATS found it much easier to deliver its books and tracts in the wealthy East than in the destitute West, where they were most needed. The problem was obvious: the strongest auxiliaries were located in the areas where they were least needed.

In 1830, the American Sunday School Union launched its version of a general supply in the American West: the Mississippi Valley Project. Again, the goal was as simple as it was audacious: "to establish a Sunday school in every destitute place where it is practicable, throughout the Valley of the Mississippi." Such a plan required libraries for every school, books for every child. "No Society is known to exist in any part of the world, which attempts to supply the whole youthful population of a country with rational and profitable books," the society's managers declared. "That this is our professed object is well understood; and that we have not been wholly unsuccessful in its prosecution, is sufficiently evident."[80]

But the American Sunday School Union was not wholly successful, either. Like the ABS and the ATS, the ASSU found its drive for universal circulation of religious publications frustrated by inefficient auxiliaries and by the sheer magnitude of the task, especially on the sprawling western frontier. By 1833, the managers claimed substantial success in their Mississippi Valley Project, with 5,000 Sunday schools operating in the West. But they admitted that three times as many were needed.[81]

Despite disappointments, the great national general supplies of the early 1830s were remarkable publishing and distribution events. Though deeply in debt and frustrated by its auxiliaries, the American Bible Society had churned out a million Bibles in three years. Though 10 million Americans were still beyond the reach of the American Tract Society, some 2 million to 3 million people *were* being reached regularly by the Systematic Monthly Distributions. In the years 1829–1831 the ATS's production of tracts never fell below 5 million annually. Counting all of its publications, the American Tract Society annually printed at least five pages for every man, woman, and child in America. Meanwhile, in the first three years of its Mississippi Valley Project, the American Sunday School Union established 4,245 new schools, revived 2,899, and placed into Sunday school libraries more than 500,000 volumes.[82]

A million Bibles, 15 million tracts, a half million Sunday school books: these were impressive numbers. All three societies pushed themselves and their machines to the limit in the years 1829 to 1833. For the American Bible Society, the American Tract Society, and the American Sunday School Union, the work of 1829–1833 demonstrated that the creation of mass media was possible in America.

The heady spirit of general supply was so intoxicating that some evangelical observers deluded themselves into believing that the task had actually been accomplished. In his 1833 book, *The Harbinger of the Millennium*, William Cogswell wrote, "And now may be said what before never could be said, that the whole nation is furnished with the word of life." With wonderful new technologies available in transportation and printing, he announced that the next logical step was to provide a copy of the Bible to *every family on earth*. "Seventy-five millions of dollars will furnish every family with a copy of the sacred Scriptures," he wrote. "Why should not the different Bible Societies in Christendom resolve at once to begin, and in a specified time, accomplish this great and glorious work?" Cogswell's millennial zeal swept through the American Bible movement in 1833, and the American Bible Society actually did resolve to supply the whole world with the Scriptures within twenty years. "It can be done," Cogswell proclaimed.[83]

The managers of the American Bible Society knew better. They agreed to support the general supply to the "whole world," but only "as rapidly as public munificence will supply funds for that purpose." With their domestic general supply stalled, with more debts than fulfilled pledges on hand, the ABS managers were wary of taking on such an astoundingly difficult and expensive task, even if "the signs of the times are propitious to exertion."[84] Seasoned by failure as well as success, schooled in business as well as evangelical Christianity, reliant on human agency as well as the outpouring of the spirit, they understood that enthusiasm was not enough.

Furthermore, not all religious Americans greeted the rapid rise of the great religious publishing societies with the giddy enthusiasm of a William Cogswell. Some erstwhile supporters of the Bible and tract movements were especially critical of the societies' turn to sales. Selling books undermined the societies' status as charities, the critics said. The author of *An Expose of the Rise and Proceedings of the American Bible Society* implied that *any* retail sales mocked the claim of publishers to furnish Scripture "without money and without price." He argued that sales instead allowed the managers to accumulate vast stores of capital in the form of stereotype plates, buildings, and real estate. "Rich in this world's goods," he said, "they are supercilious and arrogant." But more important, by spurning the indigent in favor of those who could buy, the society stole the market for Bibles from honest commercial book publishers and booksellers.[85]

In a later polemic, another critic leveled a similar complaint against all

"charity publication societies," especially the American Tract Society. This author charged that charitable donations subsidized the low prices of ATS books;
private enterprise, therefore, could not compete. He argued that charity publishing was unnecessary and wrong when people are willing and able to buy.
"What business have Christians to give their charity to do that which business
enterprise and capital would do, if let alone, quite as well and cheaply?" Help-
fully answering his own question, the author added, "None at all."[86]

The managers of the American Bible Society and the American Tract Society usually ignored criticism, but gradually they came to admit that the strategy of retail sales did distort the charitable nature of their missions. Under
such a policy, books naturally flowed to where the money was. Rich regions
produced more sales; more sales produced rich auxiliaries; rich auxiliaries produced more remittances to the national office. But the founding mission of
the publishers was altogether different. It was, as the American Tract Society's
managers liked to say, to "tender the message of the Gospel to *all*—high and
low, rich and poor."[87] Ironically, the turn to retail sales, which was designed to
produce universal circulation, not profit, had entrapped the societies in market
forces they had been founded to resist. To circulate books everywhere and to
everyone, the societies could not depend upon the financial condition of local
auxiliaries. To move supply against demand, they needed some form of centrally administered national distribution system.

5

The New Mass Media

Systematic Distribution

On May 1, 1837, the New York mercantile firm of Arthur Tappan and Co. announced a suspension of payments to creditors. The company's debt had ballooned to more than a million dollars, and the severe business contraction of 1837 made it impossible for Tappan to meet his obligations. The great benefactor of American religious charity, the financial angel of the general supplies, was bankrupt. But the bankruptcy of Arthur Tappan mattered only a little to the American Bible Society, the American Tract Society, and the American Sunday School Union. By 1837, their troubles were broader, deeper, and more systemic. Several years before his bankruptcy, Tappan had shifted his largess from purely religious evangelism to the new evangelism of antislavery, and conflicts over abolition had begun to undermine the spirit of religious unity that had given the general supplies such a boost of millennial optimism.[1] The Panic of 1837 was a punctuation mark to the end of the era of general supply, not a cause of it. The more fundamental troubles of the great national publishing societies were internal, organizational, administrative.

The main problem for the societies is simply put: selling books is one thing; giving them away is another. The failure of the general supplies taught the societies a lesson in market capitalism. By the late 1820s, the capacity of a modern, highly capitalized printing plant was astonishing; mass production of the printed word in America was possible. But efficient distribution was another matter altogether. If the goal was to reach everyone regardless of ability to pay, if the plan was to move supply against demand, then the "invisible hand" of the marketplace would not suffice. The societies' managers had always understood this in a general way. They knew they could not operate as commercial vendors in a commercial market. The system of local auxiliary societies scattered across the land, which all of the national societies adopted, was specifically designed to get books and tracts to *everyone*, especially the "destitute." The general supply campaigns of the early 1830s, however, revealed that the logic of the market worked its way even *inside* this system. Somehow, despite the efforts of the New York managers and the local auxiliaries, the books and tracts still flowed to where the money was.

For decades, the religious publishing societies struggled with this problem: how to operate as capitalist manufacturers but to move their product against the flow of the commercial market. Increasingly, they came to rely on organization and administration to sidestep market forces. In the 1840s and 1850s, the societies' managers—especially those of the American Tract Society—developed new administrative structures designed to make religious benevolence systematic. They learned to substitute what the economic historian Alfred Chandler called the "visible hand" of administration for the invisible hand of the marketplace. In doing so, they invented the national not-for-profit media corporation. In business management innovation, the religious publishers were a step ahead of commercial corporations. They were early adopters of techniques of internal organization and communication that would become, by the end of the century, standard operating procedures of the modern, large-scale business firm.[2]

The efforts of the societies to achieve "systematic Christian enterprise" passed through two phases. In phase one, society managers developed strategies to enhance and systematize the auxiliary system. In phase two, they attempted to replace the auxiliary system (or at least supplement it) with a centrally administered national organization.

In November 1829, the managers of the American Bible Society met at their offices in New York and pondered how to make their 645 auxiliary societies more efficient. They understood that the success of a general supply of the entire country, then just under way, depended on what they called "systematic organization." To this end, they approved procedures to help existing auxiliaries do their work more thoroughly and to encourage the formation of new auxil-

iaries in the new states and territories. They voted to publish books of instructions and record-keeping forms for auxiliary society officers, abstracts of ABS
policies, specimen books and price lists, and other guides and helps.[3] The ABS
managers understood that the members of the local societies played three crucial roles in the effort to circulate Bibles everywhere to everyone: (1) because
they knew their areas, they were best positioned to gather information about
local needs; (2) because they knew or could get to know the people in their
areas, they could most efficiently distribute Bibles through a system of differential pricing (i.e., selling at cost to some, selling below cost to some, and
giving freely to others); and (3) because they represented the most pious and
benevolent classes of their communities, they could most effectively raise surplus funds for the national society to use for free grants elsewhere.[4]

In a lengthy pamphlet published in 1830, titled *Brief Analysis of the System
of the American Bible Society*, the managers described what they meant by *systematic organization*. Most important was "judicious and systematic division of
labor." This meant assigning "visitors" to specific districts within the local society's area and assigning specific dates for canvasses and distributions. It
meant setting up smaller branch societies in every town, village, and even
congregation in the area. It meant carefully collecting information and reporting it to the national office. Finally, it meant fundraising. Such a "perfect organization of Auxiliary Societies," the managers explained, ". . . will secure the
discovery and judicious supply, annually, of all the destitute families within
their limits." The managers routinely reminded their many volunteers in the
field that "to encourage a wider circulation of the Holy Scriptures without note
or comment, is the sole object of Auxiliaries in connection with the American
Bible Society."[5]

Long before 1830, however, ABS officials had realized that a system of local
auxiliaries would not spring up automatically. Though the chief function of the
central office was to manufacture Bibles in great numbers, the New York-based
managers also knew that *they* had to build the auxiliary network. They tried to
do that through the application of three resources at their command: information, money, and hired agents. From the beginning, the ABS managers
viewed their office as a clearinghouse for information as well as Bibles. In their
early meetings in 1816, the managers set up procedures for placing news of
their work "in all the newspapers of the United States." They constantly solicited information from the auxiliaries, which they then published in annual
reports and a quarterly magazine founded in 1818. That quarterly became a
monthly in 1821 called *Monthly Extracts*. (In 1843, the magazine became the
Bible Society Record, which is still in publication.) Society managers also communicated to auxiliary officers and ministers through printed circular letters.

They urged that their reports, circulars, and *Monthly Extracts* be widely circulated and even read aloud at meetings of local auxiliaries.[6] The managers of the American Bible Society never lost their faith in the organizing power of information.

The managers knew that money under their direct control would be needed as well. Most of the money that flowed into the central office consisted of remittances for Bibles. In the ABS system, "Auxiliaries are allowed to receive Bibles and Testaments to the full amount of the monies remitted by them if asked for; which books, under their direction, are either sold at cost, or for part price, or gratuitously distributed, as the condition of the destitute requires, and their own rules dictate." The central office desperately hoped that the auxiliaries would *not* ask for Bibles for the full amount of their remittances. The managers needed to collect unencumbered funds from prosperous auxiliaries in order to seed new and less-prosperous auxiliaries with free grants of Bibles. They knew that free grants were essential for launching new societies and rejuvenating moribund ones, especially in relatively poor regions. To accomplish this nationwide transfer of wealth, the central office needed outright donations— "surplus revenue," the managers called it—from the wealthy auxiliaries. The treasury of the society, the managers explained, "is not a living fountain which possesses the means of its own supply, but a cistern from which nothing can be taken which has not previously been put in. The liberality of those who have enough and to spare furnishes means to meet the wants of those who want more than they have means to purchase."[7]

In addition to sharing information and encouraging the sharing of wealth, the American Bible Society in the 1820s began to employ traveling agents to organize new auxiliaries and to nurture old ones. The society appointed its first paid agent, Richard Hall, in 1821 to work in the trans-Appalachian West. In his first year of service, Hall traveled 3,000 miles through Pennsylvania, western Virginia, Ohio, Kentucky, Indiana, and Illinois, visiting thirty societies, organizing thirty-five, and laying the foundations for five more, while preaching some 300 sermons. Hall's journals were filled with accounts of "destitution," "apathy," and "languishing" local societies. ("Languishing" was a favorite word.) He complained of impassable roads and miserable accommodations. But he also came to believe that sending agents into the field was "one of the most important parts of the system." The managers in New York agreed. By 1828, the ABS had twelve agents at work.[8] In a report to the members in 1830, the managers declared:

Of the importance of such Agents your Board have long since been convinced. Auxiliaries which are already in a prosperous state may often, by the reception of your Annual Report and Monthly Extracts, and by private correspondence, be continued in this state; but when they have been imperfectly organized, and have existed through a series of years with little or no efforts, nothing but the voice of the living Agent can awake their zeal and urge them on their way.[9]

Though the American Bible Society was fond of the word *systematic*, the organization of auxiliaries and agencies was fairly haphazard in this first phase of organizational innovation in the 1820s and 1830s. Auxiliaries were provided with model constitutions specifying their duties, but essentially the only material link between the local and the national society was a financial one. The auxiliary agreed to turn over its surplus funds to the national society, and in return the ABS agreed to sell Bibles to the local at 5 percent below cost. Beyond financial obligations, the auxiliary was almost completely autonomous. And even financial obligations were often not met. Bible agents were paid stipends by the ABS, were given sheets of printed instructions, were asked to keep careful financial accounts, and were told to write to New York once a month. But beyond such general guidelines, little was specified.[10] In other words, though the managers craved a system, the strategies for achieving a system in the early years were more hortatory than administrative.[11]

Like their colleagues at the American Bible Society, the managers of the American Tract Society in the 1820s and 1830s were confident that they could manufacture millions of books and tracts—enough for the entire country—but they were less sure that they could deliver them to everyone. Once again, an efficient auxiliary system was the key, and the story of the early years of the American Tract Society runs parallel to that of the ABS. The ATS used auxiliaries in the same way the American Bible Society did: to gather information, to raise money, and to distribute publications. The ATS had nearly a thousand auxiliaries by the early 1830s; it also supplied nearly a thousand other small societies affiliated with the Boston and Philadelphia tract societies.[12] Like the ABS, the American Tract Society operated as a clearinghouse for information as well as publications. And, like the ABS, the ATS tried to pry out of its richer auxiliaries surplus income that could be used to carry tracts and books to the truly destitute.

The managers of the American Tract Society believed in the power of information. They followed the example of the ABS in urging auxiliaries to gather information about religious reading and religious practice in their areas, which they then published in their annual reports and in the *American Tract Magazine*. The New England Tract Society had founded the *American Tract Magazine* in Boston in 1824, and the new American Tract Society kept it going.

The ATS also continued publication of the *Christian Almanac,* which carried information about religious tract work collected from the auxiliaries, as well as the usual calendars and meteorological data. By 1830, the ATS was publishing the *Christian Almanac* in twenty-one different geographical editions.[13]

The American Tract Society managers also shared with the American Bible Society a fondness for the word *systematic.* They understood that careful organization and division of labor would be needed if the goal were to reach everyone. The national officers were impressed by the New York City tract society's Systematic Monthly Distribution plan, launched in 1829. The annual reports after 1829 regularly exhorted other auxiliaries to follow the example of New York, to organize systematically to carry the word to all. The reports included model plans for auxiliaries, cards of instructions for tract visitors, and "hints for Christian effort."[14] The campaign for systematic monthly distribution became the foundation for the ATS's own version of general supply of everyone in America in the early 1830s.

In its early years, the American Tract Society also followed the lead of the ABS in the deployment of traveling agents, and for the same reasons: to encourage old auxiliaries and to organize new ones, especially in the western states and territories. In 1828, the ATS dispatched its first paid agent to the Mississippi Valley. By 1830, the society had nine agents at work in the West (four in the East), and more than 5 percent of the society's expenses were going to support agents in the field.[15] In the 1830s, the society employed two types of agents: general agents, in charge of all the work in a specified region, and volume agents, in charge of the distribution of books. (The ATS had begun to publish full-length books, in addition to standard tracts, in 1827.) These agents were widely scattered. In 1833, for example, the society had sixteen agents in the field: one in Ohio, two in Indiana, two in Kentucky, three in Illinois, one in Missouri, and so on. Agents traveled constantly, but they could not hope to cover the territories assigned to them. Their reports were filled with expressions of joy in the work but despair over the magnitude of it. The society's overly optimistic plans called for only thirty agencies, each embracing a territory 100 by 180 miles, each with 300,000 people.[16]

Largely because of the size of their territories, ATS agents operated largely as middlemen, working between national and local societies and wholesaling tracts and books to auxiliaries, churches, Sunday schools, and volunteer distributors. They had no choice but to depend on auxiliaries and other volunteer support. For example, the first formal plan to distribute a book to every household over a large geographical area originated in 1834 with the local clergymen and tract men of Virginia, not with the national office. The ATS enthusiastically endorsed this plan to supply books to everyone in the southeastern states, but the national society had neither the funds nor the agents to do the job without massive local volunteer organization and support.[17]

Despite their efforts to make the auxiliary societies more efficient and the system more systematic, the New York officers of the American Tract Society found that they had little direct control over how the auxiliaries operated or how the system grew. As at the ABS, the link between the national and the local societies was chiefly financial. According to the ATS constitution, auxiliaries were supposed to donate one-fourth of their annual receipts to the national society; in return, they were allowed to purchase tracts and books at "the most reduced prices," to be resold or distributed for free. But most of the unencumbered donations to the ATS came from the national society's own members and directors, not from the auxiliaries. And most tracts were sold to auxiliaries that could pay for them, not provided as seed grants to those that could not. In no year before 1833 did the ATS have the resources to provide more than 8 percent of its tract production as free grants to struggling auxiliaries or directly to the public.[18]

The problem for both the American Bible Society and the American Tract Society was that the auxiliary system was essentially a price system. Though both societies tried to regulate and cajole their auxiliaries through constitutional provisions, shared information, and agents' exhortations, in reality the power of the central office was limited almost entirely to the setting of discounted prices for Bibles, books, and tracts. In the early years, then, the ABS and the ATS operated as wholesalers in a market separate from but analogous to the market for commercial publications. Though the "retailers" were benevolent societies, not bookstores, the relationship of the national society to them was the same: it was a price system, a marketplace.

Such a decentralized wholesale system, operating through independent auxiliaries, did not produce the results the societies desired, even with the extra prodding by traveling agents. The annual reports of the American Bible Society were filled with laments over the failure of the auxiliaries to move books to where they were really needed. Often the managers attributed this failure to the loss of evangelical zeal, but they also knew that much of the problem was systemic. The societies with money were the ones that bought the books. In 1828, the ABS managers explained how this problem undermined their efforts to reach all:

> While the issues of this year have been nearly double to those of any preceding year, but few States or Auxiliaries comparatively have contributed to this increase. It will be found too, that those Societies which have made this unusual demand on your Depository, are

mostly in the older States, and frequently in those counties which
were supposed to be already best supplied with the Bible.[19]

It is little wonder that the ABS managers were apprehensive a year later when
the society launched its first general supply.

The story was the same at the American Tract Society. In its 1827 report,
the executive committee lamented the fact that so few tracts were going to the
West. Of more than $25,000 in sales in the first two years of business, only
$107 worth of tracts had gone to Kentucky, $58 to Ohio, and $178 to Indiana,
Michigan, and Missouri combined. The problem was obvious. Though the
West was the field most destitute of religious publications, the vast majority of
auxiliaries were in the settled areas of the Northeast. The ATS believed that the
people of the western frontier needed religious publications more because they
had so few settled ministers, churches, and other religious institutions. They
also needed grants (free tracts and books) more than sales, because they were
often so poor. But for these same reasons, they lacked auxiliary societies to buy
and distribute the tracts and Bibles they needed.[20] Many local societies in the
East did contribute funds to send tracts to the West. But the overall market
forces *within* the wholesale/auxiliary system worked against the professed aim
of the society to reach those most destitute of the means of grace. Instead, the
market directed the flow of tracts and books to the East, to the wealthy local
societies—in short, to those least in need.

The employment of agents did not help much. At the ATS, the general
agents were strongly urged to get systematic monthly distributions going in
their fields. Many did. But, as usual, the work progressed more steadily in the
East than in the West and South. By 1831, some 200 to 300 towns in New
England had monthly distributions, and monthly projects were common in
New York, Pennsylvania, and New Jersey. But few were in operation in the
South and West.[21] Western agents' reports often mentioned monthly distribution efforts, but such efforts reached only a tiny fraction of the people in the
1830s. And, once again, they were usually the people in the settled towns, those
least in need. As one agent explained in 1833, "Of the nine counties already
visited, perhaps one-fifth of the population are monthly supplied, but they are
generally those best supplied with the other means of grace." This agent was
unusually lucky, by the way. One-fifth was an enormous proportion compared
with other agents' experience. One said that only one in twenty families in his
district had received any tracts; another said one in fifty. Yet another put the
situation in telling comparison: "The fact is, this field is about as much Missionary ground as Burmah."[22]

The goal of the organizational strategies of the American Bible Society and the American Tract Society was to foil the marketplace: to "tender the message of the Gospel to *all*—high and low, rich and poor." But the power of the market, like hell, was not easily overcome. Any dependence on volunteers—for financial support or for distribution—distorted the mission of the societies, directing it away from the low and the poor, away from the West and South. The ATS managers explained:

> It would be far easier and less expensive to hover around the communities now enjoying some of the means of grace, and where a ready circulation of books could be effected; but the Committee cannot disregard the more pressing wants of the border population, and they believe that the friends of the Society will cheerfully sustain them in the effort to convey the gospel to the "poor," whether they are found in the wilds of Nebraska, or among the gold-heaps of California.[23]

The leaders of all the societies recognized the problem, but the American Tract Society, more so than the others, decided to do something dramatic about it. In 1841, the ATS managers resolved that the major work of the society must be removed entirely from forces beyond their administrative control.[24] In this second phase of organizational innovation, they set about to build a national distribution system based upon salaried line employees, geographical administrative divisions, and a hierarchy of salaried managers. This was the beginning of the American Tract Society's famous system of *colportage*.

The word *colporteur* is a French term for itinerant hawker of tracts and books, and its roots reach back to the Reformation. The term derived from the pack the peddler carried (*porter*) over his shoulder or neck (*col*). In what might be called the weak form of colportage, a colporteur was simply an itinerant bookseller working on commission. Commercial book publishers had long employed traveling salesmen in this way, the most famous of whom was Parson Mason Weems, who sold books for the Philadelphia publisher Mathew Carey in the early years of the century. Another Philadelphia publisher, William Woodward, regularly recruited cash-strapped ministers to hawk his religious books in frontier settlements throughout the West. Like the national Bible and tract societies, these commercial ventures aimed to move books westward. This was a kind of "forced trade," as Carey called it, which worked to develop new markets, not just tap old ones. On at least one occasion, Weems drew a salary from Carey to cover his expenses. But the goal, of course, was always profit; and nearly always commercial colporteurs earned all of their income from commissions on sales.[25]

Traditional religious colportage differed from commercial itinerant book-selling in that religious colporteurs were usually dedicated to the cause of Christian evangelism, not pecuniary profit. Like auxiliary tract and Bible so-cieties, churches and denominations regularly relied on ministers and pious laymen to distribute the printed word. The Methodist Book Concern, founded in 1789, depended on that denomination's circuit-riding preachers to sell books as they made their rounds. Eventually, several denominational publishers, in-cluding denominational tract societies, adopted formal colportage projects for some of their work. The Baptists began colportage in the early 1840s, the Presbyterians in the late 1840s, and the Methodists in the early 1850s. Yet even these dedicated religious colporteurs usually worked on commission. Giving away publications for free was a very modest part of their mission.[26]

The American Tract Society, in contrast, tried something new. By 1841, ATS managers had grasped the idea that if a colporteur were a commission agent, his economic, if not his evangelical, incentive would always be to sell, not to give, and thus to go where the money was. The weak form of colportage suffered from the same market bias as the auxiliary system. In the ATS form of colportage, on the other hand, the colporteur was a salaried employee, not dependent on sales commissions for income, and therefore free to go to any house, every house, regardless of the potential for sales. The American Tract Society pioneered this strong form of colportage. Though much impressed by the success of the ATS colportage project, few other societies made the move to salaried colporteurs, and no one before the Civil War came close to fielding as many colporteurs as the American Tract Society.[27]

American Tract Society colportage began in August 1841, when the society commissioned its first two colporteurs and dispatched them to Indiana and Kentucky. From that small beginning, the project grew rapidly. At the end of five years, the society had 175 colporteurs in the field; after ten years, more than 500. In the first ten years, ATS colporteurs visited more than 2 million families (11 million individuals), nearly half the population of the country. They sold 2.4 million books, granted 650,000 free books, and gave away "several million" tracts.[28]

Not surprisingly, the effort did not realize the society's grandest hopes—"to visit *every abode*," to provide "the gospel for everybody." Colporteurs and agents in the West and South frequently wrote that the needs far exceeded their resources.[29] But the work that was done was impressive. By 1856, the executive committee could boast that "when we record the fact, from carefully kept sta-

tistics, that more than five millions of families have been visited at their fire-
sides on a gospel errand, and that alone—more than are embraced in the
census returns of the United States—it implies toil for Christ, such as no other
nation on the globe ever witnessed." Under the colportage system, the committee declared, tracts "have fallen like snow-flakes over the land."[30]

The fundamental premise of ATS colportage was simply stated: "True religion is aggressive." In the first full report on the project in the annual report
for 1843, the executive committee explained the idea: "Colporteurs go indiscriminately to every family; and whenever a family is found in need of a volume
to guide them to heaven, and is unable to purchase, one is furnished gratuitously." "Indiscriminately to every family"—that was the key. In an article titled
"The Power and Spirit of Colportage," published on the tenth anniversary of
the colporteur project, the American Tract Society's managers spelled out explicitly their economic and administrative reasoning:

> In effecting this general diffusion of printed truth, questions of pe-
> cuniary profit or loss are unworthy of the Christian church: nay,
> they would defeat the enterprise. Because, 1. they would keep the
> distributing agencies hovering around the communities already fur-
> nished with the means of grace, and where ready and remunerative
> sales could be effected; 2. The laborers themselves would be secular-
> ized and rendered spiritless in their work; and 3. The publications
> would be shorn of half their power for good, when the associations
> of the people receiving them are divested of the sacredness which
> attaches to books enveloped in the prayer and self-denial of their
> bearer. For these and like reasons, the Committee never connect the
> motive of profit on sales with the colporteur's labors. His salary is
> fixed and his travelling expenses defrayed by the Society; so that
> there is no pecuniary inducement for turning aside from destitute
> households.[31]

The ATS always described colportage as an effort to move supply against
demand: "By aggressive effort, at great expense, and by forced and largely
gratuitous circulation, such as benevolence alone would prompt, it deposits an
average of one or two small volumes in each family." Two years after the launching of the project, a colporteur in the wilds of Indiana wrote, in words more
concise than many of his colleagues could manage, "I visited a vile little place,
and went to every family; sold about a dozen volumes and gave several."[32] This
was precisely what the American Tract Society managers had in mind.

To make such a system work, colporteurs had to be salaried employees (no
commissions or discounts); their travel expenses had to be paid; they had to

be supplied in the field with sufficient materials; they had to have detailed information about their territories; they had to be trained and motivated; and they had to be closely supervised. In other words, colportage required systematic management, from top to bottom. The American Tract Society worked out such a management system in the 1840s. It involved eight key elements: (1) centralized budgeting and accounting; (2) decentralized middle-level management by region; (3) systematic statistical fact gathering; (4) formal recruitment and training of line workers (colporteurs); (5) in-service training; (6) printed handbooks and instructions; (7) standardized financial reporting methods and report forms; and (8) a monthly magazine and other in-house communication media.

Budgeting and Accounting

Put in fiscal terms, the business of the American Tract Society was to move wealth westward. In the 1840s, the money for benevolent work lay largely in the East; the most economical printing resources lay in the East; but the need lay in the West. Thus, the budgeting and accounting systems had to be national, and they were. All money, like all tracts and books, flowed through New York. Disbursements and receipts from both sales and donations were handled by the treasurer and assistant treasurer at the national office. Every month the accounts were published in the society's newspaper, *American Messenger*, and they were regularly audited by the executive committee. In its publications, the committee frequently reminded employees that "the same minute accuracy in all the business transactions of the Society is aimed at that to be found in systematic commercial establishments." In the 1850s, a special outside auditing committee reviewed the financial management of the ATS and declared that it had met this standard with "economy and fidelity."[33]

In its financial accounting, the ATS was typical of businesses of the era. In budgeting and cost accounting, however, the society was somewhat different and even ahead of its time. For example, in an era when most businesses were fairly conservative, the American Tract Society was a reckless spender. The society maintained no endowment, no investments, no cash reserves, no material stock reserves. It simply spent money as fast as it could get it and shipped books and tracts as fast as it could print them. "Thus the Society, with all existing facilities," the treasurer wrote in 1857, "lives 'from hand to mouth,' asking for 'daily bread,' every week's obligations being usually beyond the means at hand." Of course, many businesses, including perhaps most publishers, lived on the brink of financial disaster. But for the ATS this style of budgeting was born of policy, not exigency. At the outset, the executive committee announced that it would never look to the treasury and adjust its efforts accordingly. The managers said they would never accumulate financial reserves or large stocks of books. Instead, they vowed they would always press onward, "knowing, that the cause is God's, and that he will never suffer it to fail." The society needed "no Bank but the hearts of the people of God."[34] When money ran out, as it regularly did, the executive committee members appealed for donations, or they covered the deficits out of their own pockets.[35]

Though rash and risk taking in spending, the society was unusually careful and systematic in accounting costs. Indeed, the methods that the ATS used to standardize and measure the cost of the product and the cost of distribution were similar to the most sophisticated cost-accounting methods developed in this era by the new textile mills of New England and elaborated later by American railroad companies. The ATS routinely figured costs for all products (tracts and books) in terms of pages per cent (penny). This standardized cost measure allowed the society to make cost comparisons across product lines and over time. Just as the railroads would later speak of cost per ton/mile, the American Tract Society spoke of cost per printed page. For example, the cost of tracts as early as the 1820s was figured at 13 pages per cent and falling. Similarly, the society calculated the cost of colportage on another standard measure: cents per family visit. This permitted comparisons across individuals and regions. In 1850, for example, the average cost of colportage nationwide was 15 cents per visit.[36]

The business historian Alfred Chandler has written that not before the 1850s did American businesspeople begin to use their accounts to determine unit costs, and that the railroads led the way. Historians of accounting, however, have found evidence of the use of cost accounting as early as 1815 by the Boston Manufacturing Company of Waltham, Massachusetts, the first of the mechanized, multiprocess textile mills in New England. In these new, functionally integrated factories, cost accounting for internal administration (management accounting) grew from the same managerial pressures that were at work within the ATS, including the substitution of wage labor for market-priced labor (contract piece work). Very few businesses before the railroads, however, used cost accounting to manage geographically dispersed operations. The American Tract Society seems to have been one of the few. The society's system of cost accounting was fairly rudimentary; for example, it did not take into account depreciation of capital. But it did permit the calculation of simple and comparative unit costs, across functional departments and across vast distances.[37]

Middle-Level Management

Alfred Chandler has also argued that in the 1840s there were virtually no middle-level managers in American business.[38] This is another generalization that does not strictly apply to the American Tract Society. In the 1840s, with the growth of colportage, the society set up a managerial hierarchy of the sort that would later become standard in American businesses with national operations. Within the central office in New York, the work was divided among several functional departments, each with a manager reporting to the executive committee. The society also had regionally based "general agents," who raised funds, worked with auxiliaries, and in other ways promoted the tract cause. The key middle managers, though, were the "superintendents of colportage," also based in regional offices. By the 1850s, the society had eight large colportage agencies, including four in the West at Cincinnati, Chicago, St. Louis, and New Orleans. Each was operated by a salaried superintendent, who supervised the work of a clerk, sometimes an assistant manager, and from 42 to 120 colporteurs in the field. These superintendents of colportage were paid salaries that were substantial for benevolent work (up to $2,000); in some cases, these salaries were equal to or greater than those of department heads in New York.[39]

Statistical Fact Gathering

Like many Americans in the early nineteenth century, the managers of the American Tract Society were obsessed with statistics.[40] Not surprisingly, they found their own production statistics especially fascinating. Every annual report brimmed with numbers—numbers of books and tracts printed, numbers sold and granted, numbers of dollars donated, numbers of miles traveled, numbers of families visited. Every year, the columns of statistics grew longer, and the numbers more impressive. At the end of its first twenty-five years, the society could boast that it had raised $2.8 million and circulated 2.5 *billion* pages of tracts and books. The *American Messenger* regularly dazzled its readers with numbers. For example, feature stories about the work at society headquarters were typically built around statistics: 236 printers and binders hard at work turning out 3,500 books and 30,000 tracts and pamphlets, *every day*, at a cost of nearly $1,000. The statistical puffery never let up. In 1850, the executive committee reported that "the number of books thus placed in the hands of the people in a single year, is believed to be greater than the aggregate of volumes in all the public libraries in this country."[41]

Besides tracking its own statistics, the society also gathered a variety of statistics from the field. A good deal of effort was devoted to the compilation of what the executive committee called "a *moral census* of the United States." Annual reports and newspaper stories frequently drew on U.S. census data and other official statistics on population, immigration, trade, and welfare. But most important were the data gathered by the society's own agents and colporteurs. Each colporteur was required to report numbers of families visited, families without Bibles, families without other religious books, and so on. These data were aggregated and analyzed by the regional superintendents and the New York office to guide decisions about book allocations and colportage assignments and to support public pleas for money.[42] "Our aim," the executive committee declared in 1845, "has been in the prosecution of the colporteur enterprise, to gather authentic facts, which should in the aggregate present a fair and accurate view of *the country as it is*." The committee's simple faith in numbers never flagged. At the end of a detailed statistical report in *Home Evangelization*, a book-length overview of colportage, the author wrote, with typical nineteenth-century confidence, "We leave the naked statistics to speak for themselves."[43]

Recruitment and Training

Because colporteurs were salaried employees, not commission agents, the American Tract Society believed that close supervision was essential. This supervision began with recruitment and training. Recruitment of colporteurs was a major responsibility of both superintendents of colportage and general agents. The salary of colporteurs was deliberately set low (initially, $150 per year plus expenses) to ensure that only dedicated evangelical Christians would apply. Applicants were then screened carefully, beginning with a formal interview by the superintendent or agent. The society's handbook for agents and colporteurs lists eighteen specific questions that the candidate was required to answer in detail. The topics ranged from the candidate's education to his religious faith to his business habits. Next, each application was reviewed by the executive committee in New York. The committee made it clear to agents and superintendents that they carried great authority in hiring, but that the application must be standardized and complete: "A mere recommendation, without the data on which it is based, is insufficient; nor can the Committee act unless there is, with the data, the express recommendation of the Agent or Superintendent. No colporteur can claim compensation for services unless commissioned by the Committee."[44]

Before finally handing the candidate his commission, the superintendent was required to put him through several weeks of training, emphasizing careful study of the society's publications. Once commissioned, the new colporteur was to be eased into the work by spending a few weeks on the road with the superintendent or with an experienced colporteur. The idea was to prepare the colporteur in two ways: to teach him the substance of the books and tracts he would be distributing and to show him how the daily work of colportage must be done. The goal, of course, was to reach everyone, and the key principle, as usual, was the system. "It is only by proceeding *systematically*," the executive committee admonished new colporteurs, "that the whole work can be successfully prosecuted."[45]

In-Service Training

To tighten supervision and to boost morale, the ATS also introduced a program of formal in-service training for colporteurs. Naturally, the society urged agents and superintendents to visit informally with the workers in the field. But very early in the history of colportage, the society also began regular colporteur conventions. The first two of these were held in 1844 in Michigan and Pennsylvania, and the idea quickly caught on. By 1850, the society was organizing and funding both small meetings of colporteurs within one- or two-state areas as well as large, week-long conventions that drew colporteurs, agents, superintendents, and ATS officials from large geographical regions.[46]

The conventions mixed the inspirational and the practical. They usually began with a day or two devoted to individual narratives of faith. ("The convention was more than once bathed in tears," according to the minutes of the Cleveland convention of 1850.) Then, the participants turned to reports on the work itself. An account of a convention in Cincinnati in 1845 explained: "The design of these reports was not merely to elicit the facts respecting the spiritual condition of the population; the amount of labor performed, and the apparent results; but to draw out minutely *the manner of performing the work*, that each might profit by the experience of the other, and that any mistakes might be pointed out and corrected." At the Cincinnati convention, and at others as well, society officials then shared with the colporteurs "practical hints" on selling books, making grants, conversing with families, handling book and tract orders, keeping accounts, and filing reports.[47] The published reports suggest that the colporteurs, whose daily work was ordinarily so solitary, valued these conventions highly. And so did the executive committee, despite—as they felt the need to point out—the considerable expense involved.[48]

Handbooks and Instructions

From at least the early 1830s, the American Tract Society used formal, printed instructions to communicate with workers in the field. Even before the colportage enterprise was launched in 1841, the ATS published guides for volunteers working in local Systematic Monthly Distributions. These ranged from one-page cards to small pamphlets.[49] After 1841, the society published a substantial handbook called *Instructions of the Executive Committee of the American Tract Society, to Colporteurs and Agents.* The society also supplied colporteurs with annual reports and with copies of *Home Evangelization, Proceedings of the Public Deliberative Meeting,* and other documents. The ATS insisted that these publications be studied diligently, with pen in hand.[50]

The few surviving colporteur reports suggest that these guides were available and followed, at least in part. Several of the colporteurs who worked in the Pine Barrens of New Jersey in the summer of 1843 marked their monthly reports as "per '*Instructions*' of the Executive Committee." Though the reports were largely narratives, all supplied the kind of statistical data demanded by the executive committee, and some used the tabular format recommended in *Instructions.* Clearly, these colporteurs felt the weight of the society's directives. One wrote: "Your reporter, *according to request,* has endeavored to be very minute in this narrative—and therefore no apology is needed for its length."[51]

Reporting Methods and Forms

The ATS was very strict about how accounts were to be kept and how information was to be reported to New York. The executive committee put the matter sharply in its instructions to general agents:

> The first requisite for a successful agency is to be *qualified for the work;* the second, to *perform it;* the third, accurately to *report it when done.* The last point is utterly essential. In the neglect of it, the Committee have not the data for wisely directing the Agent's proceedings, nor judging of his usefulness, nor knowing what he has accomplished with reference to guiding the future operations of the society within the same field.[52]

Of course, the same obligations of accounting and reporting rested upon superintendents of colportage. But even the lowliest colporteur on the frontier was required to keep detailed accounts and to make monthly, quarterly, and annual reports to his superintendent. In its *Instructions* and in sessions at the colporteur conventions, American Tract Society officials explained in minute detail how records were to be kept and reported—both financial accounts and social statistics for the society's ongoing "moral census" of America.[53]

To standardize the reporting process and to ease the burden on colporteurs, who had better things to do, the society provided each man with two account books and a set of preprinted forms. One account book served as a daily log; the other as a running summary for monthly, quarterly, and annual reports. For each of these reports, the society provided blanks to be filled in and mailed to the superintendent. In its instructions, the executive committee made it clear that accounting was part of the work of colportage: "However excellent the spirit and efficient the labors of the Colporteur, he will fail in the discharge of essential duty, if, having done his work, he neglects to report his labors properly, or to adjust his accounts accurately."[54]

As might be expected, the society was most concerned to account for free grants of books—a very costly enterprise. Tracts were almost always given freely; most books were sold. But the colporteur was also expected to make free grants of books to families who had no religious books, desired them, but had no money to buy. The society insisted that free grants be made, and it left the decision to the "sound discretion" of each colporteur. At the same time, the society required an especially careful accounting and justification of all grants. In 1850, for example, ATS colporteurs sold precisely 417,939 books, granted 113,891 books, and gave away several million tracts. Altogether, the grants of books and tracts in the year leading up to the 1850 annual meeting totaled 35 million pages. The *Instructions* laid out the rules for making grants and for reporting them; these rules were also reinforced at the colporteur conventions.[55]

The surviving records suggest that colporteurs were careful to follow the rules, or at least to say they had. "In every instance where these grants have been made," wrote one of the New Jersey colporteurs, "the families had no evangelical religious books, save a Bible and hymn book: and had not the money to buy—but expressed a desire to get them." Other colporteurs wrote that they sometimes paid for a book out of their own pockets if they felt a person could afford to buy but would not. The executive committee regretted that the society's strict rules sometimes produced this extra burden on colporteurs. The committee sometimes argued that a more free distribution of books, like tracts, would be best—were the funds available.[56] But they were not. And with limited funds, strict supervision of accounts was essential for systematic management of a national operation: "The monthly or quarterly report of each [colporteur] is before the Committee, who can readily direct the contraction or expansion of the gratuitous issues, if their interposition seems necessary."[57]

Magazine and In-House Media

To support the work of colportage, the American Tract Society founded the *American Messenger*, a monthly newspaper/magazine, in 1843. The *American*

Messenger was not a house organ; indeed, it became a popular American monthly in the 1840s, achieving a circulation of 100,000 by 1848 and 200,000 by 1853.[58] It was designed to promote the colportage cause as widely as possible. But it was also aimed at colporteurs, agents, and volunteer tract workers around the country. It provided encouragement and instruction from the top down, from management to employees; it also allowed low-level employees in different parts of the country to share their experiences with each other. The paper routinely carried narratives of colportage work as well as official proceedings, reports, and announcements. The *American Messenger* became, in effect, an ongoing colporteur convention-in-print. The society also provided colporteurs with copies of a variety of other publications, which recounted the inspirational histories of tract societies, the ATS, and colportage, and in other ways drew the worker in the field into the larger community of religious publishing and benevolence.[59]

In the business practice of the American Tract Society, supervision was the word. Five years into the colportage project, the executive committee explained that "at an early period of the work it became apparent that a plan of thorough *supervision* was indispensable to the safe and successful prosecution of the enterprise." Ten years into the project, the committee declared that the goal of thorough supervision had been realized:

> With unwearied watchfulness in the investigation of the character
> and qualifications of candidates; with documents clearly defining the
> relations and duties of laborers; with a system of rigid accountability
> in all business transactions; with experienced supervisory agencies;
> with friends in all parts of the country to report any delinquency;
> and, above all, with the grace of God to direct, restrain, and control,
> we see not but there are as many safeguards around this as any
> other human agency. And with this growing conviction, we see few
> obstacles to the speedy enlistment of vastly increased numbers of
> evangelical laborers in this and various enterprises appropriate to
> laymen; thus speeding on the work of the world's conversion to
> God.[60]

The strong colportage system—the ATS model—sidestepped several of the free-rider problems that faced religious publishers. Salaried colporteurs who called on everyone, including the destitute, and who had authority to give away books were able to reach the obviously good free rider, the pious poor who merely lacked the money to buy. If giving away books had been the only task, the traveling colporteur, who knocked on every door, was clearly the best person to do it. Strong colportage also sidestepped the problem of organizational free riders in the auxiliaries. Colporteurs were employees, not volunteers, and their morale and conduct were dependent upon compensation and supervision flowing from New York. They had their own morale problems, of course, but those problems were different from the free-rider problems of voluntary organizations. The colporteur was not well equipped, however, to solve the problem of the bad free rider, the person who sought a free book but who could afford to pay or who received a free book but made poor use of it. As an itinerant outsider just passing through the neighborhood, the colporteur was in no position to sort the good free riders from the bad, that is, to administer a full-fledged system of differential pricing.

Eventually, most book and tract societies would deal with this problem by drawing a distinction between what was to be given and what was to be sold. Typically, tracts were to be given; books were to be sold. The colporteur thus would have no price decision to make. American Tract Society colporteurs, however, had the authority to give away books or to sell them at less than cost. But differential pricing was difficult in practice and was gradually replaced in the ATS by a dichotomous sell-give decision. Even so, the question of when to sell and when to give, the crucial economic decision, was not easily made. To simplify the decision-making process, the ATS colporteurs were encouraged to give away only certain small, cheap volumes (most often Richard Baxter's *Call to the Unconverted*). Those were the give-away books; the others were to be sold.[61] Though ATS colporteurs were expected to judge the recipients of their books and to sell if they could, the system increasingly looked ahead to a simpler style of religious book distribution in which some books are given, some sold, but no attempt is made to sort the good free riders from the bad. Everyone gets a free book, no questions asked. That, of course, is the modern style of print-media evangelism, the style that we routinely run into every day on the sidewalks of American cities. But it is an old ideal as well, an ideal held dear by Bible and tract society managers from the beginning. For, as the Philadelphia Bible Society managers had said in the very early years of charity Bible work, a Bible is a Bible, the word is the word, no matter how it is obtained or how it is used.

The business methods of the American Tract Society in the 1830s and 1840s were different from the methods of the commercial book trade. During this era, many book publishers did use traveling agents in a way that seems at first glance similar to the ATS's system of colportage. But in fact the methods were different. The agents for commercial booksellers (and, indeed, most religious publishers as well) worked on a discount/commission system; they received books at discounted prices and sold them at a markup. Or, more rarely, they handled "subscription" sales, taking orders for books not yet published.[62] Both types of agents were paid on commission. Thus, a good deal of risk devolved upon them, and their faithful performance was enforced by the discipline of the marketplace. The letter files of publishing houses show how the system worked: publishers fixed discounts, assigned territories to agents, took orders, and shipped books. No supervision was provided; the profit motive of the agent sufficed.[63] Indeed, many publishers in this era were moving away from the use of retail agents altogether, preferring instead to place books into the market wholesale and leave direct consumer sales to others.[64]

The American Tract Society simply operated a different sort of business. This was "no mere book-selling scheme," as the executive committee liked to put it. Indeed, the managers of the ATS held most of their fellow publishers in contempt. "It is most clear," they wrote in 1836, "that the tremendous influence of the public press in this country *may not be left* solely to the operation and influence of sales for the purpose of gain." This was the never-ending theme. In his report to the special auditing committee of 1857, the treasurer sounded it yet again: "The aim of issuing books for the sake of *profit on the sales*, has never entered into the counsels of the Committee." With immortal souls at stake, they had no choice: "If the Society might adopt the mere principles of *merchandise*, publish attractive works, and sell them to those who know their value and will come to buy, it might dispense with half its donations, and anxieties, and toils; but how then could its conductors meet souls at the day of judgment, who had perished through their criminal neglect."[65] This effort to subvert the market, to drive supply against demand, was successful enough to draw the heated criticism of commercial booksellers. In 1849, one author and marketer of religious books put out a diatribe against "charity publication societies," charging that their efforts had effectively destroyed the market for religious books in the ordinary commercial book trade. And the chief malefactor was the American Tract Society.[66]

In *Visible Hand*, his classic study of the rise of modern business in America, Alfred Chandler associated modern business practice with the extension of administrative control over market forces. He wrote that "modern business enterprise appeared for the first time in history when the volume of economic activities reached a level that made administrative coordination more efficient and more profitable than market coordination." JoAnne Yates has refined Chandler's argument by showing how this new administrative control was exercised. She defines the theory and practice of *systematic management*, which emerged in the late nineteenth century, as "control through communication." In this era, she says, American businesses learned to use middle-level managers, written instructions to employees, systematic reports, printed forms, improved record keeping, statistical analysis, meetings and conferences, in-house magazines, and other new communication techniques to impose the visible hand of management on the far-flung operations of a national firm.[67]

This, of course, describes precisely the business of the American Tract Society. And it describes, to some extent, other religious publishing societies and church organizations in the first half of the nineteenth century. The ATS was unusually systematic in its national administration, but it was not unique. Some of the same methods were used by the Presbyterian Board of Publication, the American Baptist Publication Society, the Methodist Book Concern, and other publishers. National church organizations also pioneered some of these managerial techniques. As a hierarchically managed and fast-growing denomination, the Methodist Episcopal Church was especially keen to gather and publish statistical membership data and to keep its local leaders, stewards, elders, and circuit-riders informed and energized.[68]

The American Bible Society also moved toward a bureaucratic form of national organization and administration in the 1850s. The agent system in particular was brought under more and more centralized control. By 1856, the ABS agent had fifteen different forms and documents to juggle, and the *Bible Agent's Manual* ran to thirty-five pages. (In the *Manual*, "accuracy and method" come before "piety" in the discussion of the essential personality traits of a Bible agent.) Peter Wosh sees in these years a "transformation of the American Bible Society from a missionary moral reform organization to something very new and very different: a national nonprofit corporate bureaucracy."[69]

The American Bible Society also adopted colportage, in a modest way, as early as 1848. After 1869, colportage became an increasingly important part of the ABS system.[70] But for the ABS, this change came slowly. Long after the American Tract Society had largely given up on its volunteer auxiliaries, the American Bible Society managers remained steadfast in the belief that a colporteur could never do what a local society could do. For more than fifty years, despite deep frustration and incessant complaints, the American Bible Society stuck with the auxiliary system. As late as 1860, the managers declared: "The Board have by no means lost confidence in the auxiliary system. We believe it to be the only effectual one for carrying the Word of God to every door and every individual in the land. In no other way, we believe, could the Bible be so generally and so effectually distributed, and the destitution be so thoroughly supplied."[71]

Other nonpublishing religious and benevolent organizations also drew on management techniques pioneered by the American Tract Society. The American Home Missionary Society (AHMS), for example, employed systematic accounting and reporting methods, statistical fact gathering, printed instructions, and employee periodicals. The annual reports of the AHMS and the files of the *Home Missionary* are strikingly similar to the reports and periodicals of the American Tract Society. In the 1820s, they were even printed by Daniel Fanshaw, printer to both the ABS and the ATS. The organizational structures and publication strategies of reform groups such as the American Temperance Society and the American Anti-Slavery Society were similar as well. In other words, in their business practices as well as in their ideology, these groups were indeed a great sisterhood of evangelical reform.[72]

Religious publishers and reform organizations are usually overlooked by business historians because they stood apart from the main current of market capitalism in nineteenth-century America. But precisely because they operated against the marketplace, they were very early forced to gather their entire business enterprise within the purview of administration. If this is what modern business management is all about, then these organizations—especially the American Tract Society—may well have been progenitors of it. The contribution of businessmen to benevolent reform is a common story; perhaps the contribution of systematic benevolence to business practice is an equally important one.[73]

In 1856, the American Bible Society launched a second general supply. Once again, as in 1829, success would be elusive. Once again, the society managers would be frustrated by the vast size and complexity of the country and by another economic panic, in 1857. But this time—and from this time forward—the ABS, like the American Tract Society, would no longer depend on the millennial hope that volunteers would suffice. To move books against the force of the market, the countervailing force of organization would be needed. "Wherever possible," the managers wrote, "we advise that the work shall be done by a voluntary force; for all the funds that can be spared will be needed to enable our presses to meet the increased demand. But where volunteers cannot be found, let paid agents be employed; for by whatever means the intended result must be reached."[74] "By whatever means": this was an ideology, not just of universal circulation of the word, but of business management; not just general supply, but systematic enterprise. It was the ideology of the modern not-for-profit philanthropic corporation.

6

How Readers Should Read

In the summer of 1851, twenty-five colporteurs and agents of the American Tract Society convened at Reading, Pennsylvania, to pray, to study, and to inspire each other to renewed evangelical zeal. As at all colporteur conventions, ATS leaders reserved some of the time for instruction in society policies, procedures, and paperwork. But the chief goal was to boost morale, and the way to that goal was storytelling. One after another, the colporteurs shared tales of adventure on the highways and back roads of western America—from scenes of tearful conversions to hostile attacks by dogs and guns. They also described their own religious experiences, their own life histories, their own conversion stories. At the Reading convention, one colporteur said that years ago he had "bought a copy of Pilgrim's Progress, and read and reread it in his sick-room till he became absorbed in its illustrations of divine truth." Another said he "had been awakened by reading an old copy of 'Baxter's Call,' dingy and thumbed for a hundred years."[1]

Colporteurs, whose daily lives were awash in religious publications, routinely testified to the power of the printed word. The stories the colporteurs told at Reading are standard, even archetypal, but they are more subtle and revealing than they may seem at first glance. They suggest several themes about how colporteurs, agents, and managers at the American Tract Society (and other publishing societies) understood the nature of religious reading in nineteenth-century America. First, and most simply, these stories suggest great faith in the sheer power of reading. People involved in religious book and tract work in the nineteenth century seem to have had no doubt that reading alone could save lives and souls—or destroy them. Second, though powerful, reading was not magical. For reading to work properly, the reader must work hard, especially in the realm of religion. The power of religious reading lay not in a Pentecostal outpouring of the spirit but in careful, studious, intensive reading. Cursory reading was sinful reading. The colporteur at the Reading convention read and reread his *Pilgrim's Progress*. Third, religious reading was an acquired taste. The best tracts and books were simple, plain, and attractive in style, but readers would not automatically choose them. Indeed, the more a sinner needed religious reading, the less he would seek it. Though religious reading must be voluntary, religious books and tracts must be pressed into the hands of readers, not merely left among the smorgasbord of choices of the commercial marketplace. Fourth, the colporteur stories suggest a preference for books over tracts. Tracts (and religious newspapers) could capture the fleeting attention of an inattentive sinner, but only a book could develop ideas in sufficient depth for reading to display its full transformative power. Fifth, the best books were the old books, such as John Bunyan's *Pilgrim's Progress* and Richard Baxter's *A Call to the Unconverted*. These classics of English Puritanism—"thumbed for a hundred years"—would carry the enduring virtues of religious reading into a new age of mass media: simplicity, yet depth; emotion, yet reason; cheapness, yet permanence.

The religious publishers loved and hated modern life, and this love-hate relationship rested upon a theory of reading. They believed that modern communication technologies—the steam-powered printing press, the steamship and railroad, the magnetic telegraph, all guided by market capitalism—were instruments of corruption and death. Yet these were also instruments given by God for the regeneration of the world. In an 1849 editorial, the American Tract Society's newspaper, the *American Messenger*, captured the dualism that lay at the heart of the reading experience:

> In a world where thought is unbound, and inquiry unrestricted,
> THE PRESS becomes, perhaps, the most important of human agencies for good or evil. We can neither resist nor disregard its action.
> We cannot tie up men's purses that they shall not buy, nor seal up
> their eyes that they shall not read, nor shut up their spirit of inquiry
> that they shall not investigate. The world has gone to reading, and
> read they will, for weal or woe.[2]

To provide reading material for weal not woe was the mission of the great religious publishing societies. And like their Puritan forefathers in New England, they turned to books such as Baxter's *Call*, the first book after the Bible that John Eliot had translated for his Indian mission in the 1660s. Eliot's nineteenth-century descendants employed the newest, most modern technologies and business strategies to reproduce the most traditional reading experience.

The religious publishers believed that books could kill. The *American Messenger* told lurid tales of young readers driven to madness, murder, and suicide. "Bad Books" reads the headline over a typical brief story: "An old farmer and his wife, residing near Boston, were recently murdered at night. The murderer after his arrest confessed that he had been stimulated to such deeds by reading the biographies of criminals, whose feats he desired to emulate." In another story, a young boy, possessed by wild fantasies from reading adventure books, ran away to sea, fell into debauchery and wickedness, and died of consumption: "So sunk into the grave, in his nineteenth year, one who, but for the corrupting influence of bad books, might have lived a long and happy life." In still another story, a young woman, a runaway who had assumed the name of a French novelist, was found dead beside her lover on Braintree Common (a suicide pact) "with a copy of the most vicious of the novels of her French namesake on her person." "Ye writers and publishers and venders of this vicious literature, behold your victim!" the *Messenger's* editors proclaimed. "Stand by that stiffened form, and count the gains of your unrighteous calling on that coffin-lid! Read the epitaph penned by the stricken father for the monument of a wayward child—'DELUDED BY THE WRITINGS OF_____.' "³

Writers for the American Tract Society compared the power of reading to the intoxicating, addictive power of alcohol. In its first issue of January 1843, the *American Messenger* invited submissions on a variety of topics related to religious reading, including what the editors took to be the obvious similarity between alcohol and bad books. "Do not acknowledged principles in respect to the manufacture and traffic in intoxicating liquors apply with ten-fold emphasis to writing, printing, and vending vicious books?" the editors asked. In subsequent *Messenger* articles, the answer was plain:

> Bad books are like ardent spirits; they furnish neither "aliment" nor "medicine": they are *"poison."* Both *intoxicate*—one the mind, the other the body; the thirst for each increases by being fed, and is never satisfied; both ruin—one the intellect, the other the health,

and together, the soul. . . .*Mental delirium tremens* is as certain a consequence of habitual intoxication from such reading, as is that awful
disease the certain end of the inebriate. Beware of it![4]

What did the American Tract Society mean by "bad books"? "Infidel" and
"popish" publications were part of the problem. As late as the 1840s, the ATS
managers were still as worried about Tom Paine as Elias Boudinot had been
in 1810. One society pamphlet described a faithful churchgoer who had picked
up in the road a single leaf of Paine's *Age of Reason* and was haunted for a year
by religious doubt.[5] But the American Tract Society reserved its deepest fear
and loathing for popular fiction. Novels, especially sensational French novels
by writers such as Eugene Sue, were likened to invading armies, to plagues
and pestilence. They were intoxicants, worse than rum. They were "mental and
moral poison."[6]

ATS writers imagined the effects of novels on readers in deeply psychological terms. The most obvious effect was "undue mental excitement," as one
writer explained:

> Novel reading enfeebles the mental powers. This is done by the
> excitement above described. Let the feelings be thus overwrought,
> let them be drawn up to their highest tension for hours together,
> and let this be repeated day after day, and a reaction must at length
> ensue. The mind will, in most instances, settle down into a stag
> nant, imbecile state, or else become prey to a morbid irritability of
> the most painful character.

Part of the danger, he said, was that novel-driven enthusiasm and excitement
had no anchor in the real world: "It is well, when occasion requires, to feel
emotion; but is it well for the noble mind of man thus to squander its emotions
upon vanity, and burn with a concentrated excitement over scenes that never
had existence?" For the novel reader, this kind of "overheated fantasy," like the
consumption of alcohol, would naturally spiral out of control. "Unsatisfied with
a moderate draught," the writer continued, "he hastens on with the story, from
page to page and from chapter to chapter, forgetful of other engagements and
regardless of the passing hours, his mind all the while steeped in a most
delicious intoxication." In short, as another writer put it, novel reading "is
insatiable, and leaves the mind in a perplexed and painful state and often
terminates in insanity."[7]

More common than full-blown insanity was "mental dissipation." "Novel-
reading is pernicious to man as an *intellectual* being," an ATS writer explained.
"Novels make few appeals to reason. This neglect soon engenders an aversion

to profound thought, which results in inability." For the Congregational and Presbyterian leaders of the American Tract Society, still imbued with a Calvinist faith in rationality and learning and a fear of "enthusiasm," the destruction of reason was surely the most dreadful effect of fiction upon the mind of the reader. One writer summed up the problem nicely:

> This kind of reading enfeebles the intellect. It leaves the reader little room for the investigation of truth or the exercise of a discriminating judgment. It saves him the trouble of thinking for himself. He is apt to acquire a distaste for solid instruction, and to content himself with but the show of knowledge. He becomes the mere slave of feeling, and his intellect languishes amidst the sickly sentimentalism, the dreamy extravagance, of the romantic world.[8]

The novel was noxious because it was fiction. Later, in the second half of the nineteenth century, most religious publishers came to believe that chaste, wholesome religious fiction was possible, that fiction could have a place in the Christian home. But in the antebellum era, fiction was usually decried precisely because it was "false." And not only were novels false, they undermined the taste for truth and true religion. "Popular fiction invariably gives a disrelish for simple truth," an ATS writer argued. It "engenders a habit of reading for amusement simply, which destroys all hope for mental improvement." Even the Bible lost its allure for the novel reader: "The simple and touching narratives of the New Testament will have no charm for the morbid taste you are cultivating; the story of the cross will seem insipid and tame, compared with the high-wrought scenes to which you have long been accustomed."[9]

Though the American Tract Society, in particular, was obsessed with the evils of "vicious literature," denominational publishers also sounded the alarm. The Methodists, for example, reorganized their moribund tract society in the 1850s in part to resist the "great torrent of wickedness and infidelity" flowing from the modern press and to counter "the unhappy influence exercised on the minds of the young by the yellow-covered literature."[10] Unlike the American Tract Society, the American Baptist Publication Society did not oppose "wholesome fiction," but Baptist leaders spoke in similar terms of the dreadful power of the modern press for evil.[11] Presbyterians, who were prominent in the leadership of the American Tract Society, sounded much like the ATS in the publications of their Board of Publication. "Infidelity, immorality, and error of every stamp, are poured in torrents over the land from the press, threatening to sweep away the virtue and the souls of the people," the board declared in 1849. The Presbyterian board's newspaper, the *Home and Foreign Record*, concurred: "One effect of light reading is, that it dissipates the mind, and renders it averse to serious thought, and solid and profitable reading. It also has a corrupting influence. It feeds and nourishes the depravity of our natures, and quenches the Spirit's heavenly influences. . . . Shun light reading as you would shun poison! It leads to death!" Like the ATS's *American Messenger*, the *Home and Foreign Record* relayed the sad details of youthful suicides, of death by reading.[12]

Reading, in other words, was a very dangerous activity. Its power was direct, swift, and sure. "How great is the influence of books?" the *American Messenger* asked. "Every volume you read will make impressions that will never pass away. Every one will make and leave its mark; will exert an influence now or in the future, in time or for eternity." So, again and again, the publications of the American Tract Society—and other publishers, too—urged readers to "PUT DOWN THAT NOVEL!" Novels were a libel on the very name of literature, in the judgment of the American Tract Society. "If they shine," the *Messenger* declared, "it is only 'as the rotting log, or putrescent carcase, which is phosphorescent because decaying; if brilliant, it is only as the will-o'-the-wisp, which is caused by impure and fetid gases.' " For the novel reader, the certain end was doom. "And the summing up of your sad history may all be written in the mournful sentence, 'THE NOVEL-READER IN PERDITION!' "[13]

If "bad books" were so pernicious and so powerful, what should be done? Though the religious publishers sometimes longed for the good old days when immoral literature was suppressed by Christian community consensus, they seemed to understand that public opinion no longer supported censorship.[14] Furthermore, in the modern age of democracy and religious disestablishment, they themselves had come to accept "voluntaryism in affairs of religion, republicanism in politics, and freedom in commerce." Despite all their screeds against wicked reading, they sought no Protestant inquisition. In their 1845 annual report, the American Tract Society managers explicitly renounced the "Romanist" slogan of the Reformation era: "We must put down printing, or printing will put us down." Instead, the ATS proposed the converse: "We must put *up* printing, or printing will put us down." Though rejecting censorship, the society did seek to engage the enemy in battle. "Though it would be foolhardy in us to attempt an 'index prohibitorium' or an official 'imprimatur,' yet it would be Christian prudence to make the press labor prolifically with 'the true Gospel.' "[15] Sounding much like John Milton's *Aeropagitica*, the *American Messenger* routinely published paeans to press freedom. Like Milton, the editors were confident that truth would eventually prevail: "Thank God, the press is free; and while its power for evil is tremendous, its power for good is inconceivable."[16]

To defeat the "Satanic press," the religious publishers proposed to meet the enemy on his own ground, on his own terms, with his own weapons. An early issue of the *American Messenger* asked, "Is it not time to enter the lists with Satan in this direction; and if he will thrust trash and folly under the eyes of travelers, at so cheap a rate that they can't help buying it, why should not good men press truth upon their attention in the same way, or a better one?"[17] What did they mean when they said "the same way"? In part, they meant a similar *style* of popular prose presented in a cheap, consumable format—for example, a tract.

From its earliest days, the American Tract Society had described its tracts in terms suited to the mass medium that they were: "short," "interesting," "pungent," "unassuming," "adapted to all characters and conditions." The ATS Publication Committee sought tracts "in *the most simple style*, and especially *narratives* calculated to engage and fasten the attention."[18] The American Tract Society's notions about what made a compelling religious tract harked back to the earliest days of tract work in the United States and England. In a classic essay borrowed from the Religious Tract Society of London, Jedidiah Morse's New England Tract Society, at its founding in 1814, had laid out the qualities of a good gospel tract. It must be simple, striking, entertaining, nonsectarian, and full of ideas:

> A plain didactic essay on a religious subject may be read by a Christian with much pleasure; but the persons for whom these Tracts are chiefly designed, will fall asleep over it. This will not do; it is throwing labour and money away. There must be something to allure the listless to read, and this can only be done by blending entertainment with instruction. Where *narrative* can be made the medium of conveying truth, it is eagerly to be embraced, as it not only engages the attention, but also assists the memory, and makes a deeper impression on the heart. *Dialogue* is another way of rendering a Tract entertaining. The conversation draws the reader insensibly along.[19]

A splendid exemplar of this style is *The Dairyman's Daughter*, written for the Religious Tract Society in 1805 by the Anglican evangelical cleric Legh Richmond. It became a perennial favorite of tract societies on both sides of the Atlantic throughout the nineteenth century. A first-person narrative written in the voice of a minister in rural England, *The Dairyman's Daughter* tells the story of the death by tuberculosis of Elizabeth Wallbridge, the thirty-one-year-old daughter of a poor dairy farmer. In a series of dialogues with the narrator during her final weeks of life, Elizabeth describes her selfish and thoughtless youth, her conversion to faith in Jesus Christ, and her subsequent growth in piety, humility, and contentment. While her loving parents weep, Elizabeth is serene. "Oh, sir! what a Saviour have I found!" she declares to the visiting minister. "He is more than I could ask or desire. In His fullness I have found all that my poverty could need; in His bosom I have found a resting place from all sin and sorrow; in His word I have found strength against doubt and un-belief." Like Hannah More's Cheap Repository tracts, *The Dairyman's Daughter* idealizes pious poverty. "How often is the poor man's cottage the palace of God!" the narrator exclaims. "Decency and cleanliness were manifest within and without." But *The Dairyman's Daughter* is not about class contentment or pastoral paternalism; it is simply about the good heart of one young woman and "the free mercy of God." Throughout the story, the narrator gently quizzes the dying Elizabeth on matters of doctrine: " 'Were you not soon convinced,' said I, 'that your salvation must be an act of entire grace on the part of God, wholly independent of your own previous works or deservings?' " But doctrine is not the point of the tract either. The power of *The Dairyman's Daughter* lies in the narrative and dialogue, and in the example of one woman's humble imitation of Christ:

> "My dear friend, do you not feel you are supported?"
> "The Lord deals very gently with me," she replied.
> "Are not His promises now very precious to you?"
> "They are all yea and amen in Christ Jesus."
> "Are you in much bodily pain?"
> "So little that I almost forget it."
> "How good the Lord is!"
> "And how unworthy am I!"
> "You are going to see Him as He is."
> "I think . . . I hope . . . I believe that I am."
> She again fell into a short slumber.[20]

As the tide of sentimental fiction and other secular literature rose in the mid–nineteenth century, the religious publishers redoubled their commitment to popular genre publishing. With the ATS in the lead, many societies began colportage efforts in the 1840s and 1850s, and all of them made extensive use of simple, narrative tracts. Like the fictions they fought, tracts could have direct, powerful effects on their readers—or so said the reports of the publishers. The accounts of conversions by a single tract are legion. Indeed, the societies' reports were (to borrow one of their own phrases) bathed in the tears of penitent sinners, saved by reading.[21]

The newspaper was another popular print medium promoted by religious publishers in the antebellum era. Some religious papers were denominational organs targeting narrow audiences; others—such as the ATS's *American Messenger*—were popular mass media aimed at everyone.[22] This aim required a popular style. The *Messenger* made this point clear: "Our ideal of a religious paper would not be met by giving it the method and stateliness of a sermon. We would not repel the general reader by elaborate expositions, or abstract discussions, or incessant exhortations. No; the newspaper requires varied and lively talent in a style of its own."[23]

And what was this "style of its own"? The editors of the *Messenger* laid it out for prospective writers: "The most acceptable and useful articles for our columns are simple, evangelical narratives, which unfold the plan of salvation to plain minds, in the style of 'Poor Joseph,' or 'the Dairyman's Daughter,' " two of the society's most popular tracts. Like tracts, submissions to the *Messenger* must be "brief, tersely written, highly evangelical articles, suited to claim and reward the attention of half a million of readers," the editors said.[24] The managers of the ATS believed that Americans were obsessive newspaper readers and that the United States was the greatest newspaper country on earth. To entice and capture this modern newspaper audience, the *American Messenger* must be radically condensed as well as simple and entertaining. Too many submissions were "long, hortatory, or didactic," the editors complained. Instead, they offered pithy advice to prospective writers: "Be Pithy." In the end, they hoped, "the universal disposition to newspaper reading may thus be turned to the account of direct religious instruction, and entire communities may be brought under the same evangelical influence."[25]

In style, if not in purpose, the narratives in ATS tracts and in the *American Messenger* read remarkably like the sentimental, romantic novels and story papers that the editors deplored. But beyond obvious differences in religious intent, the editors emphasized one less-apparent difference in genre: their stories were *true*. Anecdotes, narratives, dialogues, sad tales of loss, grief, and sorrow—all were needed, but all must be scrupulously true. No fiction allowed. "Our encouragement arises," a speaker told the annual meeting in 1833, "from the fact that the truth is simple—not so much a moral abstraction, as a few *great facts*."[26] As a kind of demonstration of the veracity of their publications, American Tract Society officials visited the house in England where Elizabeth Wallbridge, "the dairyman's daughter," had died such an exemplary death decades before. They checked out the facts of the tract, found them to be true, and even brought back to New York the armchair in which Elizabeth had passed her final days. They invited visitors to sit in the chair and to believe—much as the risen Jesus had invited Doubting Thomas to thrust his hand into his riven side.[27] And the ATS was not alone. Across the tract societies and the denominational publishers, the aim was to bend the popular press, to turn the genres of popular literature to the cause of "truth."

Yet the religious publishers never felt at ease with popular genre publishing, even when those genres were bent to serve the truth. They believed that religious truth, however sweetened or simplified, was difficult. As sinners, people resisted religious instruction, even when it was clothed in the most popular fashions. In the words of the Presbyterian Board of Publication, "Religious knowledge is a benefit, of which men less feel the need the less they possess of it. Here the demand does not create a supply, for the demand may not exist, however extreme the necessity. The gospel provides for its own dissemination." Similarly, the American Tract Society managers explained that their mission was to deliver the gospel message to people who resisted it, "who know not its value and would never apply for it were it issued in the usual channels of trade." The circulation of religious publications required "the principle of *aggression*—or the carrying of the Gospel to all who need it, without trusting to the uncertain hope of their coming after it."[28]

The American Tract Society seemed almost contradictory in its embrace of, yet resistance to, the genres of popular literature. Amid the flood of articles in the *American Messenger* praising the simple, touching, entertaining narrative style, the editors also denounced that style. "It would require little tact or labor to cater for the popular taste, and send abroad by millions the easily written, easily read, and never digested volume," the editors explained. "But the Tract Society was formed for a very different purpose, and has pursued widely different objects. From the outset it has repudiated the light frothy literature, which, however popular, is worthless. It has published such books, and such only, as the people, and all the people, *ought* to read."[29]

In other words, repackaging religion was insufficient. Content was not the sole problem. Even religious literature could be worthless, if it were "easily read, and never digested." The chief task of the publishers was to publish good books, but that was not enough. They must also teach readers to read properly.

In the prospectus to the *American Messenger* in 1843, the ATS editors listed the topics they would emphasize, including at the top of their list the "benefits and mischiefs" of the modern press. The new paper would condemn novels and licentious books, of course, and it would promote wholesome Christian literature. But the moral artillery of the *American Messenger* would be aimed not just at evil *content*. The American Tract Society would also target the very *style* of reading that popular genres encouraged. From its first issue onward, the *American Messenger* would be the implacable foe of "the habits of cursory reading."[30]

Cursory reading was bad reading, no matter what the content. It was bad because it was useless. Reading "for mere amusement," reading "to while away your time," and reading "at random, indiscriminately," left the reader with nothing gained. Paraphrasing Coleridge, the *American Messenger* compared casual, cursory readers to an hourglass: "their reading, like the sand, running in, and then out, and leaving not a vestige behind." Often, the religious publishers went further and argued that cursory reading was worse than useless, for a vestige, an evil vestige, could be left behind. Because readers were sinners, even cursory reading of immoral books and newspapers could plant wicked thoughts. "Light reading . . . feeds and nourishes the depravity of our natures," the Presbyterian *Home and Foreign Record* declared, "and quenches the Spirit's heavenly influences."[31]

Cursory reading, however, did not work as easily for good as for evil. Here again, the thinking of the religious publishers seemed contradictory. Though they imagined that a quick scan of a gospel tract or religious newspaper could have enormous impact, they also argued that cursory religious reading could not really succeed. The word of God required study, reflection, and prayer. It did not work by magic or even like magic. The Bible, of course, provided the best object for the application of proper reading method. In a widely reprinted devotional volume, *Letters to an Anxious Inquirer*, T. Charlton Henry included a chapter on how to read the Bible. Henry sought to impress upon his readers the idea that religious reading was difficult, that it required skill, exertion, and patience. Some careless readers expected the supernatural when they opened the Bible; they expected the Holy Spirit to guide them miraculously to understanding. Others did not expect miracles, but, habituated to light reading, they did expect the meaning of the Bible to be transparent; they expected the work of reading to be easy. Both were invariably disappointed. "He looks directly for some instantaneous operation upon his mind," Henry wrote of the cursory Bible reader. "He reads. No such result ensues. . . . A miraculous energy was anticipated from language, without its reaching him by the ordinary channel of reflection and comparison. This is a perversion of the design of the Scriptures."[32]

Instead, Henry argued in a traditional Calvinist vein that the Bible must be read in the manner that all serious works must be read: slowly and thoughtfully. The Holy Spirit did work through reading, but in the natural manner, by labor of the human intellect. "He does not make us wise above that which is written, but he makes us wise up to that which is written," Henry explained. "He gives to us the power of spiritual discernment, but that power is exerted through the medium of our own judgment." In other words, successful religious readers must be active readers: "For the most part, it will be found that the Divine assistance is furnished in proportion to our own active and sincere desires."[33]

Other writers for the societies also provided instructions for proper reading. In the introduction to his own *Anxious Inquirer*, John James laid out the proper methodology for reading a religious book. Read alone, in deep seriousness, with earnest prayer; read slowly, meditate, digest, reflect; read "regularly through in order"; don't "pick and cull particular portions"; read "calmly and coolly." He urged readers to avoid "a rambling method of reading." System and meditation were indispensable: "Salvation depends on knowledge, and knowledge on meditation."[34]

This kind of advice appeared regularly in the tracts and newspapers of the American Tract Society and the Presbyterian Board of Publication. The *American Messenger* frequently carried explicit instructions for reading, instructions designed to rescue people from the habit of cursory reading. Reading should never be random or indiscriminate; it should always be slow, attentive, and purposive:

> Let not your eyes slide thoughtlessly over your pages, like the shadows of clouds over the fields of summer. Permit not your thoughts to wander. Dream not over the printed page, but brace up, and concentrate and fix your thoughts. Attend to every statement; follow the course of every argument; mark well every illustration; notice the connection of each part with every other; leave nothing uncomprehended, but dwell upon it, and turn it over, till you fully understand the author's meaning. As well gaze at the clouds, as at the volume before you, if you give it not your fixed and earnest attention.

Slow down, readers were told. "It is not the bee's touching of the flowers that gathers honey, but her abiding for a time upon them, and drawing out the sweet," the *Home and Foreign Record* explained. "It is not he that reads most, but he that meditates most, that will prove the *choicest, sweetest, wisest*, and *strongest Christian*."[35] (See appendix.)

Given their devotion to a serious, contemplative reading style, it is not surprising that the managers of the American Tract Society turned their attention
from simple tracts to the publication of full-length books. Indeed, all of the
publishing societies invariably turned to the distribution of books. Some societies, such as the Presbyterian Board of Publication and the Methodist Book
Concern, began as book publishers and expanded into tract distribution and
colportage work—taking their books along with them. Others, such as the
American Tract Society and the American Baptist Publication Society, began
as tract societies but early moved into book publication and into what they
called "volume enterprises," the ATS in 1828 and the ABPS (then called the
Baptist General Tract Society) in 1839. The Tract Society of the Methodist Episcopal Church, founded in 1852, was from the outset committed to the circulation of books as well as tracts, and it specifically cited the volume enterprise
of the ATS as its model.[36] All of these projects involved more than the mere
manufacture of books for pastors' libraries, denominational Sunday schools,
or the regular book trade. All of them organized systematic distribution efforts
to place books into the hands of ordinary people throughout the United States.

In launching its volume enterprise, the American Tract Society stressed
the virtue of depth and completeness in books. "They do not merely draw
attention to a single point, like a small Tract; they contain matter to guide the
whole process of salvation," the organizers of the volume enterprise explained.
A religious book could not replace the Bible, but a good book could act like a
minister in regions where churches were few. With roots in Calvinist and
broadly Protestant traditions of evangelical literacy, ATS managers and supporters were confident that reading alone was a potent means of grace; priests,
preachers, and sacraments were not required. But it must be serious, learned
reading. A leading promoter of the American Tract Society's volume enterprise,
as well as a favorite author of ATS tracts, was Archibald Alexander, a professor
at the Presbyterian theological seminary at Princeton. Alexander loved cheap
tracts. He viewed them as vital "pioneers" in mission work, teaching divine
truths along with religious reading skills to people who had never seen a
preacher or a Bible. But serious religion required serious books, not just simple
tracts. "Your object should be, not only to provide *milk for babes*, but *meat for
strong men*," Alexander wrote to the managers at the American Tract Society in
1832. "Books adapted to every stage and period of Christian life are needed."[37]
And this is precisely what the ATS set out to provide in the 1830s: a full line

of Christian books, ranging from narratives and biographies for children to devotional volumes to religious histories to Jonathan Edwards's *Religious Affections*.[38]

Another virtue of books over tracts was "permanency" or "perpetuity." These terms are ubiquitous in American Tract Society discussions of its books, and mainly the society managers meant the permanence of the *content*. Once written, printed, and reprinted, the words of an author never died, and so the books published by the society could be "the choicest productions of the centuries." Turning for metaphor to the most modern technological marvels of the present, the *American Messenger* extolled the wisdom of the past: "They [ATS books] form a spiritual telegraph between the past and present, along whose wires the sanctified thoughts and emotions of Isaiah, and Paul, and Baxter, and Edwards may speed to our hearts, to quicken our faith and fire our zeal. . . . They constitute the great storehouse of truth for the world." One of the American Tract Society's most energetic colporteurs, Jonathan Cross, drew upon a humbler, biblical metaphor: "The books were like Jacob's well—the digger was gone—but they have quenched the thirst of many a weary traveller on life's journey."[39]

By *permanency*, the ATS also meant "physical durability": the book as material object. Unlike ephemeral tracts and newspapers, the volumes published by the American Tract Society and other societies were made to last. They were cheap, but they were not newsprint pamphlets or story papers; they were well printed on quality paper, nicely bound, durable, and beautiful, according to the *American Messenger*. The *Messenger* told stories of particular copies of classic books that had been read by hundreds of people over the years, even over the centuries. The editors believed that copies of ATS books would have similar longevity:

> Who can estimate the value of the operations of a Society that is
> placing *"the writings of our old solid divines"* by millions in the hands
> of the people? . . . A hundred years hence the seed the Society is
> now sowing on the virgin soil of the West and the country over, will
> spring up and bear fruit to the glory of the same grace that is even
> now making the wilderness blossom as the rose.[40]

Through books, the spiritual telegraph from the past to the present would be extended far into the future:

> The colporteur passes from the house or cabin, and his few earnest
> words may be forgotten. But a good book, perhaps it may be the

product of sanctified genius two centuries ago, having survived a
dozen generations of men, is likely to survive as many more. Good
books are rarely destroyed. They pass from one generation to another, with accumulated associations of interest clustering around
them. . . . When the valley of the Mississippi shall swarm with its
hundred millions of immortal souls, and the Pacific coast shall be as
populous as the Atlantic; when the generations who live in the noon
of the nineteenth century shall have faded away as the morning of
the twentieth century dawns upon the world, the seed of the kingdom now deposited in the abodes of the people, will perhaps germi-
nate afresh in the hearts of their children's children, and bring forth
the peaceable fruits of righteousness for a millennial day.[41]

The American Tract Society and other societies published many different
kinds of books, including recent titles, but their favorites were the classic works
of English Puritanism and dissent: Richard Baxter's *A Call to the Unconverted*
and *The Saints' Everlasting Rest*, John Bunyan's *The Pilgrim's Progress*, Joseph
Alleine's *Alarm to Unconverted Sinners*, John Flavel's *Touchstone of Sincerity*, and
Philip Doddridge's *Rise and Progress of Religion in the Soul*. The first volume to
be stereotyped by the ATS in 1828 was Doddridge's *Rise and Progress*, a book
first published in 1745. Most of the books were from an even earlier generation;
Baxter, Bunyan, Alleine, and Flavel all died before 1700. These volumes were
mass-produced at the American Tract Society's modern printing plant in New
York and sold across America for 12½ cents or less. Very often, they were
simply given away. The goal of the American Tract Society was to employ
modern technologies of printing, modern principles of business organization,
and modern methods of distribution to place into the hands of readers a collection of century-old books.[42]

These books perfectly suited the nonsectarian, evangelical posture of the
American Tract Society. The society drew from the Calvinist tradition of
English and American Puritanism, with an emphasis on the sovereignty of
God, the necessity of conversion, irresistible grace, and also the possibility of
preparation for grace. But in these very "practical works," as the ATS called
them, the most thorny doctrines of Calvinism—unconditional election and
limited atonement—were nowhere to be found. In his lifetime, Doddridge
never abandoned the doctrines of election and limited atonement, but he
downplayed them in *Rise and Progress*. Assuring his readers that the Gospel
was given for all, Doddridge urged them never to be discouraged. "Our Lord
knew into what perplexity some serious minds might possibly be thrown by

what he had before been saying, 'All that the Father hath given me shall come unto me,' " Doddridge wrote, "and therefore, as it were on purpose to balance it, he adds, those gracious words, 'him that cometh unto me, I will in no wise,' by no means, on no consideration whatsoever, 'cast out.' " In *A Call to the Unconverted*, Baxter's repudiation of the doctrine of election was explicit: "And think not to extenuate it [Christ's death on the cross] by saying, that it was only for his elect: for it was thy sin, and the sin of all the world, that lay upon our Redeemer; and his sacrifice and satisfaction is sufficient for all, and the fruits of it are offered to one as well as another." Sounding more like a Methodist or even Universalist than a Calvinist, Baxter declared, "There is mercy in God, there is sufficiency in the satisfaction of Christ, the promise is free, and full, and universal; you may have life, if you will but turn." "Turn, turn," Baxter implored his reader. "Turn and live."[43] Little surprise that these works were nearly as popular in the catalogs of the Methodist Book Concern as in those of the Presbyterian Board of Publication and the American Tract Society.

Beyond their practical, accessible, ecumenical evangelicalism, these standard works were also popular with the religious societies because the old authors loved books and believed, as the nineteenth-century publishers did, in the power of reading. They believed that reading, like grace, could infuse the heart and soul. The classic authors—Baxter, Bunyan, Doddridge—were venerated as model readers as well as model writers. Richard Baxter read so obsessively that his wife once joked that she wished she were a book so that he would pay attention to her. Philip Doddridge read Baxter and was awakened and saved. John Bunyan read everything, but especially the Bible, and the intensity of his reading was legendary: "Many have framed concordances [of the Bible], and made entire transcriptions of it; but Bunyan's concordance was his memory, and it lay all transcribed, every word and syllable of it, in his heart."[44]

In the 1840s and 1850s, the American Tract Society and other religious publishers mounted massive, well-organized campaigns to do two things: (1) to make books cheap and plentiful by turning them into a modern, mass-produced consumer good; and (2) to teach people to read and to value those books in the most traditional way. In other words, their aim was to use new mass media to encourage old reading habits—to preserve in the face of relentless change what David Hall has called "traditional literacy," the intense reading of a few standard texts.[45] Their goal, in effect, was to democratize tradition: they hoped to turn every family in the United States into an old-fashioned New England family reading circle.

In a house history published in 1849, one of the secretaries of the American Tract Society, R. S. Cook, took his readers on a tour of the society's modern printing plant in the commercial center of New York City. "The mere exhibitions of mechanical genius are wonderful," he wrote. "Ponderous presses seem to have become instinct with intelligence and Christian zeal." Letting his imagination run, Cook fancied the presses as living preachers: "Nine of these oracular machines pursue their endless task, without weariness or suffering; preaching more of Flavel's sermons in a week than he preached in a lifetime—dreaming Bunyan's Dream over a thousand times a day—reiterating Baxter's 'Call' until it would seem that the very atmosphere was vocal with, 'Turn ye, turn ye.' "[46]

Like John Eliot, the managers of the American Tract Society dearly loved Baxter's *A Call to the Unconverted*, and it became their favorite give-away volume. When an ATS colporteur met someone who was unable or unwilling to buy a book, he was usually authorized to give away a free copy of Baxter's *Call*. And year after year the *American Messenger* and ATS annual reports carried testimonials to the power of this ancient book to touch hearts and to save souls. The religious publishers spoke the language of Bunyan and Baxter. They could hear the cadences of Baxter's *Call* pounding in the pressroom and echoing through their own well-prepared minds and hearts. Steadfastly, they believed in the power of books and reading, serious books and serious reading.

But what about the people in the highways and hedges of America? Did ordinary readers respond as the publishers supposed they would or should? How did they hear Baxter's call?

7

How Readers Did Read

A poor woman in the New Jersey Pine Barrens in 1843 had heard of
the colportage work of the American Tract Society, and for a month
she hid a shilling from her husband so that she could buy a copy of
Baxter's *Call*. Another reader's eyes lit up at the sight of the *Call*.
She said she had read it in childhood and had desired a copy for
many years. She clasped it, hugged it, and bought it. Many others,
too, who had no religious books, received free copies of Baxter's *Call*—
or Alleine's *Alarm* or Flavel's *Touchstone*—with "much joy." Others
happily laid out their 12½ cents for a copy. On the other hand, many
people in the Pine Barrens refused to accept a copy of Baxter or any
other book, by purchase or gratuity. They believed that "time spent
in reading is thrown away." Others abused the colporteurs, "railed
profanely at the Society," or complained in general about the "rogu-
ery" of book peddlers. Some readers demanded free copies because
the books, they thought, were subsidized by state taxes. Others won-
dered why they should be asked to pay for books when neighbors
wealthier than they had been given books for free. They expected
their fair share of the rising river of free books and Bibles lately
flowing out of New York City.[1]

Readers responded to the new, cheap, religious literature in a
wide variety of ways, and we can catch a glimpse of their responses
in the reports of the colporteurs who fanned out across the continent in the 1840s and 1850s. The mission of colportage was the salvation of souls, and that mission depended upon the outpouring of

the spirit. But the bureaucrats at the New York offices of the American Tract Society (and the Philadelphia offices of the Presbyterian Board of Publication) knew that it also depended upon human organization, including the systematic gathering and reporting of factual information from the field. Distributing tracts and books by day, writing letters and reports by night—such was the life of the colporteur. Whether religious colportage actually hastened the flowering of religious faith in antebellum America can never be known with certainty. What is certain is that these efforts—or, more properly, the letters, reports, statistics, and other documents they generated—provide a wonderful window on readers and religious reading in that era.

Often filed from the frontiers of settlement, the colporteur reports illuminate a reading public at another kind of frontier: a frontier of publication, a borderland, both spatial and temporal, where books were at once scarce and plentiful, treasured and scorned, sacred and profane, preserved and consumed, read and unread; a borderland where readers were rooted in a tradition of reverence for books yet simultaneously drawn into a new age of literary commodification and mass consumption. Though the reports reveal an enormous diversity of reader response, some interesting patterns can be discerned. On the one hand, some responses were expected, almost formulaic. Readers often seemed to conform nicely to the societies' understanding of the power of the press and the nature of religious reading. On the other hand, some readers responded unexpectedly in ways that struck the colporteurs as remarkable. The diversity of responses suggests something about how readers in the 1840s and 1850s were negotiating the new publication frontier, the borderland where the new, cheap mass media came into contact with older print values and traditional habits of reading.

Long before the advent of colportage in 1841, the annual reports of the American Tract Society and other societies carried accounts of readers' responses. Indeed, the earliest reports of the oldest religious publication society in America included a few anecdotes of agents' encounters with readers. Daniel Little, the first agent of the Society for Propagating the Gospel among the Indians and Others in North-America, wrote about readers (and nonreaders) in the wilds of Maine in 1790. In Little's telling, many Mainers, having been corrupted by enthusiastic and illiterate preachers, were often argumentative and highly suspicious of his orthodox books and learned ways. Little's letters, though sketchy and haphazard in comparison with the later reports of nineteenth-century colporteurs, established the salient characteristics of the genre: shock at the ignorance and destitution (in money and books) of people on the American frontier, coupled with a steadfast faith in religious reading as an essential means of grace.[2]

Early accounts of reader response in American Tract Society reports followed a similar conventional form, and increasingly in the 1830s they stressed the direct and remarkable power of specific books, especially the most popular books in the ATS's volume enterprise. For example, in a section of the 1836 annual report called "Divine Blessing on the Society's Publications and Labors," ATS officials grouped together anecdotes of conversion-by-reading under the titles of specific books, the usual classics: Doddridge's *Rise and Progress*, Baxter's *Call* and *Saints' Rest*, Bunyan's *Pilgrim's Progress*, and Alleine's *Alarm*. In every case, the impact of these books on the reader was stunning and altogether conventional: one young man "found two leaves of *Baxter's Call*, and became so much interested in them, that he searched several libraries for the book, and finally sent to New-York for a copy, which he obtained and read. It was instrumental of his conversion, and he is now an eminent *Minister of the Gospel*."[3]

This kind of commentary on reader response tells us more about the commentator than the reader. The managers and agents of the American Tract Society believed that good religious literature (especially the Bible) could not fail to deliver to readers the sacred message contained in it. With eyes opened and hearts touched by the Holy Spirit, the serious reader would necessarily read out of the word what was really there. Such a theory of reader response is today disparagingly labeled the "bullet" or "hypodermic needle" theory of "media effects." It is the belief that the meaning of a text resides entirely in the text and that the text is hegemonic, that is, the reader is a passive vessel into which meaning is poured.[4] Or, to borrow the early Puritan minister Thomas Shepard's metaphor for the reception of God's grace, the reader lies like wax beneath the seal. Indeed, the nineteenth-century religious publishers shared with their seventeenth-century New England forefathers a similar understanding of the direct force of evangelical literacy. In their imagination, reading was not just a means of grace; it worked like grace: it was irresistible.

But reading is not irresistible, or so say current scholars of literature, education, mass media, and psychology. An author may write meaning into a text, but readers read out of it what they will or what they can. Scholars today routinely speak of the "active reader," a reader who brings as much meaning to a text as the author lards into it. Maybe more. But even the most blissful postmodernist does not suppose that the work of meaning-making is done by the solitary reader-as-individual. Reading is a very human practice, but not an autistic one; it is cultural. Individual readers share with other readers—and with authors—cultural codes and canons that make communication possible, though always imperfect. *Codes* and *canons* are the literary critic Norman Holland's terms. Other scholars speak of shared language, cultural frames, inter-subjectivity, interpretive strategies, and interpretive communities.[5] As Stanley Fish put the matter in the early 1980s, there are no fixed texts, only readers' interpretations, some stable and some not. A text does not produce a reader's interpretive strategy; the interpretive strategy produces the text. This is why Fish asserts that literature is in the reader, not in the text; and the reader in turn is situated in a cultural context, or what Fish calls an "interpretive community." As he explains:

> The notion of interpretive communities thus stands between an impossible ideal and the fear which leads so many to maintain it. The ideal is of perfect agreement and it would require texts to have a status independent of interpretation. The fear is of interpretive anarchy, but it would only be realized if interpretation (text making) were completely random. It is the fragile but real consolidation of interpretive communities that allows us to talk to one another, but with no hope or fear of ever being able to stop.[6]

The insight that reading is a cultural institution suggests that reading practices must vary as cultures vary and change as cultures change. In other words, reading has a history, as Robert Darnton has succinctly put it.[7] And a very elusive history it is. Literary history conceived as the history of texts and authors is much more tractable than literary history as the history of reading and readers. The act of reading, unlike the act of writing or printing, creates no physical evidence, leaves no material residue for historians to sweep up and ponder. But indirect evidence may be left behind, and in recent years historians have learned to track readers in the past and to trace their reading styles, habits, and behaviors through their surviving letters and diaries, their commonplace books and school papers, their personal libraries and book marginalia. Drawing on this kind of evidence, historians and literary scholars have cast considerable light on the varied uses of reading by relatively elite readers, those who tend to leave this kind of evidence behind.[8] Ordinary people, who typically do not preserve their personal papers for posterity, are more elusive, but even they (and evidence of their reading behaviors) may turn up in public documents or institutional records of one sort or another.[9]

One such institutional record is the colporteur report. Hundreds of colporteurs rode out with their books across America in the 1840s and 1850s, and all salaried colporteurs were required to file reports describing their experiences, including their encounters and conversations with ordinary readers. Their reports ranged from well-crafted narratives to rough statements of bare-boned facts. As one supervisor of colporteurs for the American Tract Society explained, unapologetically, "many of those good men can labor better than they can write."[10] Some colporteurs were energized by their work; others were enervated and driven down by it. All were touched—in a variety of ways—by the life-draining, life-giving intensity of meeting reader after reader in the tidy houses and miserable hovels of antebellum America. And they wrote and wrote and wrote about it.

The colporteur reports form an enormous but biased collection of evidence for the historical study of religious reading, at least thrice removed from the actual experience of the reader. Most of the reports exist today only in the form of published excerpts; a few excellent manuscript reports have survived, but most were lost, likely consumed in the editing and typesetting process.[11] Thus, readers described their experiences; colporteurs selected and described them again in reports and letters; and finally editors back in New York or Philadelphia selected, edited, and published excerpts in the societies' annual reports and magazines. In other words, readers told colporteurs, colporteurs told editors, and editors told their own readers—all, we might assume, what they wanted to hear. Indeed, a few surviving manuscript reports of colporteurs contain some evidence of such bias. One colporteur working for the Presbyterian Board of Publication wrote that he loved the work, but found it discouraging, adding, "I have not written as often as I would because you feel little inclined to hear the truth of the matter."[12]

Yet, despite their obvious limitations, these reports are useful and revealing. Unlike earlier formulaic accounts of nearly automatic conversion-by-reading, the colporteur reports, even in published form, are strikingly varied. Readers in the field were not always forced into the formula. In part, this was due to the explicit instructions that the colporteurs received, especially from the American Tract Society. ATS supervisors impressed upon their colporteurs the need for "authentic facts." Supervisors sought concrete factual narratives, not essays, sermons, or summaries. And they desired to hear bad news as well as good.[13] My own sense is that the published accounts of readers are not much different in tone or range of experience from the accounts in the few surviving manuscript reports, though the literary historian Amy Thomas is probably correct to argue that the personal voice of the colporteur is often muted in publication. Thomas's study of the manuscript report of one ATS colporteur for just one seven-week mission tour of South Carolina nicely demonstrates how much we can learn about readers and reading, even when the evidence is indirect.[14] In short, the colporteur reports have much to tell us about how ordinary readers responded to the new mass media launched by the religious publishing societies of antebellum America. As historical sources, they have one other signal virtue as well: they are what we have.

The great mission of the American Tract Society and its sister societies was to place religious books into the hands of people who had none. In particular, this was the work of colportage: to carry books "to *all the people*," especially those neglected by the commercial book trade. If people had no money, the societies would give them books. If they lived in isolated settlements, outside the marketplace of books, the colporteurs would go to them.[15] The newspapers and reports of the publishing societies were filled with sad litanies on the illiteracy, ignorance, and "moral wastes" of the United States, notably in the trans-Appalachian West and Southwest. The key word was "destitution," and it is ubiquitous in the agencies' literature. By *destitution*, they meant religious destitution: no churches, no ministers, and, perhaps most worrisome, no Bibles or religious books.[16]

But notwithstanding the incessant laments over religious destitution, most Americans *did* own books, including Bibles and religious books, as the agencies' own surveys in the 1840s and 1850s reveal. During the first twenty years of colportage by the American Tract Society, for example, from 1841 to 1861, colporteurs visited more than 8 million families across the country. Of these, only about 9 percent had no religious books except the Bible, and fewer than 6 percent had no Bible. In the early years, not surprisingly, these proportions were higher; in the first decade of colportage, 1841–1851, 17 percent of the families visited had no religious books beyond the Bible. The proportions were also considerably higher in the poor and sparsely settled regions of Appalachia and the trans-Appalachian West. ATS statistics for 1850–1851, for instance, show only 5 percent of New Jersey families destitute of religious books, compared with 25 percent in Kentucky and 27 percent in Tennessee. Yet, despite considerable variation by region, one fact is clear: the overwhelming majority of families in every state had at least some religious books. Furthermore, as the years went by, the societies' own efforts made a difference. In the 1840s and 1850s, American Tract Society colporteurs alone distributed more than 9 million volumes, and references to these very books pop up increasingly in the colporteur reports of all the agencies.[17]

These statistics on book ownership were gathered by colporteurs as they visited families across America. The American Tract Society referred to these surveys of book ownership, church and school attendance, and so on, as "moral censuses," and the managers and supervisors tried to make them as standardized and systematic as possible, with detailed instructions and preprinted forms. Indeed, one of the founding goals of colportage was to conduct a thorough moral census of the entire country, "to gather authentic facts, which should in the aggregate present a fair and accurate view of *the country as it is; especially* to explore and bring to the view of the benevolent the moral wastes of the land."[18]

Given the emphasis on "moral wastes," it is not surprising that for colporteurs out in the field the main story of book ownership remained destitution. Again and again, their reports express shock and dismay over the lack of religious reading material in the homes of hundreds of thousands of American families. In a typical report, an ATS colporteur wrote from the West in 1847:

> In my field nearly two-thirds of the families visited were destitute of all religious books. About one-fourth were without the Bible. The mass of people have no books of any kind. They have never been in the habit of reading. Not one man in twenty takes even a newspaper of any sort. Many cannot read, and those who are able exhibit no desire to do so. The people are in the grossest darkness and spiritual ignorance.

Another wrote from Virginia:

> I have found great destitution of the Bible. In 31 days, I found 41 families without the Bible. Traveling down a rough creek five miles in length, I found nine families destitute; a woman who told me that she had plenty of good books, had not even a Bible. I furnished a man about fifty years of age with the first Bible he ever owned. I sometimes found persons in good standing, and possessing property, destitute of the Bible, and a few of them were unwilling to buy. There is also great destitution of religious books in general. A great many were entirely destitute, while many others have one or two small books lying about in the smoke and dust, as though they had not been moved for months. . . . Ignorance prevails to an alarming extent.

Similar commentaries run throughout the reports, like a melancholy chorus: "Gross ignorance," "wretched ignorance," "deplorable ignorance," "no book in the house, not even a Bible."[19]

The societies also drew on the federal census for statistics, especially for data on illiteracy. In 1843, the *American Messenger* reported the "astounding disclosure" of the census of 1840: "*Seven hundred thousand white persons over twenty years of age, in the United States, unable to read!*" In some poor regions of the country, ranging from the Pine Barrens of New Jersey to the isolated prairies of Illinois, colporteurs found illiteracy rates of 50 percent and more. "Many families have no readers in them," a colporteur wrote from eastern Kentucky, "and seem as stupid on the subject of religion as the stones of the street."[20]

Destitution and illiteracy, however, were not the only unpleasant surprises. Colporteurs also wrote in amazement of the indifference of many people who *did* own books. Typically, during a visit, the colporteur would ask to see the family's Bible and religious books. The response could be revealing. As an Arkansas colporteur wrote, "Frequently when I ask for a Bible that I may read a chapter before prayer and singing, many minutes are spent in hunting for it, and when found it is covered with dust, which has been months in accumulating on its cover." It was the same story elsewhere. "I asked her if she had a Bible," a colporteur wrote of a visit with a woman in Kentucky. "She replied, 'I *do not know*, we have several books but I don't know what they are about.' After searching for a while she found an old Bible and a Testament. This is one specimen out of many of the utter ignorance of many in this country." Some people at first said they had no Bible or religious books, but then remembered that they did, squirreled away amid the "dust and rubbish." Others were sure they had books but, when they looked, could not find them.[21]

Perhaps most shocking to the colporteurs were the people who mistook other books for the Bible. One woman in the New Jersey Pine Barrens told two student colporteurs from Princeton Theological Seminary that she guessed she had two or three Bibles and then handed them a history of the Baptists and a Greek lexicon. "These were her Bibles!" they exclaimed. A woman in Virginia had a life of Washington that she thought was a Bible. Although these stories imply a kind of reverence for the Bible even among people who apparently could not read it, the colporteurs were horrified nonetheless. "I have visited many families without finding a Bible," a Baptist colporteur wrote from Illinois. "Some of them when asked if they had a Bible answered, yes; and showed me another book. They did not even know the Holy Book, nor anything of Him of whom it speaks."[22]

These stories suggest that a book could have meaning for a person, including a nonreader, purely as a physical object. Indeed, people often owned books, especially Bibles, as totems. This, too, surprised and disturbed the colporteurs, who were imbued with a Protestant devotion to the word itself, not to the vessel that contained it. A colporteur in Pennsylvania wrote disparagingly of a woman who wanted a Bible that looked exactly like the one a neighbor had, because it had been such a comfort to her. The Princeton colporteurs encountered several people who owned (or desired) Bibles only to write their children's names in them. The colporteurs viewed such use of the Bible as non-use, much like the man in the New Testament who tied up his coin in a napkin and hid it rather than investing it wisely.[23]

Colporteurs were equally, though more pleasantly, surprised by some other habits of book ownership. All of the agencies promoted the active *use* of books, and therefore colporteurs were most impressed by people who used their books intensely yet cared for them intensely as well. Hundreds of anecdotes about old books, worn books, disassembled books, rebound books, personalized books, shared books, and long-lost books run through the colporteur letters.

For the colporteurs, it was high praise to describe a book as "worn out," and this descriptor crops up again and again in the letters. In western Virginia in 1854, a colporteur found most of the people too poor to buy even his cheapest books. The good and pious people owned books, but they were usually old and worn out from use. Not all worn books were old, however; more impressive were those that had been worn out in a year or two. One young man proudly showed a colporteur on the Mississippi River a well-worn copy of Baxter's *Call*, which he had been given two years before. He carried it with him in his pocket.[24] Sometimes the extent of wear on books in the West surprised the colporteurs. They often remarked on seeing *pieces* of books in regular use; sometimes a scrap of a book was all a family had. Occasionally, books, especially Bibles, were intentionally disassembled in order to distribute the parts to various family members—a communal yet still individual style of book ownership. The colporteurs who told these stories seemed surprised to find Bibles in pieces, but they also were moved by the idea of cutting up a precious possession in order to share the parts with children or grandchildren.[25]

More common than dividing books into individual pieces was a kind of communal ownership through extensive lending. Indeed, books were often worn out because they were in constant circulation. One woman in North Carolina laid aside $5 for a colporteur's return visit because her neighbors had worn out the books she had bought just the year before. Similar stories came in from the river towns of the Mississippi and the mountains of Kentucky. A Kentucky colporteur wrote that "an old woman walked five miles on foot to return Baxter's Call, which brother M. sent out a year before. When it came back it was literally *worn out*—scores having read it; and she returned it because it had written on the blank leaf, 'Let hundreds read it, and then let it come home.' "[26]

Neighbors sometimes set up lending libraries for books or tracts. And some nosy neighbors expected no less, as a colporteur in Canada discovered.

"The people were generally very thankful for any book given to them," he wrote. "Two days after giving a copy of Baxter's Call to one, I heard of it eight miles distant. Another to whom I gave a copy of Alleine's Alarm, followed me from house to house for about a mile, to see what books his neighbors had got." Another wrote, "I have frequently met with books several miles from where I sold or gave them, having been read and loaned from one to another, with the name of each reader marked on the cover." A colporteur in Florida came across a worn copy of Baxter's *Call* that had traveled forty miles since he had given it away, loaned from neighbor to neighbor. Readers sometimes owned a favorite book only in memory. It had been loaned and loaned and finally lost.[27]

Colporteurs were impressed by careful as well as by utilitarian ownership. The reports carry many anecdotes of books repaired and book pieces carefully rebound and preserved. A woman proudly showed a colporteur a copy of Baxter's *Saints' Rest*, the pages of which she had sewn together where torn. A man in Rhode Island had made a little leather bag for his copy of J. G. Pike's *Persuasives to Early Piety*. Even simple tracts, which were scattered freely by colporteurs everywhere, were sometimes kept for years and repaired by sewing and binding in homemade deerskin covers. A woman in Virginia happily brought out her whole library for the colporteur to see: a part of a New Testament and several little books and tracts, all carefully sewn into several small volumes.[28]

Colporteurs were alert to these details of wearing out, cutting up, lending, repairing, and binding books because they illuminated for them (and for us) the sharp contrast between the book-rich environment of the East and the book-poor environment of Appalachia and the expanding West. Both environments simultaneously existed in the 1840s and 1850s, and it was the colporteurs' mission to try to bring them together. Most colporteurs simply noted the contrast; they did not reflect much upon it. But a few did reflect. One of the American Tract Society's most effective colporteurs, Jonathan Cross, wrote a memoir that was plainly aimed at an eastern audience fascinated by the backwoods frontier. In his conclusion, he asked his readers to ponder the contrast in media environments that his book makes so vividly clear:

> As to the rich blessing that has attended the reading of books and
> tracts, it is well for those reared in the midst of church privileges
> and good libraries to consider how different the influence of a good
> book may be on such as have few books, or none at all. Take, if you
> please, a prosperous family in the interior of the country, far from
> any book-store, who may have an old family Bible, a few school-
> books, or perhaps some other old books moral and religious. A col-

porteur enters with his saddle-bags of beautiful books. The children
are almost frantic with joy. Each member of the family gets a book.
It is devoured with greediness—not by a gospel-hardened sinner,
but by one who has few or no gospel privileges.[29]

Not everyone valued reading, of course. But for those who did, especially
in the destitute West, a book could still be a pearl of great price—even if it
were mass produced for 6¼ cents by the latest manufacturing technologies of
New York City.

Whether they owned books or not, people had to decide, when the colporteur
arrived, how to receive them. At this moment of meeting between book and
reader, the colporteur hoped and expected that the power of the Holy Spirit
and the virtues of the book itself would carry the day, that people would respond
with hospitality and perhaps with a little money, that they would receive the
books with joy, enthusiasm, and thanksgiving. And sometimes they did. But
often, people responded to the offer of books in ways that surprised the colporteurs. Sometimes their resistance or indifference was striking; sometimes
their joy and enthusiasm were overwhelming. These disproportionate responses, which the colporteurs found remarkable enough to record, suggest
the complexity and intensity of the interaction between the new mass media
and readers in antebellum America.

"I prayed with him, sold him eighteen volumes of good books, and left the
whole family in tears."[30] This was the colporteur's dream, the ideal encounter
with a reader: hospitality, piety, money. It is also a common enough story told
in the colporteur letters, though eighteen volumes in one visit was an extraordinarily rare sales performance. Colporteurs routinely told of people greeting
them with joy, rarely charging them for food or lodging, and showing great
eagerness to see the books—whether they could afford to buy them or not.
Annual reports and newspapers such as the *American Messenger* are so filled
with reports of such happy encounters that they define the clichés of the colporteur report-as-genre, a genre in which tears are as common as books.

But it was not always so. The colporteurs also told of abuse and cold indifference. Failure and disappointment were not the messages the editors
wanted to convey in the published reports, so such themes are not so common
as themes of hospitality and success. But they are common enough to suggest
that resistance, abuse, and failure were frequent outcomes of encounters be-

tween colporteurs and readers. Indeed, sometimes, violence erupted. Colporteurs were threatened with sticks and sledges, attacked by dogs, and bodily thrown out of houses and taverns. Some wrote of their bitter discouragement. "I have been many a time treated so badly that if it were not for the cause I am engaged in, I would lay aside my pedlar's basket for ever," a Presbyterian colporteur wrote from the West. "I often find myself so worn down, that I have to go home and recruit my strength," an ATS colporteur wrote. Even the American Tract Society's most famous colporteur, Jonathan Cross, described numerous episodes of abuse and resistance, and he too, at one point, fell into despair and nearly gave up the work.[31]

Some abusive people resisted on religious grounds. They hated a particular denomination, or churches in general, or they opposed the interdenominational evangelicalism of the American Tract Society. More stunning to the colporteurs was hostility or indifference to learning and reading in general. Some people said they wanted no books because books cause trouble. The Bible seemed everywhere enmeshed in controversy, so they did not want one in the house. Some thought that societies such as the ATS simply had no right to give people books. A woman in New Jersey said she "had only a Bible & hymn book & *that was enough.*" Most commonly, people believed that reading was simply a waste of time, and they said so to the colporteurs. A "prejudice against education" was one of the main impediments to the work in western Virginia, according to Jonathan Cross. "Almost every day," he wrote, "I had to meet this objection: 'Oh, I don't want my children learned to read; it will spoil them. I have got along very well without reading, and so can they.' " Another man said he was against education because he once knew a man accused of forgery, who never would have been accused if he had been ignorant of letters.[32]

People also resisted accepting books because they believed colportage was a confidence scam. For some, a free book was too good to be true; they feared they would be billed for it later. Conversely, some thought *all* religious books from publishing societies were free, and therefore they refused to pay if asked to pay. The Princeton students in the Pine Barrens ran into both of these problems, and they cropped up in other parts of the country as well. A colporteur in the South nicely summarized a range of rationales for resistance:

> Many have refused to receive my books as a gift, fearing that they would have to pay for them afterwards; and others have demanded their share, saying that they had paid for them in their taxes, and the government had sent me to distribute them. I visited thirteen families in one day who had no Bible. Often those who are destitute and able to buy, require much persuasion before they will buy one.

Others who have a Bible and hymn-book, think they are well supplied and need no other books. One preacher whom I believe to be a
good man, and the pastor of several churches, said he did not ap-
prove of reading any book but the Bible.

Jonathan Cross so frequently ran into the fear of the delayed bill that he developed a standard trick for allaying it. He "lent" books instead of giving them
away, writing inside the cover, "Loaned til I call for it"—which, of course, he
never did.[33]

Even plain indifference could be surprising. Sometimes people gave no
reason at all for their lack of interest. "I asked the lady of the house if she did
not want a good book," a Presbyterian colporteur wrote. "I think not, was the
reply." Sometimes resisters gave reasons that could startle a pious colporteur.
The Princeton students told of a man who said that "during these hard times
he could scarce find money enough to buy rum much less a Bible."[34]

If the range and intensity of resistance to books could surprise the colporteurs, the enthusiasm for them could be equally striking. Jonathan Cross
wrote of books being "devoured with greediness" by book-starved readers. William Schenck, the corresponding secretary of the Presbyterian Board of Publication, wrote that the colporteurs' letters vividly reveal everywhere readers'
"hunger of the mind." An American Tract Society colporteur in Indiana wrote
that "many have seemed like persons starving: when they get the books, they
know not how to be denied the privilege of reading them."[35] The reports and
letters frequently resort to such vivid and visceral imagery. The specific stories
and anecdotes told in the letters suggest why.

Colporteurs were often struck, for example, by people traveling long distances to obtain tracts and books. Though they tried to go door to door, colporteurs obviously had to follow some path through a region, and word of their
presence would sometimes drift to households passed by. Some readers would
come from over the next ridge or beyond the next creek, seeking the man with
the books. Cross told several such stories, including this one:

> A young woman came up to me, having just reached the place, and
> asked me for a book. I told her I had given away all that I had
> brought with me. She burst into tears, and said, "I left my babe,
> three weeks old, in the field where my husband was hoeing corn,
> and walked five miles in my bare feet to get a book; and now I am
> disappointed." In a few minutes an old woman who had seen sev-
> enty winters came to me with a crutch under one arm, and a cane
> in the other hand, and told me she had come two miles to get books
> for her sons, who were raising large families over the mountains,

that were as wild as deers. I returned soon, and gave the necessary supply.

Similar stories abound in the reports and papers of the societies.[36]

But probably the response that most impressed the colporteurs was the eagerness of some people to give *all* their money for a book. Though most colporteurs, notably those employed by the American Tract Society, usually had the authority to give books away, these free grants were costly—to the overall effort and to the colporteurs themselves if they were paid a percentage of sales, as many non-ATS colporteurs were. Therefore, most colporteurs made an initial effort to sell, though always at a very low price. But many people had no money at all, and colporteurs often suffered through days of travel without selling a single book.[37] The memorable cases, however, involved people who had just a little money but were willing to spend it all on books. "I have spent several weeks along the eastern spurs of the Allegheny mountains," a colporteur in Pennsylvania wrote. "The people are very poor in both temporal and spiritual things, and sometimes they offer me all the money they have for a book: what shall I do in such cases?" The ATS sanctioned free grants in such cases, but sometimes readers insisted on paying, even if they obviously could not afford to. A colporteur described such an encounter with a poor family in western New York: "One of them got the last money they had and offered it to me for the Bible, but when I saw that they had neither bed nor table nor chair in their log cabin, I could not take it. The man said I must take it, for he must pay for his Bible. He wept and would not let me go without the money." Other colporteurs told similar tales: families "parting with their last shilling"; a young man going some distance to labor and earn twenty-five cents to buy a book; another going through the neighborhood hoping to borrow enough money to buy a coveted volume. Jonathan Cross debated at length with a man in a tavern over how he would spend the last six cents he had: on a drink or a book. The man finally decided, reluctantly, in favor of a copy of Baxter's *Call*.[38]

Some pious but penurious readers offered to trade goods for books. Colporteurs needed currency to settle their accounts in New York or Philadelphia, so they were chary of barter. But sometimes they could not resist the pleas, and they ended a day's work with an extra pair of socks, a piece of buckskin, or a scarf of homespun silk. A Wisconsin colporteur traded Baxter's *Call* for a deck of playing cards, which he promptly shredded with his knife. On a few occasions, an intensely if perversely pious reader simply robbed the colporteur in order to haul off a supply of books and tracts to a community that had been passed by.[39]

How people received books, then, suggests how they valued them and how they understood the place of books in their communities and in their own personal lives. Some cared not at all for books, even free ones. Some thought religious books should be free and were annoyed to be asked to pay. To them, a book was a cheap, manufactured product of little value. To others, a book was an object of inestimable value, and they were willing to give all the money they had to get one. As with owning books, receiving them illuminates the interplay between the new and the old in the world of books: new availability, old values.

The ultimate goal of religious publication was conversion. Both publishers and colporteurs believed that reading could bring about that great end. Obviously, owning books or accepting books was not enough. People must read them and read them properly. Not surprisingly, therefore, the colporteurs' reports were filled with observations on the reading process: how people read and how their reading affected them. Typically, these observations fell into the standard, general account of the conversion-by-reading experience, the cliché of the genre: reader reads, reader weeps, reader is saved. But some of the experiences of individual readers were remarkable enough to prompt the colporteurs to describe them in more specific detail. These accounts provide some insight into how readers responded to the new religious media of the 1840s and 1850s.

"I gave the 'Call' to a young man, and at midnight he cried aloud to God for mercy."[40] If the letters of colporteurs are to be trusted, this response—so simple, so pure—was common among readers of religious books in antebellum America. Again and again, Baxter, Alleine, Bunyan, or one of the other standard authors in the colporteur's bag brought tears to the reader's eyes and salvation to his soul. This is what society officials in New York and Philadelphia wanted to hear, and the colporteurs told it to them. In reality, of course, given their endless itinerancy, colporteurs rarely had any idea of how a book was read, though they tried to find out. Two of the Princeton colporteurs in the Pine Barrens said they believed that ATS books had contributed to the revival of religion in their field, but they could not be sure. "We have not been able it is true after much inquiry," they confessed, "to learn that there were any cases of conversion to be traced to some of the vol[ume]s." Sometimes the response to a book was more obvious, if even less encouraging. "He rubbed his fist under my nose, and swore he would smash my face into a jelly," Jonathan Cross wrote of one reader's response to an offer of Baxter's *Call.* "I never saw the place or the man afterwards, but I heard he soon went to ruin," Cross added, with a touch of weary colporteur satisfaction.[41]

Fortunately, some of the colporteurs' descriptions of reading were more specific and, therefore, more revealing than the standard conversion-by-reading cliché. For example, the letters contain numerous accounts of the kind of intense, obsessive reading that the publishing societies promoted. Many people, upon receiving tracts or books, simply stopped what they were doing, sat down, and read them through on the spot. One western colporteur described how pleasing it was "to see a wicked, careless man chained to his seat for a whole day in reading one of these volumes, the first time it was opened." Another told of a farmer who took his book into the field, reading while he rested and thinking while he worked. Finally, he gave up working altogether to read steadily. One man complained that his wife would read the *American Messenger* through on the afternoon it arrived, neglecting to make his supper. Frequently, the letters mention people reading half the night or all night on the day they got their books. One poor couple said they burned a whole candle to finish a new book—a great sacrifice for them. Readers read intently in their houses, in the fields and woods, in carriages, on horseback, and beside the road. One young man, in a scene the colporteur took as delightfully ironic, read his Baxter's *Call* late into the night by the light of a distillery fire.[42]

Some people read even more intensely. They read their books repeatedly until they knew them by heart. Students in school memorized the *Tract Primer* and chapters of Baxter's *Call*. A "profane drunkard" began reading a tract while riding home from a tavern, then read it again and again until he had memorized it. A colporteur in Virginia reported that "one old man who had not read 400 pages in 40 years, told me he was reading 'The Saints' Rest' for the fourth time." Another man had read Baxter's *Saints' Rest* so regularly and intently that he actually spoke like Baxter. The colporteur was fascinated and impressed. "I have sometimes thought one might nearly tell what book was in the house by the tone of the remark," he wrote. "Where they have Bunyan, they use his language; and so with Baxter, Doddridge, Payson, and others. Where they have but few books, the impression is deep."[43]

Sometimes a less-salubrious intensity in reading impressed the colporteurs. They wrote often of readers actively struggling with their books. The incessant flow of tears that pours through the letters was the most common testimony. Readers also fought over and fought with their books. Not surprisingly, a hostile family member sometimes destroyed a reader's book or tract— for example, the drunken husband who burned his wife's New Testament and threw her out into the snow. But more fascinating for the colporteurs were the readers who attacked their own books: the man who drowned his Bible in a pond, another who tore up his tracts. A farmer in Texas carried a copy of David Nelson's *Cause and Cure of Infidelity* in his pocket. He would read for a while, then throw it down on the ground in anger, swearing not to read another page. But then he would go back to it, take it up, and read on, until he had finally finished it. Another reader verbalized his struggle for the colporteur's journal: "A young Roman-catholic to whom I sold the tract 'Colporteur and Roman-catholic,' said, 'It knocks us down as fast as we get up.' He meant to throw it into the fire, but somehow he still kept it."[44]

These were private struggles of individual readers. The colporteurs also wrote regularly of intense communal reading. According to the letters, people regularly read to each other and, especially, to nonreaders. Husbands read to wives, wives to husbands, parents to children, and not uncommonly literate children to illiterate adults. Sometimes the colporteur read to a family or gathering of families. In a typical case from North Carolina, an illiterate woman, whose husband bitterly opposed religious reading, persuaded a neighbor to read Baxter's *Call* to her on the sly. Equally common were the cases of one neighbor reading to a group of neighbors—at home, in a lumbering camp, in a tavern. The letters report examples from different parts of the country of groups of neighbors gathering regularly on Sundays to hear chapters from *Pilgrim's Progress*. The widespread practice of passing books around the neighborhood often prompted oral reading but even silent reading could have a communal aspect. A colporteur in Georgia left some tracts at a grog shop. "The next day," he said, "as I passed, I saw them nailed up, with the leaves open, so that all could read"—like Luther's Ninety-Five Theses nailed to the castle church door.[45]

Colporteurs encouraged oral communal reading, just as they supported preaching, teaching, hymn singing, and religious conversation. But perhaps because they were solitary travelers and silent readers themselves, they seemed especially attentive to intense private reading, even within a communal setting. One colporteur told the story of a young man at a religious camp meeting who stole off into the woods by himself to read Alleine's *Alarm*. "This was during the progress of the meeting," the colporteur wrote, "and I mention this fact as a specimen of many which occurred, and to show the importance of books on these occasions. Sometimes you may see between services a large portion of the encampment reading the books."[46]

Another indicator of intense interest in reading was the oft-expressed desire of illiterates to learn to read. Most striking were those who set to work immediately to learn so that they could read the very book or tract the colporteur had given them. The letters report many such cases. A colporteur in North Carolina met a man shaving shingles; he was illiterate but eager to learn. The two men sat right down on the draw-horse with the *Tract Primer* and had a first lesson on the alphabet. A colporteur in Virginia read *The Dairyman's Daughter* to an illiterate man, who then determined to learn to read so that he could read it himself. And he did. Later, he told the colporteur that he always carried the tract in his pocket. Some colporteurs ran into so many nonreaders who had a passion to read that they took to setting up Sunday schools to teach basic literacy.[47]

The ideology of the religious publishers declared intense reading to be a virtue and cursory reading a vice. And the colporteurs sometimes reported on the evil effects of cursory reading in terms that must have brought knowing nods to the heads of society leaders in New York and Philadelphia. For example, colporteurs described encounters with young novel readers, whose ability to read serious books had been squandered. "I asked a young man to look at some books I had," a colporteur wrote from Michigan, and "he replied, I have read too many novels to look at such books as you have; one has no taste for such when he gets into the way of reading novels." And yet, like their super-visors, the colporteurs were also fascinated by the power of cursory reading, for good as well as evil. Certainly, the model reader was the steady, careful, thoughtful reader. But the letters also tell of people who picked up Baxter for a quick glance, just to pass the time—and were gripped, arrested, convicted, and converted. Most marvelous of all—and not uncommon—was the occa-sional power of a single, gospel tract: salvation in four easy-to-read pages.[48]

Like their supervisors in the East, the colporteurs in distant fields had great faith in the power of reading, and they looked for—and saw—its results among the people they visited. But often there were no results, and the colporteurs were forced to confess that "the people were not much interested in our un-dertaking" or "they are not a reading people generally." Some readers took a tract or book merely to humor the colporteur. Many books lay unread.[49] Despite their obvious bias in favor of serious reading, the colporteur letters portray a great diversity in reading styles and reader responses. Still, the style they de-scribed most fully was the one that interested them most: intensity. The end of reading could be miraculous, but the method rarely was. It was serious, careful, thoughtful, obsessive, absorbed. And the colporteurs saw this kind of reading often in antebellum America.

In the summer of 1844 in the New Jersey Pine Barrens, one of the student colporteurs from Princeton seminary met a poor woman who said she had long been eager to have a particular book. The student said he was surprised that she had not been given a copy of that book the year before when several other Princeton students had come through the village. This set her to thinking, and she remembered that she had indeed received a book and "had been *mighty* careful of it," the student reported. "She then produced a linen cloth containing the book, & when this was unwrapped, lo! it was a copy of the very work she had been soliciting, with every appearance of having lain unread."[50]

This encounter amused the Princeton colporteurs, and they wrote it up as another example of the pathetic ignorance of the people of the Pine Barrens. Yet this odd encounter may suggest something more. The idea of a free book obviously fascinated this woman; she wanted one; she thought she needed one; and she was willing to take care of one. But she had forgotten that she had already been given one by a colporteur just the summer before. In other words, this episode shows a person with a traditional reverence for books responding to a new world of publishing in which books were so plentiful and easily available that they were delivered regularly and freely door to door.

In the 1840s and 1850s, the American Tract Society and other religious publishers launched colportage projects against the tide of secularism and commercialism in the new mass media. They employed the latest technologies and business strategies to foster the most traditional of religious experiences: the intense, meditative reading of a few classic evangelical texts. They resolved to use the tools of modernity to resist modernity; they embraced the market revolution in order to thwart it. They proposed to make good books *both* cheap and dear.

This meeting of the new and the old produced a wonderful mixture of reader responses out on the publication borderlands of antebellum America. In the mountains of Appalachia, in the great valley of the Mississippi, and beyond, readers encountered books—cheap books shipped in from New York and Philadelphia and carried door to door by itinerant colporteurs. Some readers were hostile, some skeptical, some merely indifferent. Some readers took these cheap books for what they were: throw-away consumer goods. Some treasured them and wrapped them in linen or buckskin; some treasured them and used them up. Some glanced at them; some read them with savage intensity. Some forgot they had books; some read their books as Bunyan had read his two centuries before, with passages "hammering at his mind, striking him across the face, pursuing him relentlessly."[51]

Certainly, the great national religious publishing societies did not succeed in supplanting the novel or the sensational newspaper with Baxter's *Call*, nor could they manufacture a nation of readers like John Bunyan. But the evidence suggests that the style of reading they favored was, if not resurgent, at least not lost in the new world of mass publication. In antebellum America, as today, even the cheap book could become a priceless treasure. The consumer good could consume its buyer.

Epilogue

Fragmentation and Denomination

At midcentury, the great national religious publishing societies were flourishing. In 1850, the American Tract Society's 569 colporteurs visited 505,422 families, sold nearly a half million volumes, and gave away 35 million pages of books and tracts. In 1855, the American Sunday School Union, with 300 missionaries in the field, sold $185,000 worth of books and periodicals. In 1855, the American Bible Society opened an opulent new building in New York to house a modern printing plant, stereotype foundry, and bindery capable of churning out 1.5 million volumes per year—enough Bibles, the managers believed, to complete a second general supply of the United States.[1]

But trouble loomed. In 1853, one of the founding fathers of the Bible and tract movement in America, William Jay, dropped his financial support of the American Tract Society. In an open letter to Russell S. Cook, the society's long-time corresponding secretary, Jay praised the society for its many years of service to Christian evangelism but also declared that "painful doubts" had intruded upon his mind. "There is a giant, and in its influence an all-pervading sin in our land," he wrote. "Yet the American Tract Society has publicly and officially announced through you, as its organ, that it does not intend to recognize even the existence of this sin!" The all-pervading sin was slavery.[2] In the 1850s, all of the national religious publishing societies, like the national churches before them, were wracked by sectional tensions and religious/political controversy over slavery.

The founding confidence in the unity of Christendom was severely shaken. The postmillennial faith in steady progress through nondenominational Christian enterprise was shattered.

Pressed by strident partisans from both the South and the North, the managers of the societies struggled mightily in the 1850s to preserve what they, like the political leaders of the time, fondly called "the bond of union." Like other national institutions, including the political parties and the U.S. Congress, the societies had long sought to avoid controversy by deferring to local interests any issues that touched on slavery, while imposing upon themselves a virtual gag rule at the national level. The American Bible Society, for example, though not disputing the claim that slaves deserved the opportunity to read the Bible, steadfastly maintained that all decisions about Bible distribution must be made by local auxiliaries, including the conservative, slaveholder-dominated auxiliaries of the South. The national office regularly chose to sidestep its auxiliaries, but not on this issue. To northern abolitionists clamoring for "Bibles for slaves," the ABS managers replied that there was nothing they could do. Such decisions, they said, "must as heretofore be left wholly to the wisdom and piety of those who compose these local associations in the different States and Territories." In the 1850s, the American Bible Society tried to expand its operations in the South, and as late as 1862, after war had commenced, one ABS official could still proclaim, more wistfully than accurately, that "this Society retains its national name and character."[3]

The ABS's troubles lay only in distribution, for the text they published "without note or comment" was, by definition, Holy Scripture, acceptable in both the North and the South. In the South, the Bible sanctioned slavery; in the North, at least among evangelical abolitionists, the same Bible condemned slavery. But though it seemed to speak in regional dialect, the Bible unalterably said what it said.[4] Not so the publications of the American Tract Society and the American Sunday School Union. Those societies commissioned, selected, edited, abridged, and sometimes expurgated their very human publications. And their favored approach to the problem of slavery was to ignore it, to exclude it from their books and tracts, right up to the dissolution of the American nation and the firing on Fort Sumter.[5]

Given the hothouse atmosphere of the 1850s, such strategies of avoidance could not succeed. In 1857, the managers of the American Tract Society learned how their agonized efforts to offend no one on the issue of slavery seemed to offend everyone. The crisis came in the summer and fall, following an attempt by the annual convention in May to stake out a compromise position on the handling of slavery in society publications. Abolitionists had long badgered the ATS to condemn the sin of slavery, just as it had condemned other sins, such as intemperance, gambling, and sabbath breaking. Southern tract leaders, on the other hand, had long opposed any discussion of slavery in society publications. At the 1857 convention, the society adopted a resolution to permit ATS books and tracts to address "moral duties" and "moral evils and vices" that may arise from the existence of slavery, while continuing to avoid altogether any discussion of the "political aspects" of slavery.[6]

Though supposedly an honest compromise adopted in the spirit of Christian brotherhood, the new policy was hailed as a victory by both sides. Antislavery northerners interpreted the policy as the first step on the path to righteousness; southerners portrayed it as an official repudiation of abolitionism. The incompatibility of these interpretations and the intractability of the slavery issue were immediately revealed when the ATS Publishing Committee actually considered publishing a small volume of tracts on *The Duties of Masters.* Though the tracts were written mainly by southern clergymen and urged masters to little more than Christian benevolence toward their slaves, the announcement of plans to publish this book produced an outcry of opposition in the South. In response, the committee decided not to release *The Duties of Masters,* and that act of "suppression" sparked outrage in the North. By the autumn of 1857, the managers of the American Tract Society admitted publicly what they must have known in their hearts all along: that "the *moral* and the *political* bearings of slavery are inseparable." To publish *anything* on slavery would be "fratricide and suicide in one act." So they resolved to fall back on their previous policy of complete silence.[7]

In a half dozen pamphlets and circulars, the managers argued their case on grounds of constitutionality and practicality. The society's constitution envisioned a national union and required that ATS publications be "calculated to receive the approbation of all evangelical Christians"—not some Christians, not some sections, but *all.* And it was clear by the fall of 1857, if there had been any doubt before, that *no* publication on slavery could find approbation in the South. In a circular letter to "our endeared fellow-workers," the ATS managers explained and lamented their dilemma:

> The issue of a single book upon that subject now, would instantly
> array one half our friends against the other half; drive out of the
> whole South our nearly three hundred colporteurs, superintendents,
> and agents; exclude our laborers and volumes from the seven or

eight millions in the South who are neither slaveholders nor respon-
sible for the system; and effectually close up the ten thousand channels through which our other issues are now flowing freighted with
blessings to millions there.[8]

Many northern friends of the society agreed that a self-imposed gag rule
offered the only hope of saving the union they loved. In a long pamphlet published early in 1858, the Boston secretary of the ATS, Seth Bliss, argued that
silence was the only viable option. "Will not each party, in its heat, use a religious or moral tract on slavery . . . to promote the objects of the party?" he
wrote. "Will not each party desire to increase its strength among religious men,
by showing, from these tracts, that even so great and good and impartial an
institution as the Tract Society is on its side? The Society which expects to
stand between these stones thrown from opposite sides, must be ground to
powder."[9]

The American Tract Society was not ground to powder by the ordeal of the
union; nor was the American Bible Society nor the American Sunday School
Union. But they were transformed. In response to the crisis of 1857, the American Tract Society of Boston (the successor to Jedidiah Morse's New England
Tract Society) seceded from the national organization, thus sundering the
union of the New England and New York tract movements that had given birth
to the national American Tract Society in 1825.[10] Waves of local secessions and
lost contributions, exacerbated by the financial Panic of 1857, hobbled the ABS
and the ASSU as well. The secession of the Confederate states freed the societies from their subservience to the South, and all three eventually came to
support a moral war as well as a military war on slavery. But, in the process,
they saw their national pretensions evaporate, along with tens of thousands of
dollars worth of books and other publications, which were lost in the fog of
civil war.[11]

Though slavery and sectional hostility were direct and immediate crises, those
crises were linked to more gradual and more fundamental transformations
in American religion, including the hardening of denominationalism. The
three major evangelical Protestant denominations—Presbyterians, Baptists,
and Methodists—had split over slavery (or at least in part over slavery) long
before the climax of the 1850s.[12] Those schisms had far-reaching implications
for religious publishing. Though the schisms created temporary financial

troubles for the churches and for the churches' publishing operations, they also seemed to energize the denominational tract and book work of Presbyterians, Baptists, and Methodists—traditionally major supporters of the American Bible Society, the American Tract Society, and the American Sunday School Union. Even the Congregationalists and Unitarians, essentially northern churches from the start, increased their own denominational publishing efforts in the 1850s.

Historians disagree over whether the largely doctrinal split of the Presbyterians into Old School and New School factions in 1837 also involved the issue of slavery.[13] The split did, however, have a sectional flavor—very few southern presbyteries were New School—and it certainly had an impact on denominational publishing. Before the schism, the publishing activities of the Presbyterian church were scattered and unsystematic. The most important agency was the Presbyterian Tract and Sabbath-School Book Society, operated by the Synod of Philadelphia. After the schism, that operation was taken over by the General Assembly, and in 1839 its name was changed to the Presbyterian Board of Publication. This Old School enterprise stepped up its tract and book work dramatically in the 1840s and 1850s, publishing many of the titles long cherished by the American Tract Society, including Baxter's *Call*, Doddridge's *Rise and Progress*, and Bunyan's *Pilgrim's Progress*. The board also published doctrinal works with a decidedly "denominational complexion," works that the nondenominational ATS could not publish or could publish only in watered-down form. In 1847, the Presbyterian Board of Publication launched a colportage project and by the mid-1850s had more than 200 colporteurs in the field, visiting 100,000 families and selling more than 100,000 books a year.[14] The New School faction lagged behind, but even it began a modest publishing operation in 1852 with the formation of the Presbyterian Publication Committee. New School leaders praised the work of the union societies, such as the ATS and the ASSU, but they were also impressed by the recent rise of denominational publishing, and they argued for liberal Presbyterianism to enter the fray.[15]

The Baptist schism of 1845 was directly related to slavery and sectional animosity, but because Baptist churches were governed locally (congregational polity) there were no presbyteries or national church to split. What split after 1844 were national Baptist missionary and educational societies, which were independent voluntary associations, and the Baptist General Convention. Disaffected southerners in 1845 organized the Southern Baptist Convention, a more centralized organization to handle their own missionary, educational, and benevolent work.[16] The denomination's publishing arm, the American Baptist Publication Society, like the Presbyterian Board of Publication, continued to serve southern as well as northern churches in the 1840s and 1850s; and like the Presbyterian board, the ABPS stepped up its denominational efforts in spite of sectional tensions. The society published many of the usual evangelical works, but a favorite volume was Richard Pengilly's *Scripture Guide to Baptism*, a doctrinal brief against infant baptism. The American Baptist Publication Society also climbed aboard the colportage bandwagon. In 1856, the society had 109 colporteurs, who visited 67,000 families, sold 37,000 volumes, and gave away nearly a half million pages of tracts. By its own account a "meagre publishing business," the ABPS launched a major campaign in the mid-1850s to raise $100,000 for a new building and for a stock of working capital. Shortly after the Civil War, the American Baptist Publication Society was circulating more than a million books a year.[17]

Organized more hierarchically than the Baptists, the Methodist Episcopal Church also wrecked on the issue of slavery, specifically on whether a bishop could be a slave owner. When the Methodist General Conference of 1844 decided that he could not, the church split, and the next year southerners founded a new denomination, the Methodist Episcopal Church, South. Because of the centralized polity of the church, the Methodist Book Concern, which had been founded in New York City in 1789 and had expanded to Cincinnati in 1820, became a disputed church property, a valuable spoil of doctrinal and sectional warfare. A Plan of Separation agreed upon in 1844 provided for an equitable division of Methodist Book Concern assets between the new MEC, South, and the old MEC, but a decade of litigation was required to settle the southerners' claims, eventually in their favor.[18] In 1854, the MEC, South, established its own book concern at Nashville. The bickering over the property of the original Methodist Book Concern only slightly slowed the publishing work of the northern church. In 1852, the General Conference launched a new tract society to compete with the ATS, which Methodists viewed as insufficiently Arminian. Meanwhile, the northern Methodist Book Concern was prospering. By 1856, the New York and Cincinnati printing plants were turning out more than 6 million books and pamphlets a year, an output comparable to that of the American Tract Society and the American Bible Society. By 1863, the Methodist Book Concern claimed to be the largest publishing house in the world.[19]

Other churches followed the parade into denominational publishing. Even the Congregationalists and the Unitarians, though neither very sectarian nor very evangelical, sought to bolster via publishing their denominational presence in the 1840s and 1850s. The Doctrinal Tract and Book Society, largely a supplier of books for Congregational pastors' libraries from its founding in 1829, changed its name in 1854 to the Congregational Board of Publication and changed its mission from publishing purely doctrinal works to a broader denominational outreach, along the lines of the Presbyterian Board of Publication. The Congregational Board of Publication even hired a couple of colporteurs in the late 1850s. Though the output of the board was minuscule, the idea was expansive: to follow the trend toward a full-service denominational publishing operation.[20] The Unitarians launched the Unitarian Book and Pamphlet Society in 1827 and stepped up their efforts in the 1830s and 1840s to get their message of liberal Christianity out into the religious marketplace. Though the publishing activities of the Congregationalists and the Unitarians were overshadowed by the work of the Presbyterians, Baptists, and Methodists, these descendants of John Eliot still held fast to the old faith in the "wonderful engine of the press." "Books are no longer the costly and infrequent possession they were," Unitarian Henry Ware, Jr., declared. "When God reformed his church, he summoned into existence the press; and the question, 'by what method shall we diffuse Christianity?' is no longer to receive one answer,— 'by sending abroad its preachers'; it requires another,—'by sending abroad its books.' "[21]

In an age of sectionalism, denominationalism, and civil war, the old union societies—the American Bible Society, the American Tract Society, and the American Sunday School Union—soldiered on. During the Civil War and Reconstruction, the demand for books and tracts for the army and for freed slaves temporarily stimulated production. But times had changed. In the late nineteenth century, even the most general of the big three organizations, the American Bible Society, became a kind of niche publisher. Though the ABS continued to print hundreds of thousands of copies of ordinary English Bibles, the society turned increasingly to foreign-language translations and overseas missions. The ABS became more an international business bureaucracy than a vital force in the local communities of America. Meanwhile, the appearance of new English translations, diverse Bible editions, and vast quantities of denominational literature made the simple Scripture, "without note or comment," seem somehow less central, less unifying, to the American Protestant experience.[22] The American Tract Society also turned more to overseas missions and to specialty publications, and its fortunes fell in the decades after 1860. The managers blamed the decline on the "rise and progress of various denominational societies, each undertaking for its separate constituency some part of the catholic work of this society."[23] The American Sunday School Union was similarly eclipsed by denominational Sunday schools and publishers. The centralized society was succeeded by ad hoc cross-denominational conventions of Sunday school teachers and administrators, who affirmed, rather than rejected, the new reality of denominational loyalty.[24]

In every sense—doctrinal, denominational, technological, and organizational—the religious landscape of late nineteenth-century America was too rich and pluralistic for any one national agency to dominate.[25] Protestants kept their faith in the power of the press and the voluntary association, and they kept their eye out for the second coming of Christ. But the era of the great union society and of the general supply was over.

Today, nearly two centuries after their founding, the American Bible Society, the American Tract Society, and the American Sunday School Union live on. Of the three, the ASSU has changed the most. Overshadowed for a century by denominational Sunday schools and publishing houses, the ASSU finally ended its publishing activities in 1968 and in 1974 changed its name to the American Missionary Fellowship. The AMF is now located in Villanova, Pennsylvania, outside Philadelphia. Though out of publishing and now a much smaller operation than the ASSU was in its antebellum heyday, the fellowship still employs missionaries to organize vacation Bible schools and Bible Learning Communities, as it calls them, throughout the United States.[26] The American Bible Society and the American Tract Society never abandoned their commitments to religious print; indeed, they remain large-scale publishers. Still based in Manhattan and still a major player in Bible translation and overseas work, the ABS also produces for the American market a wide variety of Bible guides and commentaries along with English-language Bibles in dozens of styles and translations.[27] The American Tract Society, which languished in the early twentieth century, was rejuvenated in the 1960s, when it returned to its oldest historical mission: the publication of brief, simple tracts. The ATS moved from New York to suburban New Jersey in 1962 and then to Garland, Texas, a Dallas suburb, in 1978. Today the American Tract Society describes itself as "one of the largest producers of electronic and printed gospel tracts in the world." Proud of its history, the ATS frequently reminds its supporters of its roots in the New England Tract Society (1814), the New-York Tract Society (1812), and even the Religious Tract Society of London (1799). "Since 1825," a recent news release declared, "the ATS has published over 10 billion tracts, CD-ROMs, Bibles and Christian books worldwide."[28]

Talk of CD-ROMs and electronic tracts suggests the technological distance from the early nineteenth century to the early twenty-first century. Like the culture in which they swim, the ABS and the ATS have gone digital. For example, the American Bible Society's new *Learning Bible*, which in its printed form is packed with maps, charts, pictures, commentaries, and lessons, also comes as a CD-ROM, for searching the Scriptures (never merely browsing) and for comparing translations in a way that Richard Baxter or John Bunyan would have loved. The ABS also operates a Web consulting service called ForMinistry to help local churches set up Websites and online Bible-based ministries. On a more technical level, the ABS is the leader of the Bible Technologies Group, an international effort to produce what it calls an "open scriptural information standard" for common XML coding and markup of Bible texts and annotations across translations and digital systems worldwide.[29] The American Tract Society, which has for some time produced videos and interactive CD-ROMs, is moving steadily into electronic tract publication through a partnership with an online not-for-profit company called DigiTracts. Electronic tracts (e-tracts), most of which follow the style of printed tracts jazzed up a bit with animation and inspirational background music, are produced in a variety of formats, from simple PowerPoint to Macromedia Flash. Like ATS tracts of old, these new technological wonders can be scattered like snowflakes across the land—but with no marginal cost at all.[30] Samuel Mills and Jedidiah Morse would be impressed.

While the technology is new, the fascination with new technology is as old as the societies themselves. Indeed, what may be most striking about the American Bible Society and the American Tract Society in the twenty-first century is how true they remain to the old faiths—faith in communications technology, in literacy and reading, in noncommercial business enterprise, and, of course, in the Christian gospel message. Though Baxter, Bunyan, and Doddridge have been retired, the Bible, the devotional volume, and the simple evangelical tract are still at work. At the ATS, Princess Di and the life of football coach Tom Landry have replaced *The Dairyman's Daughter* and the *Life of David Brainerd*, but the new narrative tracts tell the same old stories and affirm the same traditional values. At the ABS, some Bibles are now bound in denim, and the *Extreme Faith Bible* has photos of teenage skaters and rock climbers on the cover, but the Bible is still the Bible.[31] Though dressed in modern fashion, the message is the same message that was carried in the first tracts printed by the New England Tract Society and in the first Bibles stereotyped by the Bible Society of Philadelphia. And though fascinated by new visual media, both societies remain committed to the experience of *reading* the word—serious, contemplative reading. The ABS, in fact, recently launched a new project, Read All about It, to teach basic literacy. The lessons are based on the Contemporary English Version of the Bible.[32] Thus, in the early twenty-first century, as in the early nineteenth century, basic literacy and Bible literacy are one. Print remains paramount. Faith in reading endures.

Another important continuity is the societies' undiminished commitment to the voluntary principle in evangelism wedded to the noncommercial business enterprise. The American Tract Society and the American Bible Society today are part of a vast not-for-profit sector of the mass media industry, a sector that they helped to create two centuries ago. From the beginnings of Bible and tract work in America, the entrepreneurs of religious print imagined themselves at work in a marketplace of ideas and a marketplace of media. They proposed to compete vigorously in both, but not by fitting supply to demand. In the words of the Presbyterian Board of Publication: "Religious knowledge is a benefit, of which men less feel the need the less they possess of it. Here the demand does not create a supply, for the demand may not exist, however extreme the necessity. The gospel provides for its own dissemination. It was never contemplated that men would 'seek,' and hence the command is 'to send,' 'to go,' and 'to preach.' "[33]

And to print. From the seeds sown by the Society for Propagating the Gospel among the Indians and Others in North-America, by the Massachusetts Society for Promoting Christian Knowledge, by the New England Tract Society, and by all the other societies that populate this book, a verdant noncommercial religious media industry has flowered.[34] In two hundred years much has changed, but the goal and the strategy have not. Religious publishers still aim to use the media against the media, to turn commerce against commerce, to employ the visible hand of organization against the invisible hand of the marketplace, to save souls through what the American Tract Society in 1851 called "systematic Christian enterprise."

Appendix

*American Tract Society: Commentaries on
Proper Reading Methods*

Habits of Reading

Character is formed more as the result of habits of daily reading
than we are accustomed to think. Scarcely less depends on these
than on the character of the books read. One man will glance over a
dozen books, gaining some general conception of their contents, but
without mastering a single thought and making it his own; while
another in the perusal of a single work will gather materials of
thought and conversation for a lifetime. Grimke, of South Carolina,
an eminent scholar and orator, attributed his distinction to the influence of the thorough reading and study of a single book—Butler's
Analogy: while thousands, if they would confess the truth, might as-
cribe their mental dissipation and imbecility to the indiscriminate
and cursory reading of whatever comes in their way.

There is an evil in this direction that lies back of the character
of the popular literature, and that could not but work immense mis-
chief, even if what is so universally read were a great deal better
than it is. We allude to the habit of reading for amusement or excitement. There are multitudes who have no other or higher object in
reading. If the book is only "interesting" it suffices. No matter
whether it contains a single valuable thought, fact or principle: no
matter if it is true or false. It is enough that a morbid love of what is

wonderful or amusing is gratified. It helps to "kill time," and satisfies an appetite that is as craving and about as healthful as that of the drunkard for his cups.

It is truly melancholy to see so many minds employed in catering for the risibles and lachrymals of weak men and silly women, who spend the best part of a lifetime in an imaginary world, living in "castles in the air" and feeding on husks of sentimentality. If there were no duties to be performed in this matter-of-fact world; and if men had no immortal souls; and if there were no day of final account, it might be well enough, perhaps, to yield one's self to the control of fancy, and surrender the mind to become the plaything of every literary harlequin who chooses to amuse and delight us: but we have duties, and we have souls, and there will be a judgment-day, and we protest solemnly against the prevalent neglect of all these in the habit of reading simply for amusement. We object,

1. Because it is a wanton and wicked *waste of time.*
2. Because it *enervates* and *dissipates the mind.*
3. Because it *unfits the mind for solid and instructive reading.*
4. Because it engenders such a false taste, that even the Bible, and serious books, and the preached Gospel become powerless, or are only valued in the degree that they excite or amuse.
5. Because *eternity is a sober world;* and the mind that has given itself up to amusement in this life will find itself poorly prepared for the *realities* of another. It will be a sad meeting when the writers and readers of amusing fiction stand before the Judge![1]

The Manner of Reading

We should read *correctly,* but that is not enough. Some read over a book like a child looking for pictures; that is not the way to read so as to be profited.

We should read with *diligence*—give attendance to it—striving to improve and endeavoring to remember what we read.

We should read with *attention,* laboring to understand what we read and thoroughly to digest it.

We should read with *reflection*—think of what we read—ponder it—compare it—weigh it—make our observations—form our own conclusions. It is a good thing to *take notes* when we read, mark what is important, that we may refer to it as occasion may require. We are not to take opinions on trust, or because this or that man says so, but to examine and investigate for ourselves. Hence the necessity of reflection, comparison and review.

We should read with *practice*—adopt as our own what is good, and reduce it at once to practice. Especially should we do this in reading religious authors and the Bible. They who *do* his will shall know of the doctrine.

We should read with *prayer*. Prayer is the best preparation for reading and study. How can we expect to arrive at truth unless we seek wisdom from the All-wise in humble and devout prayer? Dr. [Isaac] Watts, in his excellent work on the improvement of the mind, which ought to be more read and studied and practised than it is, quotes from Bishop [Robert] Saunderson, "Study without prayer is atheism, as prayer without study is presumption."[2]

Notes

1. Samuel J. Mills and Daniel Smith, *Report of a Missionary Tour through that Part of the United States which Lies West of the Allegany Mountains; Performed under the Direction of the Massachusetts Missionary Society* (Andover, Mass.: Flagg and Gould, 1815), 28. This pamphlet is reprinted in facsimile in *To Win the West: Missionary Viewpoints, 1814–1815*, ed. Edwin S. Gaustad (New York: Arno, 1972).

2. The best account of the mythic importance of the battle of New Orleans remains John William Ward, *Andrew Jackson: Symbol for an Age* (New York: Oxford University Press, 1955). See also Robert V. Remini, *The Battle of New Orleans* (New York: Viking, 1999).

3. Mills and Smith, *Report of a Missionary Tour*, 21. The report of Mills's first tour of the West is John F. Schermerhorn and Samuel J. Mills, *A Correct View of that Part of the United States which Lies West of the Allegany Mountains, with Regard to Religion and Morals* (Hartford, Conn.: Gleason, 1814). This report is also reprinted in Gaustad, *To Win the West*.

4. Mills and Smith, *Report of a Missionary Tour*, 20–21, 42.

5. Letter from William Dickey to Samuel Mills, April 1, 1815, quoted in ibid., 53.

6. Mills and Smith, *Report of a Missionary Tour*, 6; Bible Society of Philadelphia, *Sixth Annual Report* (1814), 9–11.

7. Charles Sellers, *The Market Revolution: Jacksonian America, 1815–1846* (New York: Oxford University Press, 1991); Daniel Feller, *The Jacksonian Promise: America, 1815–1840* (Baltimore, Md.: Johns Hopkins University Press, 1995); and Sean Wilentz, "Society, Politics, and the Market Revolution, 1815–1848," in *The New American History*, rev. ed., ed. Janet Flammang

and Eric Foner (Philadelphia, Pa.: Temple University Press, 1997). For critical discussions of the market revolution idea, see Melvyn Stokes and Stephen Conway, eds., *The Market Revolution in America: Social, Political, and Religious Expressions, 1800–1880* (Charlottesville: University Press of Virginia, 1996. The related issue of how capitalism came to America is explored in Joyce Appleby, "The Vexed Story of Capitalism Told by American Historians," *Journal of the Early Republic* 21 (Spring 2001): 1–18; Michael Merrill, "Putting 'Capitalism' in Its Place: A Review of Recent Literature," *William and Mary Quarterly*, 3d ser., 52 (April 1995): 325, and "Special Issue on Capitalism in the Early Republic," *Journal of the Early Republic* 16 (Summer 1996): 159–308.

8. Recent historians of print culture are wary of the term *reading revolution*, though they still tend to see the early nineteenth century as an important era in the history of reading as well as the history of printing and publishing. See, for example, Isabelle Lehuu, *Carnival on the Page: Popular Print Media in Antebellum America* (Chapel Hill: University of North Carolina Press, 2000), 15–18; William J. Gilmore, *Reading Becomes a Necessity of Life: Material and Cultural Life in Rural New England* (Knoxville: University of Tennessee Press, 1989), 354–59; David D. Hall, "Introduction" and "The Uses of Literacy in New England, 1600–1850," in *Cultures of Print: Essays in the History of the Book* (Amherst: University of Massachusetts Press, 1996); and Ronald J. Zboray, *A Fictive People: Antebellum Economic Development and the American Reading Public* (New York: Oxford University Press, 1993).

9. R. Laurence Moore, *Selling God: American Religion in the Marketplace of Culture* (New York: Oxford University Press, 1994), 5–6; Roger Finke and Rodney Stark, *The Churching of America, 1776–1990: Winners and Losers in Our Religious Economy* (New Brunswick, N.J.: Rutgers University Press, 1992), 5–6, 59; John H. Wigger, *Taking Heaven by Storm: Methodism and the Rise of Popular Christianity in America* (New York: Oxford University Press, 1998), 5; Nathan O. Hatch and John H. Wigger, introduction to *Methodism and the Shaping of American Culture*, ed. Hatch and Wigger (Nashville, Tenn.: Abingdon, 2001), 14; Peter J. Wosh, *Spreading the Word: The Bible Business in Nineteenth-Century America* (Ithaca, N.Y.: Cornell University Press, 1994), 250. See also Jon Butler, *Awash in a Sea of Faith: Christianizing the American People* (Cambridge, Mass.: Harvard University Press, 1990), chap. 8; Nathan O. Hatch, *The Democratization of American Christianity* (New Haven, Conn.: Yale University Press, 1989), chap. 5; and Mark A. Noll, *America's God: From Jonathan Edwards to Abraham Lincoln* (New York: Oxford University Press, 2002), chap. 9.

10. Daniel Walker Howe, "The Market Revolution and the Shaping of Identity in Whig-Jacksonian America," and Richard Carwardine, " 'Antinomians' and 'Arminians': Methodists and the Market Revolution," both in Stokes and Conway, *Market Revolution in America*.

11. Alfred D. Chandler, Jr., *The Visible Hand: The Managerial Revolution in American Business* (Cambridge, Mass.: Belknap, 1977), 8–12; JoAnne Yates, *Control through Communication: The Rise of System in American Management* (Baltimore, Md.: Johns Hopkins University Press, 1989), chaps. 1–2.

12. Peter Dobkin Hall, "Religion and the Organizational Revolution in the United States," in *Sacred Companies: Organizational Aspects of Religion and Religious Aspects of Organizations*, ed. N. J. Demerath III et al. (New York: Oxford University

Press, 1998), 99–101; Peter Dobkin Hall, *Inventing the Nonprofit Sector and Other Essays on Philanthropy, Voluntarism, and Nonprofit Organizations* (Baltimore, Md.: Johns Hopkins University Press, 1992), 35–36. See also Lawrence J. Friedman and Mark D. McGarvie, eds., *Charity, Philanthropy, and Civility in American History* (Cambridge: Cambridge University Press, 2003).

13. Robert Darnton, "First Steps toward a History of Reading," in *The Kiss of Lamourette: Reflections in Cultural History* (New York: Norton, 1990); David D. Hall, "Readers and Reading in America: Historical and Critical Perspectives," in *Cultures of Print;* Roger Chartier, *The Order of Books* (Stanford, Calif.: Stanford University Press, 1994), chap. 1; Norman N. Holland, "Reader-Response Criticism," in *The New Princeton Encyclopedia of Poetry and Poetics,* ed. Alex Preminger and T. V. F. Brogan (Princeton, N.J.: Princeton University Press, 1993).

14. Mills and Smith, *Report of a Missionary Tour,* 45–47.

15. Ibid., 47.

CHAPTER 1

1. Martin Luther, quoted in Elizabeth L. Eisenstein, *The Printing Revolution in Early Modern Europe* (Cambridge: Cambridge University Press, 1983), 147; John Foxe, quoted in Stephen Greenblatt, *Renaissance Self-Fashioning: From More to Shakespeare* (Chicago, Ill.: University of Chicago Press, 1980), 98–99. See also Harry Y. Gamble, *Books and Readers in the Early Church: A History of Early Christian Texts* (New Haven, Conn.: Yale University Press, 1995); and Mark U. Edwards, Jr., *Printing, Propaganda, and Martin Luther* (Berkeley: University of California Press, 1994). The best study of the creation of print culture in sixteenth- and seventeenth-century Europe is Adrian Johns, *The Nature of the Book: Print and Knowledge in the Making* (Chicago, Ill.: University of Chicago Press, 1998).

2. David D. Hall, "The Chesapeake in the Seventeenth Century," in *A History of the Book in America,* vol. 1: *The Colonial Book in the Atlantic World,* ed. Hugh Amory and David D. Hall (Cambridge: Cambridge University Press, 2000), chap. 2. See also Richard D. Brown, *Knowledge Is Power: The Diffusion of Information in Early America, 1700–1865* (New York: Oxford University Press), chap. 2.

3. Perry Miller, *The New England Mind: The Seventeenth Century,* 2d ed. (Cambridge, Mass.: Harvard University Press, 1954), 20–22; David D. Hall, introduction to Amory and Hall, *History of the Book,* 1:2–3; Hugh Amory, "Printing and Bookselling in New England, 1638–1713," in Amory and Hall, *History of the Book,* 1:108–9. See also Arthur G. Dickens, *The English Reformation,* 2d ed. (London: Batsford, 1989); and Christopher Haigh, ed., *The English Reformation Revised* (Cambridge: Cambridge University Press, 1987).

4. David D. Hall, *Worlds of Wonder, Days of Judgment: Popular Religious Belief in Early New England* (New York: Knopf, 1989), 31; Harry S. Stout, *The New England Soul: Preaching and Religious Culture in Colonial New England* (New York: Oxford University Press, 1986), 105–6. See also Harry S. Stout, "Word and Order in Colonial New England," and Nathan O. Hatch, "*Sola Scriptura* and *Novus Ordo Seclorum,*" both in *The Bible in America: Essays in Cultural History,* ed. Nathan O. Hatch and Mark A. Noll

(New York: Oxford University Press, 1982); Jill Lepore, "Literacy and Reading in Puritan New England," in *Perspectives on American Book History: Artifacts and Commentary*, ed. Scott E. Casper, Joanne D. Chaison, and Jeffrey D. Groves (Amherst: University of Massachusetts Press, 2002); Julie Hedgepeth Williams, "Evangelism and the Genesis of Printing in America," in *Media and Religion in American History*, ed. Wm. David Sloan (Northport, Ala.: Vision, 2000); and Julie Hedgepeth Williams, *The Significance of the Printed Word in Early America: Colonists' Thoughts on the Role of the Press* (Westport, Conn.: Greenwood, 1999), chaps. 1 and 3.

5. Thomas Shepard and Thomas Hooker, quoted in Perry Miller, *The New England Mind: From Colony to Province* (Cambridge, Mass.: Harvard University Press, 1953), 64–65. See also Sydney E. Ahlstrom, *A Religious History of the American People* (New Haven, Conn.: Yale University Press, 1972), 152–53.

6. Miller, *New England Mind*, 67.

7. Janice Knight, *Orthodoxies in Massachusetts: Rereading American Puritanism* (Cambridge, Mass.: Harvard University Press, 1994), 2–3, 8–9; Samuel Willard, quoted in David D. Hall, "On Common Ground: The Coherence of American Puritan Studies," *William and Mary Quarterly*, 3d ser., 44 (April 1987): 202; David D. Hall, "Narrating Puritanism," in *New Directions in American Religious History*, ed. Harry S. Stout and D. G. Hart (New York: Oxford University Press, 1997), 66. See also Stephen Foster, *The Long Argument: English Puritanism and the Shaping of New England Culture, 1570–1700* (Chapel Hill: University of North Carolina Press, 1991); and John Morgan, *Godly Learning: Puritan Attitudes towards Reason, Learning, and Education, 1560–1640* (Cambridge: Cambridge University Press, 1986).

8. Hall, "Narrating Puritanism," 67–68; Charles E. Hambrick-Stowe, *The Practice of Piety: Puritan Devotional Disciplines in Seventeenth-Century New England* (Chapel Hill: University of North Carolina Press, 1982), chap. 7.

9. Andrew Delbanco, *The Puritan Ordeal* (Cambridge, Mass.: Harvard University Press, 1989), 50–51. See also Sacvan Bercovitch, *The American Jeremiad* (Madison: University of Wisconsin Press, 1978), 47–51.

10. Knight, *Orthodoxies in Massachusetts*, 130–31.

11. Hall, "Narrating Puritanism," 55.

12. Mark A. Noll, *A History of Christianity in the United States and Canada* (Grand Rapids, Mich.: Eerdmans, 1992), 34–35. See also Jack P. Greene, *Pursuits of Happiness: The Social Development of Early Modern British Colonies and the Formation of American Culture* (Chapel Hill: University of North Carolina Press, 1988), chaps. 1–3; Knight, *Orthodoxies in Massachusetts*, chaps. 4–5.

13. Hall, *Worlds of Wonder*, 34; Edmund S. Morgan, *The Puritan Family: Religion and Domestic Relations in Seventeenth-Century New England*, rev. ed. (New York: Harper and Row, 1966), 88–89; John Demos, *A Little Commonwealth: Family Life in Plymouth Colony*, 2d ed. (New York: Oxford University Press, 2000), 183; Gloria L. Main, *Peoples of a Spacious Land: Families and Cultures in Colonial New England* (Cambridge, Mass.: Harvard University Press, 2001), chap. 2. For an overview of family history in New England, see Helena M. Wall, "Notes on Life since *A Little Commonwealth*: Family and Gender History since 1970," *William and Mary Quarterly*, 3d ser., 57 (October 2000): 807–25.

14. E. Jennifer Monaghan, "Literacy Instruction and Gender in Colonial New England," in *Reading in America: Literature and Social History*, ed. Cathy N. Davidson (Baltimore, Md.: Johns Hopkins University Press, 1989), 54–61; E. Jennifer Monaghan, "Reading for the Enslaved, Writing for the Free: Reflections on Liberty and Literacy," *Proceedings of the American Antiquarian Society* 108 (October 1998): 311–15. See also Joel Perlmann and Dennis Shirley, "When Did New England Women Acquire Literacy?" *William and Mary Quarterly*, 3d ser., 48 (January 1991): 50–67; and Gloria L. Main, "An Inquiry into When and Why Women Learned to Write in Colonial New England," *Journal of Social History* 24 (Spring 1991): 579–89.

15. Kenneth A. Lockridge, *Literacy in Colonial New England: An Enquiry into the Social Context of Literacy in the Early Modern West* (New York: Norton, 1974), 4–5, 27, 97–101; Linda Auwers, "Reading the Marks of the Past: Exploring Female Literacy in Colonial Windsor, Connecticut," *Historical Methods* 13 (1980): 209; William J. Gilmore, *Reading Becomes a Necessity of Life: Material and Cultural Life in Rural New England* (Knoxville: University of Tennessee Press, 1989), 122–23.

16. Monaghan, "Literacy Instruction," 62, 66–69; Hall, *Worlds of Wonder*, 34–35; Main, *Peoples of a Spacious Land*, 140–43. See also Bernard Bailyn, *Education in the Forming of American Society* (Chapel Hill: University of North Carolina Press, 1960); and Lawrence Cremin, *American Education: The Colonial Experience, 1607–1783* (New York: Harper and Row, 1970).

17. Robert A. Gross, "Giving in America: From Charity to Philanthropy," in *Charity, Philanthropy, and Civility in American History*, ed. Lawrence J. Friedman and Mark D. McGarvie (New York: Cambridge University Press, 2003), 33–35; Peter Dobkin Hall, "Religion and the Organizational Revolution in the United States," in *Sacred Companies: Organizational Aspects of Religion and Religious Aspects of Organizations*, ed. N. J. Demerath III et al. (New York: Oxford University Press, 1998), 100–101. See also Conrad Edick Wright, *The Transformation of Charity in Postrevolutionary New England* (Boston: Northeastern University Press, 1992), chap. 1.

18. Peter Dobkin Hall, *Inventing the Nonprofit Sector and Other Essays on Philanthropy, Voluntarism, and Nonprofit Organizations* (Baltimore, Md.: Johns Hopkins University Press, 1992), 16–17; E. Digby Baltzell, *Puritan Boston and Quaker Philadelphia: Two Protestant Ethics and the Spirit of Class Authority and Leadership* (New York: Free Press, 1979), 94. One of the great institution builders of eighteenth-century America, Benjamin Franklin of Philadelphia, was an expatriate New Englander. See, for example, Edmund S. Morgan, *Benjamin Franklin* (New Haven, Conn.: Yale University Press, 2002). On the founding of Harvard College, see Samuel Eliot Morison, *Three Centuries of Harvard, 1636–1936* (Cambridge, Mass.: Harvard University Press, 1936).

19. Amory, "Printing and Bookselling," 86–87, 105–7; Hugh Amory, "The New England Book Trade, 1713–1790," in Amory and Hall, *History of the Book*, 1:314–15. See also George Parker Winship, *The Cambridge Press, 1638–1692: A Reexamination of the Evidence concerning the "Bay Psalm Book" and the Eliot Indian Bible as Well as Other Contemporary Books and People* (Philadelphia, Pa.: University of Pennsylvania Press, 1945).

20. Hall, introduction to Amory and Hall, *History of the Book*, 18–19; Neal Salisbury, "Red Puritans: The 'Praying Indians' of Massachusetts Bay and John Eliot," *Wil-*

liam and Mary Quarterly, 3d ser., 31 (January 1974): 27–54. See also Amanda Porterfield, "Protestant Missionaries: Pioneers of American Philanthropy," in Friedman and McGarvie, *Charity, Philanthropy, and Civility*; Richard W. Cogley, *John Eliot's Mission to the Indians before King Philip's War* (Cambridge, Mass.: Harvard University Press, 1999); and Jean M. O'Brien, *Dispossession by Degrees: Indian Land and Identity in Natick, Massachusetts, 1650–1790* (Cambridge: Cambridge University Press, 1997), chaps. 1–2.

21. Amory, "Printing and Bookselling," 89; Hall, introduction to Amory and Hall, *History of the Book*, 18–19. See also Jill Lepore, *The Name of War: King Philip's War and the Origins of American Identity* (New York: Knopf, 1998), chap. 1; and William Kellaway, *The New England Company, 1649–1776* (London: Longmans, 1961).

22. John Eliot, quoted in Winship, *Cambridge Press*, 242.

23. Richard Baxter, *A Call to the Unconverted* (New York: American Tract Society, n.d.), 41, 44, 59, 61–63, 74–75, 93; N. H. Keeble, *Richard Baxter: Puritan Man of Letters* (Oxford: Clarendon, 1982), 71–72, 148. The American Tract Society edition of Baxter's *Call* was published throughout the 1830s and 1840s in cheap format, often as a volume to be given away for free.

24. Baxter, *Call to the Unconverted*, 35–36, 45; Keeble, *Richard Baxter*, 1, 6, 30–33, 45 (quotation).

25. Susan O'Brien, "Eighteenth-Century Publishing Networks in the First Years of Transatlantic Evangelicalism," in *Evangelicalism: Comparative Studies of Popular Protestantism in North America, the British Isles, and Beyond, 1700–1990*, ed. Mark A. Noll, David W. Bobbington, and George A. Rawlyk (New York: Oxford University Press, 1994), 43–44. See also Frank Lambert, " 'Pedlar in Divinity': George Whitefield and the Great Awakening, 1737–1745," *Journal of American History* 77 (December 1990): 812–37.

26. On the survival of Baxter's *Call* into the nineteenth century, see chapters 6 and 7 of this book. See also David D. Hall, "The Uses of Literacy in New England, 1600–1850," in *Cultures of Print: Essays in the History of the Book* (Amherst: University of Massachusetts Press, 1996). The only book that rivaled the *Call* in the repertoire of nineteenth-century religious publishing in America was John Bunyan's *Pilgrim's Progress*, another English Puritan classic.

27. Keeble, *Richard Baxter*, 46–47 (quotation, p. 46); Hall, *Worlds of Wonder*, 24–25. On the doctrine of *sola scriptura* and reading the Bible, see Mark A. Noll, *America's God: From Jonathan Edwards to Abraham Lincoln* (New York: Oxford University Press, 2002), chap. 18.

28. Stanley E. Fish, "Interpreting the Variorum," in *Reader-Response Criticism: From Formalism to Post-Structuralism*, ed. Jane P. Tompkins (Baltimore, Md.: Johns Hopkins University Press, 1980), 183. See also Stanley E. Fish, *Is There a Text in This Class? The Authority of Interpretive Communities* (Cambridge, Mass.: Harvard University Press, 1980); Norman N. Holland, *The Critical I* (New York: Columbia University Press, 1992); and David Morley, "Active Audience Theory: Pendulums and Pitfalls," *Journal of Communication* 43 (Autumn 1993): 13–19.

29. Roger Chartier, *The Order of Books: Readers, Authors, and Libraries in Europe between the Fourteenth and Eighteenth Centuries* (Stanford, Calif.: Stanford University

Press, 1994), 3. See also Robert Darnton, "First Steps toward a History of Reading," in *The Kiss of Lamourette: Reflections in Cultural History* (New York: Norton, 1990).

30. Charles L. Cohen, "The Post-Puritan Paradigm of Early American Religious History," *William and Mary Quarterly*, 3d ser., 54 (October 1997): 697. See, for example, Jon Butler, *Awash in a Sea of Faith: Christianizing the American People* (Cambridge, Mass.: Harvard University Press, 1990); Patricia U. Bonomi, *Under the Cope of Heaven: Religion, Society, and Politics in Colonial America* (New York: Oxford University Press, 1986); and Hall, *Worlds of Wonder.* I discuss an analogous rise of "heresy" in seventeenth- and eighteenth-century journalism in David Paul Nord, "Teleology and News: The Religious Roots of American Journalism, 1630–1730," in *Communities of Journalism: A History of American Newspapers and Their Readers* (Urbana: University of Illinois Press, 2001).

31. Hall, *Worlds of Wonder*, 241–45. The classic account of this intermingling of literary and folk culture in religion is Carlo Ginzburg, *The Cheese and the Worms: The Cosmos of a Sixteenth-Century Miller*, trans. John Tedeschi and Anne Tedeschi (Baltimore, Md.: Johns Hopkins University Press, 1980).

32. Frank Lambert, *"Pedlar in Divinity": George Whitefield and the Transatlantic Revivals, 1737–1770* (Princeton, N.J.: Princeton University Press, 1994), 137. See also Harry S. Stout, *The Divine Dramatist: George Whitefield and the Rise of Modern Evangelicalism* (Grand Rapids, Mich.: Eerdmans, 1991); and Frank Lambert, *Inventing the Great Awakening* (Princeton, N.J.: Princeton University Press, 1999).

33. Erik R. Seeman, "Reading Indians' Deathbed Scenes: Ethnohistorical and Representational Approaches," *Journal of American History* 88 (June 2001): 20–21, 38–39; Salisbury, "Red Puritans," 42–43. See also Hilary E. Wyss, *Writing Indians: Literacy, Christianity, and Native Community in Early America* (Amherst: University of Massachusetts Press, 2000), chap. 1.

34. Jill Lepore, "Dead Men Tell No Tales: John Sassamon and the Fatal Consequences of Literacy," *American Quarterly* 46 (December 1994): 504–5; Lepore, *Name of War*, 41–44. See also Cogley, *John Eliot's Mission*, chap. 7.

CHAPTER 2

1. *Brief Account of the Society for Propagating the Gospel among the Indians and Others in North-America* ([Boston]: n.p., 1798), 2.

2. Ibid., 2–4; *A Brief Account of the Present State of the Society for Propagating the Gospel among the Indians and Others in North-America,—with a Sketch of the Manner in Which They Mean to Pursue the Objects of Their Institution* ([Boston: Adams, 1791]), 1–2. See also James F. Hunnewell, ed., *The Society for Propagating the Gospel among the Indians and Others in North-America, 1787–1887* (Cambridge, Mass.: Society for Propagating the Gospel, 1887); and Richard D. Pierce, ed., *Handbook of the Society for Propagating the Gospel among the Indians and Others in North-America, 1787–1964* (Boston: Society for Propagating the Gospel, 1964).

3. Ruth Bloch, *Visionary Republic: Millennial Themes in American Thought, 1756–1800* (New York: Cambridge University Press, 1985), 75–78, 103–4; Jon Butler, *Awash in a Sea of Faith: Christianizing the American People* (Cambridge, Mass.: Harvard Uni-

versity Press, 1990), 217; Sacvan Bercovitch, *The American Jeremiad* (Madison: University of Wisconsin Press, 1978), 128–29. For overviews of American religion in this period, see Gordon S. Wood, "Religion and the American Revolution," in *New Directions in American Religious History*, ed. Harry S. Stout and D. G. Hart (New York: Oxford University Press, 1997); James H. Hutson, ed., *Religion and the New Republic: Faith in the Founding of America* (Lanham, Md.: Rowman and Littlefield, 2000); and Ronald Hoffman and Peter J. Albert, eds., *Religion in a Revolutionary Age* (Charlottesville: University Press of Virginia, 1994).

4. Bloch, *Visionary Republic*, 131–32, 229–30. See also Nathan O. Hatch, *The Sacred Cause of Liberty: Republican Thought and the Millennium in Revolutionary New England* (New Haven, Conn.: Yale University Press, 1977); and Jonathan D. Sassi, *A Republic of Righteousness: The Public Christianity of the Post-Revolutionary New England Clergy* (New York: Oxford University Press, 2001).

5. Samuel Hopkins, *A Treatise on the Millennium* (Boston: Thomas and Andrews, 1793), 41, 44–46; Bloch, *Visionary Republic*, 125.

6. Jedidiah Morse, *The American Geography; or, A View of the Present Situation of the United States of America* (Elizabethtown, N.J.: Shepard Kollock, for the author, 1789), 469; Richard J. Moss, *The Life of Jedidiah Morse: A Station of Peculiar Exposure* (Knoxville: University of Tennessee Press, 1995), 38–39, 43–45, 74–75; Joseph W. Phillips, *Jedidiah Morse and New England Congregationalism* (New Brunswick, N.J.: Rutgers University Press, 1983), 31–33.

7. Jedidiah Morse, *A Sermon, Exhibiting the Present Dangers, and Consequent Duties of the Citizens of the United States of America* (Charlestown, Mass.: Etheridge, 1799), 31–32; Moss, *Life of Jedidiah Morse*, 64–66; Phillips, *Jedidiah Morse*, chap. 3; Sassi, *Republic of Righteousness*, 104–5. See also Peter S. Field, *The Crisis of the Standing Order: Clerical Intellectuals and Cultural Authority in Massachusetts, 1780–1833* (Amherst: University of Massachusetts Press, 1998), chap. 5.

8. Morse, *A Sermon*, 32; Jedidiah Morse, *Signs of the Times: A Sermon Preached before the Society for Propagating the Gospel among the Indians and Others in North-America, at Their Anniversary, Nov. 1, 1810* (Charlestown, Mass.: Armstrong, 1810), 26–29. See also Bloch, *Visionary Republic*, chap. 9; and James H. Moorhead, "Between Progress and Apocalypse: A Reassessment of Millennialism in American Religious Thought, 1800–1880," *Journal of American History* 71 (December 1984): 524–42.

9. Hopkins, *Treatise on the Millennium*, 152; Morse, *Signs of the Times*, 26, 29, 36.

10. *Brief Account* (1798), 3; *Brief Account* (1791), 1.

11. John Lathrop, *A Discourse before the Society for "Propagating the Gospel among the Indians and Others in North-America": Delivered on the 19th of January, 1804* (Boston: Manning and Loring, [1804]), 6, 13, 17. On the broader tendency to link knowledge and virtue in early America, see Richard D. Brown, *The Strength of a People: The Idea of an Informed Citizenry in America, 1650–1870* (Chapel Hill: University of North Carolina Press, 1996).

12. *Brief Account* (1791), 1; *Report of the Select Committee of the Society for Propagating the Gospel among the Indians and Others in North-America, Presented at the Sixty-Seventh Annual Meeting, May 31, 1855* (Boston: Wilson and Son, 1856), 21–22.

13. Letter from Daniel Little, Nov. 24, 1790, reprinted in *Brief Account* (1791), 2–4.

14. *A Brief Account of the Present State, Income, Expenditures, &c. of the Society for Propagating the Gospel among the Indians, and Others, in North-America* ([Boston]: n.p., 1795), 3; *Brief Account* (1798), 4.

15. Pauline Maier, "The Revolutionary Origins of the American Corporation," *William and Mary Quarterly*, 3d ser., 50 (January 1993): 51–84. See also Peter Dobkin Hall, *Inventing the Nonprofit Sector and Other Essays on Philanthropy, Voluntarism, and Nonprofit Organizations* (Baltimore, Md.: Johns Hopkins University Press, 1992), chap. 1; and David C. Hammack, ed., *Making the Nonprofit Sector in the United States: A Reader* (Bloomington: Indiana University Press, 1998).

16. Conrad Edick Wright, *The Transformation of Charity in Postrevolutionary New England* (Boston: Northeastern University Press, 1992), 56.

17. *Brief Account* (1795), 1–2; *Brief Account* (1798), 2–3; "Annual Report of the Society for Propagating the Gospel among the Indians and Others in North-America" (1809), in Morse, *Signs of the Times*, 67–68. See also Mark A. Noll, introduction to *God and Mammon: Protestants, Money, and the Market, 1790–1860*, ed. Mark A. Noll (New York: Oxford University Press, 2002).

18. *Brief Account* (1798), 4–7; *Report of the Select Committee of the Society for Propagating the Gospel among the Indians and Others in North-America: Read and Accepted VIII November MDCCCXVI* (n.p., [1816]), 23.

19. Thomas Barnard, *A Discourse before the Society for Propagating the Gospel among the Indians and Others in North-America, Delivered November 6, 1806* (Charlestown, Mass.: Etheridge, 1806), 10. See also Wright, *Transformation of Charity*, 72–76.

20. Cyprian Strong, *A Sermon, Preached at Hartford, before the Board of Trustees, of the Missionary Society, in Connecticut, at the Ordination of the Rev. Jedediah [sic] Bushnell, as a Missionary to the New Settlements; January 15th, A.D. 1800* (Hartford, Conn.: Hudson and Goodwin, 1800), 9; Nathaniel Emmons, *A Sermon, Delivered before the Massachusetts Missionary Society, at Their Annual Meeting in Boston, May 27, 1800* (Charlestown, Mass.: Etheridge, 1800), 38. On Congregational home missions, see James R. Rohrer, *Keepers of the Covenant: Frontier Missions and the Decline of Congregationalism, 1774–1818* (New York: Oxford University Press, 1995); and Colin Brummitt Goodykoontz, *Home Missions on the American Frontier* (Caldwell, Idaho: Caxton, 1939).

21. Journal of Caleb Alexander, in "Annual Report of the Trustees," in Samuel Spring, *A Sermon, Delivered before the Massachusetts Missionary Society, at Their Annual Meeting May 15, 1802* (Newburyport, Mass.: Blunt, 1802), 42.

22. Anne Stott, *Hannah More: The First Victorian* (Oxford: Oxford University Press, 2003), 169, 208–9; Patricia Demers, *The World of Hannah More* (Lexington: University Press of Kentucky, 1996), 109–10. The founders of the MSPCK preferred the somewhat more doctrinal RTS tracts to Hannah More's moralistic popular narratives. See also William Jones, *The Jubilee Memorial of the Religious Tract Society* (London: Religious Tract Society, 1850); and James Raven, "Sent to the Wilderness: Mission Literature in Colonial America," in *Free Print and Non-Commercial Publishing since 1700*, ed. James Raven (Aldershot, England: Ashgate, 2000).

23. *An Account of the Massachusetts Society for Promoting Christian Knowledge*

(Cambridge, Mass.: Hilliard, 1806), 17–18, 31–32; *An Account of the Massachusetts Society for Promoting Christian Knowledge* (Andover, Mass.: Flagg and Gould, 1815), 13–15.

24. *Constitution of the Massachusetts Society for Promoting Christian Knowledge* (Charlestown, Mass.: Etheridge, 1803); *Account of the Massachusetts Society* (1815), 75–76.

25. *Account of the Massachusetts Society* (1806); *Account of the Massachusetts Society* (1815). On such reports in a later age, see chapter 7 of this book.

26. *Account of the Massachusetts Society* (1815), 32–37, 70–74. On the rise of new religious groups and denominations in this era, see Butler, *Awash in a Sea of Faith*, chaps. 7–8; Nathan O. Hatch, *The Democratization of American Christianity* (New Haven, Conn.: Yale University Press, 1989); John H. Wigger, *Taking Heaven by Storm: Methodism and the Rise of Popular Christianity in America* (New York: Oxford University Press, 1998); and Roger Finke and Rodney Stark, *The Churching of America, 1776–1990: Winners and Losers in Our Religious Economy* (New Brunswick, N.J.: Rutgers University Press, 1992).

27. In England, the religious tract movement was also founded as "an antidote to the poison continually flowing thro' the channel of vulgar and licentious publications," in the words of the prospectus for Hannah More's Cheap Repository. Quoted in Stott, *Hannah More*, 174. See also Demers, *World of Hannah More*, 109.

28. Eliphalet Pearson, *A Sermon Delivered in Boston before the Massachusetts Society for Promoting Christian Knowledge, Nov. 27, 1811* (Cambridge, Mass.: Hilliard and Metcalf, 1811), 23–24; "To the Friends of Religion in New England," in *Proceedings of the First Ten Years of the American Tract Society, Instituted at Boston, 1814* (Andover, Mass.: Flagg and Gould, 1824), 8; *An Address to Christians Recommending the Distribution of Cheap Religious Tracts, with an Extract from a Sermon, by Bishop Porteus, before the Yearly Meeting of the Charity Schools, London* (Charlestown, Mass.: Etheridge, 1802), 23. See also Phillips, *Jedidiah Morse*, 117–18.

29. *Account of the Massachusetts Society* (1806), 21; *Account of the Massachusetts Society* (1815), 38–39. See also Rohrer, *Keepers of the Covenant;* and Paul K. Conkin, *The Uneasy Center: Reformed Christianity in Antebellum America* (Chapel Hill: University of North Carolina Press, 1995), chaps. 3–4.

30. Phillips, *Jedidiah Morse*, 108–9, 118, 137; Field, *Crisis of the Standing Order*, chap. 5. See also Leo P. Hirrel, *Children of Wrath: New School Calvinism and Antebellum Reform* (Lexington: University of Kentucky Press, 1998).

31. *Constitution of the Massachusetts Society* (1803), 3–5; *Account of the Massachusetts Society* (1806), 34; *Account of the Massachusetts Society* (1815), 14.

32. Jonathan D. Sassi, "The First Party Competition and Southern New England's Public Christianity," *Journal of the Early Republic* 21 (Summer 2001): 267–68, 298; Peter Dobkin Hall, *The Organization of American Culture, 1700–1900: Private Institutions, Elites, and the Origins of American Nationality* (New York: New York University Press, 1982), 87–88. See also Conrad Wright, "The Controversial Career of Jedidiah Morse," in *The Unitarian Controversy: Essays on American Unitarian History* (Boston: Skinner House, 1994); and John G. West, Jr., *The Politics of Revelation and Reason: Religion and Civic Life in the New Nation* (Lawrence: University Press of Kansas, 1996), chap. 2.

33. Field, *Crisis of the Standing Order*, 145–46, 151–52, 163–67; Phillips, *Jedidiah Morse*, 135–39; Moss, *Life of Jedidiah Morse*, 48–49, 88–89, 93–94.

34. *Account of the Massachusetts Society* (1815), 76.

35. "To the Friends of Religion in New England," 10.

36. Hopkins, *Treatise on the Millennium*, 75–77. See also James H. Moorhead, "The Millennium and the Media," in *Communication and Change in American Religious History*, ed. Leonard I. Sweet (Grand Rapids, Mich.: Eerdmans, 1993).

37. William Cogswell, *The Harbinger of the Millennium* (Boston: Peirce and Parker, 1833), 34, 59, 298–99. On the changing nature of Calvinist-based theology in this era, see Mark A. Noll, *America's God: From Jonathan Edwards to Abraham Lincoln* (New York: Oxford University Press, 2002), chaps. 7 and 14.

CHAPTER 3

1. Matt. 10:8; 2 Thess. 3:1.

2. Connecticut Bible Society, *Report of the Directing Committee of the Connecticut Bible Society* (Hartford: Hudson and Goodwin, 1810), 7; Connecticut Bible Society, *Address, Constitution, and Subscription Proposal of the Connecticut Bible Society* (n.p., 1808), 1, 4; Bible Society of Philadelphia, *The First Report of the Bible Society Established at Philadelphia* (Philadelphia, Pa.: Fry and Kammerer, 1809), 11; Massachusetts Bible Society, *A Circular Address from the Bible Society of Massachusetts* (Boston: Belcher, 1809), 4–5, 14.

3. Connecticut Bible Society, *Address* (1808), 2; Bible Society of Philadelphia, *An Address of the Bible Society Established at Philadelphia to the Public* (Philadelphia, Pa.: Fry and Kammerer, 1809), 3–4; New York Bible Society, *The [First] Annual Report of the New-York Bible Society* (New York: Seymour, 1810), 1; Elias Boudinot, *An Address Delivered before the New-Jersey Bible Society at Their Annual Meeting* (Burlington, N.J.: Allinson, 1811), 5; Bible Society of Philadelphia, *First Report* (1809), 8. On the British and Foreign Bible Society, see Leslie Howsam, *Cheap Bibles: Nineteenth-Century Publishing and the British and Foreign Bible Society* (Cambridge: Cambridge University Press, 1991); and William Canton, *A History of the British and Foreign Bible Society*, vol. 1 (London: Murray, 1904).

4. Leslie Howsam, "The Nineteenth-Century Bible Society and 'the Evil of Gratuitous Distribution,' " in *Free Print and Non-Commercial Publishing since 1700*, ed. James Raven (Aldershot, England: Ashgate, 2000), 121; Bible Society of Philadelphia, *Address* (1809), 9. See also Howsam, *Cheap Bibles*.

5. Bible Society of Philadelphia, *Address* (1809), 6–7; Bible Society of Philadelphia, *First Report* (1809), 7–8.

6. Howsam, "Nineteenth-Century Bible Society," 119–20, 122–23, 128, 131; Howsam, *Cheap Bibles*, 35–37, 42–43, 50–51.

7. Bible Society of Philadelphia, *Address* (1809), 10, 22; See also Massachusetts Bible Society, *Circular Address* (1809), 19.

8. Connecticut Bible Society, *Address* (1808), 4–5; Bible Society of Philadelphia, *Address* (1809), 18.

9. Bible Society of Philadelphia, *First Report* (1809), 4, 8–9. Other state societies

were also surprised by the extent of the destitution. See, for example, Connecticut Bible Society, *Report of the Directing Committee of the Connecticut Bible Society* (Hartford: Hudson and Goodwin, 1812), 6; and New York Bible Society, *[First] Annual Report*, 4. On Mathew Carey and the commercial Bible business in this era, see James N. Green, *Mathew Carey: Publisher and Patriot* (Philadelphia, Pa.: Library Company, 1985), 18–20; and Paul C. Gutjahr, *An American Bible: A History of the Good Book in the United States, 1777–1880* (Stanford, Calif.: Stanford University Press, 1999), 23–29.

10. Howsam, *Cheap Bibles*, 77–79. On the stereotype process in American publishing, see Michael Winship, "Printing with Plates in the Nineteenth Century," *Printing History* 4 (1983): 15–27; Rosalind Remer, *Printers and Men of Capital: Philadelphia Book Publishers in the New Republic* (Philadelphia: University of Pennsylvania Press, 1996), 94–98; and John Bidwell, "Joshua Gilpin and Lord Stanhope's Improvements in Printing," *Papers of the Bibliographical Society of America* 76 (Second Quarter 1982): 143–58. On the broader history of the process, see George A. Kubler, *A New History of Stereotyping* (New York: Little and Ives, 1941). Two early pamphlets on the process have been reprinted; see Charles Brightly, *The Method of Founding Stereotype*, and Thomas Hodgson, *An Essay on the Origin and Progress of Stereotype Printing* (New York: Garland, 1982). Brightly's pamphlet was originally published in 1809; Hodgson's in 1822.

11. Bible Society of Philadelphia, *The Second Report of the Bible Society Established at Philadelphia* (Philadelphia, Pa.: Fry and Kammerer, 1810), 10–11; Bible Society of Philadelphia, *The Third Report of the Bible Society Established at Philadelphia* (Philadelphia, Pa.: Fry and Kammerer, 1811), 7. The plates arrived in October 1812 and were turned over to the Philadelphia printer William Fry, who immediately struck off an edition of 1,250 copies, the first stereotyped Bible printed in America. By 1816, the Philadelphia society had printed more than 55,000 Bibles and New Testaments from several sets of plates. See Bible Society of Philadelphia, *The Fifth Report of the Bible Society Established at Philadelphia* (n.p., 1813), 9; Bible Society of Philadelphia, *The Eighth Report of the Bible Society Established at Philadelphia* (Philadelphia, Pa.: Fry, 1816), 3–4. See also Margaret T. Hills, *The English Bible in America: A Bibliography of Editions of the Bible and the New Testament Published in America, 1777–1957* (New York: American Bible Society and New York Public Library, 1961), 37; and Gutjahr, *American Bible*, 29.

12. In the Philadelphia book trade in this era, the role of the publisher was splitting away from the role of the printer. See James N. Green, "From Printer to Publisher: Mathew Carey and the Origins of Nineteenth-Century Book Publishing," in *Getting the Books Out: Papers of the Chicago Conference on the Book in Nineteenth-Century America*, ed. Michael Hackenberg (Washington, D.C.: Library of Congress, 1987). See also Remer, *Printers and Men of Capital*. In Bible work, this distinction existed as well, but the long-term trend turned out to be in the opposite direction; printer and publisher came together. From the beginning, some Bible societies owned their own plates. Later they owned their own presses, even though their printers worked as independent contractors. In 1845, the American Bible Society took over its own printing; in 1848, its own binding; and in 1851, its own stereotype-plate founding.

13. Bible Society of Philadelphia, *The Sixth Report of the Bible Society of Philadelphia* (Philadelphia, Pa.: n.p., 1814), 7.

14. Bible Society of Philadelphia, *Fifth Report* (1813), 11–12; Bible Society of Philadelphia, *Sixth Report* (1814), 13.

15. Bible Society of Philadelphia, *An Address of the Bible Society of Philadelphia to the Friends of Revealed Truth in the State of Pennsylvania* (Philadelphia, Pa.: Fry and Kammerer, 1810), 6, 8–9.

16. Ibid., 4, 9.

17. Bible Society of Philadelphia, *Third Report* (1811), 4.

18. Bible Society of Philadelphia, *Eighth Report* (1816), 3–4; Bible Society of Philadelphia, *Address* (1810), 5.

19. New York Bible Society, [*First*] *Annual Report*, 4–5; New York Bible Society, *Fourth Report of the New-York Bible Society* (New York: Seymour, 1813), 3; Bible Society of Philadelphia, *Sixth Report* (1814), 13–14.

20. Green, *Mathew Carey*, 18–20; Remer, *Printers and Men of Capital*, 52.

21. Gutjahr, *American Bible*, 29–30; Remer, *Printers and Men of Capital*, 95–99; Rebecca Bromley, "The Spread of the Bible Societies, 1810–1816," Historical Essay No. 8 (New York: American Bible Society, 1963), 54–55. In 1809, Carey published ads in New York newspapers for Bibles with prices ranging from $3.50 to $25. See Margaret T. Hills, "Bible Publication in America to 1816," Historical Essay No. 5 (New York: American Bible Society, 1963), 8.

22. Connecticut Bible Society, *Report of the Directing Committee of the Connecticut Bible Society* (Hartford: Hudson, 1816), 5–6, 8.

23. On genres and reading styles, see chapter 6 of this book.

24. "The Constitution" and "To the Friends of Religion in New England," in *Proceedings of the First Ten Years of the American Tract Society, Instituted at Boston, 1814* (Andover, Mass.: Flagg and Gould, 1824). This volume includes the first ten annual reports of the New England Tract Society. It was reprinted in facsimile in *The American Tract Society Documents, 1824–1925* (New York: Arno, 1972). The New England Tract Society changed its name in 1823 to the American Tract Society, and it retained that name even after the founding of the larger American Tract Society of New York in 1825.

25. "To the Friends of Religion," 9; "First Report, 1815," in *Proceedings of the First Ten Years*, 27, 29. On the formation of auxiliary societies, see "Second Report, 1816," in ibid., 38–39.

26. "Third Report, 1817," in ibid., 42–43; "Seventh Report, 1821," in ibid., 78.

27. "Fifth Report, 1819," in ibid., 55.

28. "Seventh Report, 1821," in ibid., 80–85.

29. "Constitution," in ibid., 6; "Second Report, 1816," in ibid., 38–39; "Fifth Report, 1819," in ibid., 62; "Sixth Report, 1820," in ibid., 64; "Seventh Report, 1821," in ibid., 74–75.

30. "Seventh Report, 1821," in ibid., 76; "Eighth Report, 1822," in ibid., 92; "Tenth Report, 1824," in ibid., 129–31; *The Christian Almanack, for the Year of Our Lord and Saviour Jesus Christ, 1822* (Boston: New England Tract Society [1821]). On the Pa-

nic of 1819, see Charles Sellers, *The Market Revolution: Jacksonian America, 1815–1846* (New York: Oxford University Press, 1991), chaps. 4–5.

31. "Ninth Report, 1823," in *Proceedings of the First Ten Years*, 112–13; *History of Tracts* (Andover, Mass.: Flagg and Gould, 1820), 28.

32. "Seventh Report, 1821," in *Proceedings of the First Ten Years*, 85.

33. "Tenth Report, 1824," in ibid., 128.

34. "Summary of the Operations of the American Tract Society, during the First Ten Years," in ibid., 178; *History of Tracts*, 28.

35. "Table of Religious Tract Societies," in *Proceedings of the First Ten Years*, 208.

36. New-York Religious Tract Society, *The First Annual Report of the New-York Religious Tract Society* (New York: Seymour, 1813), 3; New-York Religious Tract Society, *The Sixth Annual Report of the New-York Religious Tract Society* (New York: Seymour, 1818), 33; New-York Religious Tract Society, *The Twelfth Annual Report of the New-York Religious Tract Society* (New York: Fanshaw, 1824), 16.

37. These terms appear in Rodney Stark and Roger Finke, *Acts of Faith: Explaining the Human Side of Religion* (Berkeley: University of California Press, 2000); Laurence R. Iannaccone, "Rational Choice: Framework for the Scientific Study of Religion," in *Rational Choice Theory and Religion: Summary and Assessment*, ed. Lawrence A. Young (New York: Routledge, 1997); and Laurence R. Iannaccone, "Voodoo Economics? Reviewing the Rational Choice Approach to Religion," *Journal for the Scientific Study of Religion* 34 (1995): 76–88. See also Rodney Stark and William Sims Bainbridge, *A Theory of Religion* (New York: Lang, 1987).

38. Roger Finke and Rodney Stark, *The Churching of America, 1776–1990: Winners and Losers in Our Religious Economy* (New Brunswick, N.J.: Rutgers University Press, 1992); R. Stephen Warner, "Work in Progress toward a New Paradigm for the Sociological Study of Religion in the United States," *American Journal of Sociology* 98 (March 1993): 1044–93.

39. Iannaccone, "Rational Choice," 26. The new paradigm is explained in Stark and Finke, *Acts of Faith*, part 1; R. Stephen Warner, "Convergence toward the New Paradigm: A Case of Induction," in Young, *Rational Choice Theory and Religion;* and Roger Finke, "The Consequence of Religious Competition: Supply-Side Explanations for Religious Change," in ibid. For a friendly critique of the new paradigm, see Mary Jo Neitz and Peter R. Mueser, "Economic Man and the Sociology of Religion: A Critique of the Rational Choice Approach," in ibid. For a generally hostile critique, see Steve Bruce, *Choice and Religion: A Critique of Rational Choice Theory* (Oxford: Oxford University Press, 1999).

40. Laurence R. Iannaccone, "Why Strict Churches Are Strong," *American Journal of Sociology* 99 (March 1994): 1184; Stark and Finke, *Acts of Faith*, 148.

41. Finke and Stark, *Churching of America*, 252–55. See also Iannaccone, "Why Strict Churches Are Strong," 1182–83; and Carl L. Bankston III, "Rationality, Choice, and the Religious Economy: The Problem of Belief," *Review of Religious Research* 43 (2002): 311–25.

42. Connecticut Bible Society, *Report* (1816), 6.

CHAPTER 4

1. Samuel J. Mills, "Plan of a General Bible Society," *Panoplist* (October 1813): 357.

2. Samuel J. Mills and Daniel Smith, *Report of a Missionary Tour through that Part of the United States which Lies West of the Allegany Mountains* (Andover, Mass.: Flagg and Gould, 1815), 21, 28. See also Robert V. Remini, *The Battle of New Orleans* (New York: Viking, 1999), chap. 9.

3. Charles Sellers, *The Market Revolution: Jacksonian American, 1815–1846* (New York: Oxford University Press, 1991); Daniel Feller, *The Jacksonian Promise: America, 1815–1840* (Baltimore, Md.: Johns Hopkins University Press, 1995); and Sean Wilentz, "Society, Politics, and the Market Revolution, 1815–1848," in *The New American History*, rev. ed., ed. Janet Flammang and Eric Foner (Philadelphia, Pa.: Temple University Press, 1997). See also Melvyn Stokes and Stephen Conway, eds., *The Market Revolution in America: Social, Political, and Religious Expressions, 1800–1880* (Charlottesville: University Press of Virginia, 1996).

4. Samuel J. Mills, *Communications relative to the Progress of Bible Societies in the United States* (Philadelphia, Pa.: n.p., 1813), 9–10; Thomas C. Richards, *Samuel J. Mills: Missionary, Pathfinder, Pioneer and Promoter* (Boston: Pilgrim Press, 1906), 130, 273; Gardiner Spring, *Memoirs of the Rev. Samuel J. Mills, Late Missionary to the South Western Section of the United States* (New York: Seymour, 1820), 94, 97; Eric M. North, "The Pressure toward a National Bible Society, 1808–1816," Historical Essay No. 9 (New York: American Bible Society, 1963), 9, 25. On the Age of Reform, see Steven Mintz, *Moralists and Modernizers: America's Pre–Civil War Reformers* (Baltimore, Md.: Johns Hopkins University Press, 1995).

5. Elias Boudinot, *The Age of Revelation* (Philadelphia, Pa.: Dickins, 1801), xx; George Adams Boyd, *Elias Boudinot: Patriot and Statesman, 1740–1821* (Princeton, N.J.: Princeton University Press, 1952), 257–60. See also Peter Dobkin Hall, *The Organization of American Culture, 1700–1900: Private Institutions, Elites, and the Origins of American Nationality* (New York: New York University Press, 1982), chap. 5.

6. The circular letter published by the Bible Society of Philadelphia has been lost, but the Philadelphians' arguments are reproduced in Elias Boudinot, *An Answer to the Objections of the Managers of the Philadelphia Bible-Society, against a Meeting of Delegates from the Bible Societies in the Union* (Burlington, N.J.: Allinson, [1815]). See also North, "Pressure toward a National Bible Society," 41–76.

7. Boudinot, *Answer to the Objections*, 10; Boyd, *Elias Boudinot*, 260.

8. Mills and Smith, *Report of a Missionary Tour*, 44–46; Connecticut Bible Society, *Report of the Directing Committee of the Connecticut Bible Society* (Hartford: Hudson, 1815), 16–19; Elias Boudinot, *To the Several Bible Societies in the United States of America* (Burlington, N.J.: n.p., 1816).

9. [William Jay], *A Memoir on the Subject of a General Bible Society for the United States of America, by a Citizen of the State of New-York* (Burlington, N.J.: n.p., 1816), 11–13. Jedidiah Morse also preferred a powerful, independent organization to a confederacy of existing Bible societies. See *Panoplist* (February 1816): 91–92.

10. *New York Evening Post*, Feb. 13, 14, and 28, 1815. See also Sellers, *Market Revolution*, 19–20.

11. Sellers, *Market Revolution*, 20; Robert G. Albion, *The Rise of New York Port* (New York: Scribner's, 1939), 10, 13–14; Charles King, *Progress of the City of New York during the Last Fifty Years* (New York: Appleton, 1852), 74–75. See also Allan R. Pred, *Urban Growth and the Circulation of Information: The United States System of Cities, 1790–1840* (Cambridge, Mass.: Harvard University Press, 1973).

12. *Constitution of the American Bible Society, Formed by a Convention of Delegates, Held in the City of New-York, May, 1816, Together with Their Address to the People of the United States* (New York: Hopkins, 1816), 16. The best study of the business practices of the American Bible Society is Peter J. Wosh, *Spreading the Word: The Bible Business in Nineteenth-Century America* (Ithaca, N.Y.: Cornell University Press, 1994). General histories of the ABS include Henry Otis Dwight, *The Centennial History of the American Bible Society* (New York: Macmillan, 1916); and Creighton Lacy, *The Word-Carrying Giant: The Growth of the American Bible Society* (South Pasadena, Calif.: Carey Library, 1977).

13. American Bible Society, *Seventh Annual Report* (1823), 8; Lewis Tappan, *The Life of Arthur Tappan* (New York: Hurd and Houghton, 1871), 74–75; Bertram Wyatt-Brown, *Lewis Tappan and the Evangelical War against Slavery* (Cleveland, Ohio: Press of Case Western Reserve University, 1969), chaps. 3–4. See also John M. Gibson, *Soldiers of the Word: The Story of the American Bible Society* (Philadelphia, Pa.: Philosophical Library, 1958), 57–58.

14. American Bible Society, *Eleventh Annual Report* (1827), 8. The commercial publishers' drive for the high end of the Bible market culminated in Harper and Brothers' publication in the 1840s of a spectacular *Illuminated Bible*, a thirteen-pound folio volume printed on the finest paper with 1,600 engravings. See Paul C. Gutjahr, *An American Bible: A History of the Good Book in the United States, 1777–1880* (Stanford, Calif.: Stanford University Press, 1999), 36–37, 70–71.

15. American Bible Society, *First Annual Report* (1817), 10. See also American Bible Society, Minutes of the Board of Managers, July 3 and 15, Aug. 7 and 17, 1816, in American Bible Society Archives, New York. See also Eric M. North, "The Production and Supply of Scriptures, 1816–1820," Historical Essay No. 18, part 1 (New York: American Bible Society, 1963), 1–2.

16. American Bible Society, *First Annual Report* (1817), 11; American Bible Society, *Third Annual Report* (1819), 10–11; *Brief View of the American Bible Society* (New York: Paul, 1823), 2–3. See also Margaret T. Hills, *The English Bible in America: A Bibliography of Editions of the Bible and the New Testament Published in America, 1777–1957* (New York: American Bible Society and New York Public Library, 1961), 50–51; and Margaret T. Hills, "The Production and Supply of Scriptures, 1821–1830," Historical Essay No. 18, part 2 (New York: American Bible Society, 1964).

17. Stereotypography advanced more slowly in commercial book printing. Philadelphia publishers moved into stereotyping in the 1820s. New York's largest book publisher, Harper and Brothers, did not adopt stereotyping until 1830. See Rosalind Remer, *Printers and Men of Capital: Philadelphia Book Publishers in the New Republic*

(Philadelphia: University of Pennsylvania Press, 1996), 95–98; Eugene Exman, *The Brothers Harper: A Unique Publishing Partnership and Its Impact upon the Cultural Life of America from 1817 to 1853* (New York: Harper and Row, 1965), 20; Gutjahr, *American Bible*, 30.

18. American Bible Society, Minutes of the Board of Managers, Aug. 7 and Dec. 4, 1816ērican Bible Society, *First Annual Report* (1817), 10, 21; American Bible Society, *Second Annual Report* (1818), 11–12; American Bible Society, *Third Annual Report* (1819), 10. See also Hills, *English Bible in America*, 60.

19. American Bible Society, Minutes of the Board of Managers, July 15 and Nov. 18, 1819, and Feb. 1, 1821; American Bible Society, *Fourth Annual Report* (1820), 8. On the Panic of 1819, see Sellers, *Market Revolution*, chaps. 4–5.

20. American Bible Society, *Twelfth Annual Report* (1828), 28–29; *An Abstract of the American Bible Society, Containing an Account of Its Principles and Operations* (New York: Fanshaw, 1830), 12. Discussions of printing costs and techniques are common in the minutes of the late 1810s and 1820s of the ABS Standing Committee, which was composed of five members of the Board of Managers appointed in the society's first year to conduct daily business between monthly board meetings.

21. James Moran, *Printing Presses: History and Development from the Fifteenth Century to Modern Times* (Berkeley and Los Angeles: University of California Press, 1973), 113–16; Robert Hoe, *A Short History of the Printing Press* (New York: Hoe, 1902), 10–11. Jonas Booth is sometimes credited with introducing the power press in America, also about 1822, but he produced very few machines.

22. Daniel Treadwell, letter to American Bible Society, Sept. 20, 1823, in American Bible Society Archives; American Bible Society, Minutes of the Standing Committee, Jan. 27, 1827, in American Bible Society Archives; *Address of the Board of Managers of the American Bible Society to the Friends of the Bible of Every Religious Denomination, on the Subject of the Resolution for Supplying All the Destitute Families in the United States with the Bible in the Course of Two Years* (New York: Seymour, 1829), 13; *Abstract of the American Bible Society*, 12. See also Hills, "Production and Supply of Scriptures," 11–15.

23. J. Leander Bishop, *A History of American Manufactures from 1608 to 1860*, 2 vols. (Philadelphia, Pa.: Young, 1864), 2:380; Exman, *Brothers Harper*, 17.

24. "Daniel Fanshaw," in *American Dictionary of Printing and Bookmaking* (1894; reprint, New York: Lenox Hill, 1970), 184; Moran, *Printing Presses*, 114. Fanshaw's relationship with the ABS is discussed in North, "Production and Supply of Scriptures," and Hills, "Production and Supply of Scriptures." In the 1830s, Fanshaw fell behind in the race for mechanical improvements in printing and was dismissed by the American Bible Society in 1844. As ABS historian Peter Wosh puts it, "He became a victim of the technological revolution he helped foster." See Wosh, *Spreading the Word*, 24.

25. Robert quoted in Dard Hunter, *Papermaking: The History and Technique of an Ancient Craft*, 2d ed. (New York: Knopf, 1947), 344, 346. See also Robert H. Clapperton, *The Papermaking Machine: Its Invention, Evolution, and Development* (New York: Pergamon, 1968).

26. On prices, see Donald C. Coleman, *The British Paper Industry, 1495–1860*

(Oxford: Clarendon, 1958), 202–4; and Lyman H. Weeks, *A History of Paper Manufacturing in the United States, 1690–1916* (New York: Lockwood Trade Journal, 1916), 195, 223–24.

27. Hunter, *Papermaking*, 351–56; David C. Smith, *History of Papermaking in the United States, 1691–1969* (New York: Lockwood, 1970), 32; Harold B. Hancock and Norman B. Wilkinson, "The Gilpins and Their Endless Papermaking Machine," *Pennsylvania Magazine of History and Biography* 81 (October 1957): 391–405. See also Judith A. McGaw, *Most Wonderful Machine: Mechanization and Social Change in Berkshire Paper Making, 1801–1885* (Princeton, N.J.: Princeton University Press, 1987).

28. "Memorial to Congress," draft, American Bible Society, Minutes of the Board of Managers, Jan. 1, 1817, and May 7, 1818, American Bible Society Archives; American Bible Society, *Second Annual Report* (1818), 21.

29. American Bible Society, *Fourteenth Annual Report* (1830), 23; and American Bible Society, *Fifteenth Annual Report* (1831), 24; Hills, "Production and Supply of Scriptures," 47–48.

30. Letters from Amos Hubbard to American Bible Society, Aug. 8 and 11, Sept. 4 and 11, 1830, American Bible Society Archives.

31. James Milnor, speech text, in *Monthly Extracts of the American Bible Society* 17 (May 1829): 239.

32. American Bible Society, *Fourth Annual Report* (1820), 8.

33. Milnor, speech text, 239.

34. American Bible Society, *Third Annual Report* (1819), 15; Eric M. North, "The Great Challenge: Distribution in the United States, 1816–1820," Historical Essay No. 14, part 1 (New York: American Bible Society, 1963), 2; Mary F. Cordato, "The Relationship of the American Bible Society to Its Auxiliaries: A Historical Timeline Study," Historical Working Paper Series No. 1991–1 (New York: American Bible Society, 1991), 1–5. See also Wosh, *Spreading the Word*, chap. 3.

35. The idea of differential pricing is explored in more detail in chapter 3 of this book.

36. "Circular Letter of the Committee on Auxiliary Societies," in American Bible Society, *Third Annual Report* (1819), 74; American Bible Society, *Fifth Annual Report* (1821), 30; American Bible Society, *Sixth Annual Report* (1822), 32–33. Though the managers sometimes cited the sales policy of the British and Foreign Bible Society as a precedent for their own, it was in fact different. Within Great Britain, the BFBS policy was to sell only, never to give. And the poor who received Bibles were, in a sense, members of centrally administered Bible associations who received their books through small weekly subscriptions. See Leslie Howsam, *Cheap Bibles: Nineteenth-Century Publishing and the British and Foreign Bible Society* (Cambridge: Cambridge University Press, 1991), 43, 50–51.

37. Leslie Howsam, "The Nineteenth-Century Bible Society and 'the Evil of Gratuitous Distribution,'" in *Free Print and Non-Commercial Publishing since 1700*, ed. James Raven (Aldershot, England: Ashgate, 2000), 126–27.

38. *An Expose of the Rise and Proceedings of the American Bible Society, during the Thirteen Years of Its Existence, by a Member* (New York: n.p., 1830), 13–14, 17–18. See also Wosh, *Spreading the Word*, 124–26.

39. American Bible Society, *Seventh Annual Report* (1823), 24; American Bible Society, *Eighth Annual Report* (1824), 28–29.

40. American Bible Society, *Eleventh Annual Report* (1827), 37.

41. American Bible Society, *Ninth Annual Report* (1825), 63.

42. American Bible Society, *Fifth Annual Report* (1821), 28; American Bible Society, *Seventh Annual Report* (1823), 11; American Bible Society, *Eighth Annual Report* (1824), 27; American Bible Society, *Thirteenth Annual Report* (1829), 43–44. The problem of the organizational free rider in the realm of religion is discussed in Laurence R. Iannaccone, "Why Strict Churches Are Strong," *American Journal of Sociology* 99 (March 1994): 1180–1211; and Rodney Stark and Roger Finke, *Acts of Faith: Explaining the Human Side of Religion* (Berkeley and Los Angeles: University of California Press, 2000), 147–52. See also chapter 3 of this book.

43. American Bible Society, Minutes of the Board of Managers, June 18 and July 3, 1829, American Bible Society Archives. See also Wosh, *Spreading the Word*, 68–70.

44. *Address of the Board of Managers of the American Bible Society . . . on the Subject of the Resolution for Supplying All the Destitute Families in the United States with the Bible*, 2–3.

45. *Address of the Executive Committee of the American Tract Society to the Christian Public: Together with a Brief Account of the Formation of the Society, Its Constitution and Officers* (New York: Fanshaw, 1825), 4; *Address of the Managers of the American Sunday School Union, to the Citizens of Philadelphia* (Philadelphia, Pa.: Ashmead, 1826), 4–5.

46. Some denominations, notably the Methodists, also expanded their publishing operations in the 1820s. Founded in 1789, the Methodist Book Concern opened a branch in Cincinnati in 1820, while Nathan Bangs guided the New York office into a new era of printing and stereotyping after 1824. See Nathan Bangs, *A History of the Methodist Episcopal Church*, vol. 4 (New York: Carlton and Porter, 1857), chap. 16; Abel Stevens, *Life and Times of Nathan Bangs, D.D.* (New York: Carlton and Porter, 1863); and James Penn Pilkington, *The Methodist Publishing House: A History*, vol. 1 (Nashville, Tenn.: Abingdon, 1968), chap. 4. Also, many reform organizations such as the American Temperance Society (1826) and the American Anti-Slavery Society (1833) were organized on the model of the evangelical religious publishing house. See David Paul Nord, "Benevolent Books: Printing, Religion, and Reform," in *An Extensive Republic: Print, Culture, and Society in the New Nation*, ed. Robert A. Gross and Mary Kelley, vol. 2 of *A History of the Book in America* (Cambridge: Cambridge University Press, forthcoming).

47. *Address of the Executive Committee of the American Tract Society*, 4, 13; American Tract Society, *First Annual Report* (1826), 18; American Tract Society, *Twenty-Fifth Annual Report* (1850), 22–23.

48. *Address of the Executive Committee of the American Tract Society*, 12–13.

49. Ibid., 12.

50. American Tract Society, *First Annual Report* (1826), 11–12, 18; American Tract Society, *Second Annual Report* (1827), 10.

51. *American Tract Magazine* 1 (April 1826): 275; "Daniel Fanshaw," in *American Dictionary of Printing and Bookmaking*, 184; Moran, *Printing Presses*, 114. See also

Lawrence Thompson, "The Printing and Publishing Activities of the American Tract Society from 1825 to 1850," *Papers of the Bibliographical Society of America* 35 (Second Quarter 1941): 81–114.

52. *Address of the Executive Committee of the American Tract Society*, 14; American Tract Society, *First Annual Report* (1826), 22; American Tract Society, *Second Annual Report* (1827), 23.

53. "Prospectus," in *American Messenger*, January 1843; *American Messenger*, October 1851; *American Messenger*, June 1851; [R. S. Cook], *Home Evangelization: View of the Wants and Prospects of Our Country, Based on the Facts and Relations of Colportage* (New York: American Tract Society, [1849]), 140. The ATS newspaper *American Messenger* was founded in 1843.

54. *Christian Advocate*, Sept. 9, 1826; Bangs, *History of the Methodist Episcopal Church*, 4:452; Methodist Episcopal Church, *Journal of the General Conference* (1844), 167. The Methodist newspaper *Christian Advocate* was founded in 1826.

55. *Home and Foreign Record*, September 1851; Presbyterian Board of Publication, *Twelfth Annual Report* (1850), 39–40; Presbyterian Board of Publication, *Seventeenth Annual Report* (1855), 4–5. The Presbyterian newspaper *Home and Foreign Record* was founded in 1850.

56. American Baptist Publication Society, *Thirty-First Annual Report* (1855), 7, 58–59; American Baptist Publication Society, *Thirty-Second Annual Report* (1856), 49.

57. American Baptist Publication Society, *Thirty-Second Annual Report* (1856), 41; *American Messenger*, February 1844. On the rise of popular print culture in nineteenth-century America, see Cathy N. Davidson, *Revolution and the Word: The Rise of the Novel in America* (New York: Oxford University Press, 1986); and Isabelle Lehuu, *Carnival on the Page: Popular Print Media in Antebellum America* (Chapel Hill: University of North Carolina Press, 2000). On popular print culture in Britain in this era, see James A. Secord, *Victorian Sensation: The Extraordinary Publication, Reception, and Secret Authorship of Vestiges of the Natural History of Creation* (Chicago, Ill.: University of Chicago Press, 2000).

58. American Tract Society, *Eighteenth Annual Report* (1843), 25; [Cook], *Home Evangelization*, 139–40.

59. [Cook], *Home Evangelization*, 107; *American Messenger*, February 1844.

60. American Tract Society, *Fourth Annual Report* (1829), 17; American Tract Society, *Fifth Annual Report* (1830), 28–29; American Tract Society, *Seventh Annual Report* (1832), 20; "Address of the Rev. Justin Edwards," in American Tract Society, *First Annual Report* (1826), 32; "Address on the Formation of an Auxiliary Society," bound with American Tract Society, *Second Annual Report* (1827).

61. American Tract Society, *Eleventh Annual Report* (1836), 41–44. See also *Proposed Circulation of the Standard Evangelical Volumes of the American Tract Society to the Southern Atlantic States* (New York: American Tract Society, 1834).

62. *Address of the Managers of the American Sunday School Union*, 5, 10; American Sunday School Union, *Eighth Annual Report* (1832), 36. For an overview of the ASSU, see Anne M. Boylan, *Sunday School: The Formation of an American Institution, 1790–1880* (New Haven, Conn.: Yale University Press, 1988).

63. American Sunday School Union, *Ninth Annual Report* (1833), 3.

64. *Address of the Managers of the American Sunday School Union*, 8–9; American Sunday School Union, *Third Annual Report* (1827), iii; American Sunday School Union, *Fourth Annual Report* (1828), iv–v; American Sunday School Union, *Seventh Annual Report* (1831), 18.

65. *Address of the Managers of the American Sunday School Union*, 9; American Sunday School Union, *Second Annual Report* (1826), 4; American Sunday School Union, *Sixth Annual Report* (1830), 16–17; American Sunday School Union, *Eleventh Annual Report* (1835), 17.

66. American Sunday School Union, *Second Annual Report* (1826), 4; American Sunday School Union, *Fifth Annual Report* (1829), 4; American Sunday School Union, *Sixth Annual Report* (1830), 15–16; Willard Hall, *A Defence of the American Sunday School Union, against the Charges of Its Opponents* (Philadelphia, Pa.: Clarke, 1828), 6–7.

67. American Sunday School Union, *Sixth Annual Report* (1830), 15–19; American Sunday School Union, *Eighth Annual Report* (1832), 36.

68. *Address of the Board of Managers of the American Bible Society . . . on the Subject of the Resolution for Supplying All the Destitute Families in the United States with the Bible*, 12–13.

69. Ibid., 3. For narrative overviews of the ABS general supply, see Lacy, *Word-Carrying Giant*, chap. 4; and Dwight, *Centennial History*, chap. 12.

70. American Bible Society, *Twelfth Annual Report* (1828), 28; American Bible Society, *Thirteenth Annual Report* (1829), 41–42; Dwight, *Centennial History*, 88; and Tappan, *Life of Arthur Tappan*, 75.

71. *Address of the Board of Managers of the American Bible Society . . . on the Subject of the Resolution for Supplying All the Destitute Families in the United States with the Bible*, 7.

72. American Bible Society, *Fifteenth Annual Report* (1831), 3–4, 17–18, 47–48; American Bible Society, *Seventeenth Annual Report* (1833), 14. For more detailed data on ABS Bible production in this era, see David Paul Nord, "The Evangelical Origins of Mass Media in America, 1815–1835," *Journalism Monographs* No. 88 (May 1984).

73. *Monthly Extracts of the American Bible Society* 26 (March 1830): 325; American Bible Society, *Fifteenth Annual Report* (1831), 6–7, 17–18; American Bible Society, *Seventeenth Annual Report* (1833), 16–17; American Bible Society, Minutes of the Board of Managers, June 18 and July 3, 1829, American Bible Society Archives; American Bible Society, *Twenty-Fourth Annual Report* (1840), 25–26. See also Eric M. North, "Distribution of Scriptures in the United States, 1831–1840," Historical Essay No. 14, part 3 (New York: American Bible Society, 1964), 21.

74. American Bible Society, *Seventeenth Annual Report* (1833), 16–17.

75. American Tract Society, *Fourth Annual Report* (1829), 28–29. See also Charles I. Foster, "The Urban Missionary Movement, 1814–1837," *Pennsylvania Magazine of History and Biography* 75 (January 1951): 58–59; and Paul S. Boyer, *Urban Masses and Moral Order in America, 1820–1920* (Cambridge, Mass.: Harvard University Press, 1978), chap. 2.

76. American Tract Society, *Fourth Annual Report* (1829), 74–76; American Tract Society, *Eighth Annual Report* (1833), 31–32; American Tract Society, *Ninth Annual Report* (1834), 126–28. See also Wyatt-Brown, *Lewis Tappan*, 53.

77. American Tract Society, *Sixth Annual Report* (1831), 16; American Tract Society, *Eighth Annual Report* (1833), 23.

78. American Tract Society, *Sixth Annual Report* (1831), 24–27; American Tract Society, *Ninth Annual Report* (1834), 126–28. See also *Proposed Circulation of the Standard Evangelical Volumes.*

79. American Tract Society, *Sixth Annual Report* (1831), 28; American Tract Society, *Eighth Annual Report* (1833), 24–28.

80. American Sunday School Union, *Sixth Annual Report* (1830), 3, 15; American Sunday School Union, *Seventh Annual Report* (1831), 5.

81. American Sunday School Union, *Ninth Annual Report* (1833), 32–39.

82. American Tract Society, *Sixth Annual Report* (1831), 28; American Tract Society, *Eighth Annual Report* (1833), 24–28; American Sunday School Union, *Ninth Annual Report* (1833), 10. See also Boylan, *Sunday School*, 68–77.

83. William Cogswell, *The Harbinger of the Millennium* (Boston: Peirce and Parker, 1833), 34; *Resolutions of the American Bible Society, and an Address to the Christian Public, on the Subject of Supplying the Whole World with the Sacred Scriptures; within a Definite Period* (New York: Fanshaw, 1833).

84. *Resolutions of the Amercan Bible Society*, 3.

85. *Expose of the Rise and Proceedings of the American Bible Society*, 13, 17.

86. [Herman Hooker], *An Appeal to the Christian Public, on the Evil and Impolicy of the Church Engaging in Merchandise; Setting Forth the Wrong Done to Booksellers, and the Extravagance, Inutility, and Evil-Working, of Charity Publication Societies* (Philadelphia, Pa.: King and Baird, 1849), 5–6.

87. American Tract Society, *Fifth Annual Report* (1830), 28–29.

CHAPTER 5

1. Bertram Wyatt-Brown, *Lewis Tappan and the Evangelical War against Slavery* (Cleveland, Ohio: Press of Case Western Reserve University, 1969), 70, 115, 174; Charles Sellers, *The Market Revolution: Jacksonian America, 1815–1846* (New York: Oxford University Press, 1991), 54–55.

2. Alfred D. Chandler, Jr., *The Visible Hand: The Managerial Revolution in American Business* (Cambridge, Mass.: Belknap Press of Harvard University Press, 1977), 8–12; JoAnne Yates, *Control through Communication: The Rise of System in American Management* (Baltimore, Md.: Johns Hopkins University Press, 1989), 9–13.

3. American Bible Society, Minutes of the Board of Managers, Nov. 19, 1829, in American Bible Society Archives, New York.

4. *Brief Analysis of the System of the American Bible Society, Containing a Full Account of Its Principles and Operations* (New York: Fanshaw, 1830), 34–36.

5. Ibid., 81–83.

6. American Bible Society, Minutes of the Board of Managers, May 21, June 5, and July 15, 1816; *Quarterly Extracts*, August 1818; *Monthly Extracts*, July 31, 1821, all in

American Bible Society Archives. See also Eric M. North, "Public Relations, Financial Promotion and Support," Historical Essay No. 17, part 1: "1816–1820" (New York: American Bible Society, 1963); Dorothy U. Compagno, "Public Relations, Financial Promotion and Support," Historical Essay No. 17, part 2: "1821–1830" (New York: American Bible Society, 1964); and Dorothy U. Compagno, "Public Relations, Financial Promotion and Support," Historical Essay No. 17, part 3: "1831–1860" (New York: American Bible Society, 1964).

7. *Brief Analysis* (1830), 34–35; American Bible Society, *Seventh Annual Report* (1823), 11.

8. American Bible Society, Minutes of the Board of Managers, Nov. 8, 1821, American Bible Society Archives; American Bible Society, *Seventh Annual Report* (1823), 20–21, 73–74; American Bible Society, *Twelfth Annual Report* (1828), 30–31; "Journal of R. D. Hall, 1822," in American Bible Society Archives, New York, transcribed in Eric M. North, "Distribution in the United States," Historical Essay No. 14, part 2: "1821–1830" (New York: American Bible Society, 1964), special section A.

9. *Brief Analysis* (1830), 28.

10. Ibid., 34, 84–86; *Instructions of the Auxiliary Society Committee of the American Bible Society to Their Agent Mr. _____* (New York: n.p., 1830). This is a printed broadside to be filled in with the name of the agent.

11. Peter J. Wosh, *Spreading the Word: The Bible Business in Nineteenth-Century America* (Ithaca, N.Y.: Cornell University Press, 1994), 65–71.

12. American Tract Society, *Seventh Annual Report* (1832), 20.

13. American Tract Society, *First Annual Report* (1826), 12–13; American Tract Society, *Fifth Annual Report* (1830), 9. Collecting and publishing information was a major concern of individual denominations as well, perhaps especially the Methodists. See John H. Wigger, *Taking Heaven by Storm: Methodism and the Rise of Popular Christianity in America* (New York: Oxford University Press, 1998), 191–92.

14. American Tract Society, *Fourth Annual Report* (1829), 28–29, 74–76; American Tract Society, *Fifth Annual Report* (1830), 31; American Tract Society, *Sixth Annual Report* (1831), 24–27; American Tract Society, *Eighth Annual Report* (1833), 128. The New York society's "Card of Instructions to Tract Missionaries" is reprinted in American Tract Society, *Eighth Annual Report* (1833), 32–33. See also chapter 4 in this book.

15. American Tract Society, *Fourth Annual Report* (1829), 22; American Tract Society, *Fifth Annual Report* (1830), 21, 34–41.

16. American Tract Society, *Eighth Annual Report* (1833), 32–38.

17. *Proposed Circulation of the Standard Evangelical Volumes of the American Tract Society to the Southern Atlantic States* (New York: American Tract Society, 1834). For a general account of evangelical work in the South, see John W. Kuykendall, *Southern Enterprize: The Work of National Evangelical Societies in the Antebellum South* (Westport, Conn.: Greenwood, 1982).

18. American Tract Society, "Constitution of the American Tract Society," in *Address of the Executive Committee of the American Tract Society to the Christian Public* (New York: Fanshaw, 1825), 24, reprinted in facsimile in *American Tract Society Documents, 1824–1925* (New York: Arno, 1972); American Tract Society, *Second Annual Report* (1827), 15; American Tract Society, *Twenty-Fifth Annual Report* (1850), 30.

19. American Bible Society, *Twelfth Annual Report* (1828), 27.

20. American Tract Society, *Second Annual Report* (1827), 19–23; American Tract Society, *First Annual Report* (1826), 20; American Tract Society, *Third Annual Report* (1828), 14. The problems of the American Sunday School Union with its auxiliaries, agents, and internal market forces were so similar that it would be redundant to describe them here. See Anne M. Boylan, *Sunday School: The Formation of an American Institution, 1790–1880* (New Haven, Conn.: Yale University Press, 1988), 74.

21. American Tract Society, *Sixth Annual Report* (1831), 24–28.

22. American Tract Society, *Eighth Annual Report* (1833), 33–37; American Tract Society, *Sixth Annual Report* (1831), 20–23; American Tract Society, *Thirteenth Annual Report* (1838), 18.

23. American Tract Society, *Fifth Annual Report* (1830), 28–29; American Tract Society, *Twenty-Fifth Annual Report* (1850), 65.

24. In its report to a special auditing committee appointed in 1857, the American Tract Society Executive Committee admitted that by 1841 the system of auxiliaries, agents, and monthly distributions had failed and that "millions of the most destitute, neglected, and needy of our population were not thus reached." See *Report of the Special Committee Appointed at the Annual Meeting of the American Tract Society, May 7, 1857, to Inquire into and Review the Proceedings of the Society's Executive Committee* (New York: American Tract Society, 1857), 15. See also the American Tract Society's *Home Appeal*, June 23, 1841, excerpted in American Tract Society, *Twenty-Sixth Annual Report* (1851), 47.

25. Rosalind Remer, *Printers and Men of Capital: Philadelphia Book Publishers in the New Republic* (Philadelphia: University of Pennsylvania Press, 1996), chap. 6; James N. Green, *Mathew Carey: Publisher and Patriot* (Philadelphia, Pa.: Library Company, 1985); James N. Green, "From Printer to Publisher: Mathew Carey and the Origins of Nineteenth-Century Book Publishing," in *Getting the Books Out: Papers of the Chicago Conference on the Book in Nineteenth-Century America*, ed. Michael Hackenberg (Washington, D.C.: Library of Congress, 1987).

26. James Penn Pilkington, *The Methodist Publishing House: A History*, vol. 1: *Beginnings to 1870* (Nashville, Tenn.: Abingdon, 1968), 109, 138, 142–43, 213; J. Newton Brown, *History of the American Baptist Publication Society, from Its Origin in 1824, to Its Thirty-Second Anniversary in 1856* (Philadelphia, Pa.: American Baptist Publication Society, [1856]), 156–57, 170–71; American Baptist Publication Society, *Sixth Annual Report* (1845), 38–39; American Baptist Publication Society, *Seventh Annual Report* (1846), 17–18; *Instructions for Colporteurs of the Presbyterian Board of Publication* (Philadelphia, Pa.: Presbyterian Board of Publication, n.d.); *Presbyterian Board of Publication: Its Present Operations and Plans* (Philadelphia, Pa.: Presbyterian Board of Publication, [1848]); Abel Stevens, comp., *Documents of the Tract Society of the Methodist Episcopal Church* (New York: Carlton and Phillips, 1853), 22; Methodist Episcopal Church, *Journal of the General Conference* (1852), 120, 123; Methodist Episcopal Church, *Journal of the General Conference* (1856), 229.

27. One of the few denominational societies to employ the strong form of colportage was the Presbyterian Board of Publication, though its colportage project was a

modest affair. Correspondence and some business records of the Presbyterian Board of Publication are located in the Presbyterian Historical Society, Philadelphia, Pa.

28. American Tract Society, *Twenty-First Annual Report* (1846), 21; American Tract Society, *Twenty-Sixth Annual Report* (1851), 46–47, 64–65. Each annual report after 1841 reviewed the colportage effort for the year. For general accounts of ATS colportage, see the special report "Ten Years of Colportage in America," in American Tract Society, *Twenty-Sixth Annual Report* (1851), 45–72; *The American Colporteur System* (New York: American Tract Society, [1843]), reprinted in facsimile in *American Tract Society Documents;* [R. S. Cook], *Home Evangelization: View of the Wants and Prospects of Our Country, Based on the Facts and Relations of Colportage* (New York: American Tract Society, [1849]); R. S. Cook, "The Colporteur System," in *Proceedings of a Public Deliberative Meeting of the Board and Friends of the American Tract Society, Held in Broadway Tabernacle, New-York, October 25, 26, and 27, 1842* (New York: American Tract Society, 1843); [Jonathan Cross], *Five Years in the Alleghanies* (New York: American Tract Society, 1863); and [John McMillan Stevenson] *Toils and Triumphs of Union Missionary Colportage for Twenty-Five Years, by One of the Secretaries of the American Tract Society* (New York: American Tract Society, [1866]).

29. [Cook], *Home Evangelization,* 19; *American Messenger,* September 1851, 34. For examples of laments from the South and West, see American Tract Society, *Twenty-Third Annual Report* (1848), 70, 73.

30. American Tract Society, *Thirty-First Annual Report* (1856), 42; American Tract Society, *Twenty-Seventh Annual Report* (1852), 53. By 1854 the American Tract Society had more than 600 colporteurs in the field; the Presbyterian Board of Publication had about 150; the Tract Society of the Methodist Episcopal Church about 100; the American Baptist Publication Society about 60. These figures appear routinely in the societies' annual reports.

31. American Tract Society, *Fifteenth Annual Report* (1840), 24–25; American Tract Society, *Eighteenth Annual Report* (1843), 28, 46; *American Messenger,* June 1851, 22.

32. [Cook], *Home Evangelization,* 109; American Tract Society, *Eighteenth Annual Report* (1843), 46.

33. *American Colporteur System,* 22; *Report of the Special Committee,* 5–7. This 1857 report includes a letter from three prominent New York publishers (John Harper, Robert Carter, and John Wiley), who examined the printing operations of the society and concluded that "great care and economy are exercised in each department."

34. *Report of the Special Committee,* 13; American Tract Society, *First Annual Report* (1826), 17; American Tract Society, *Third Annual Report* (1828), 15; [Cook], *Home Evangelization,* 61.

35. *American Messenger,* February 1846, 7; January 1847, 1; January 1850, 2; American Tract Society, *Third Annual Report* (1828), 14–15; *Report of the Special Committee,* 13.

36. Every annual report included cost data of this sort. See, for example, American Tract Society, *Third Annual Report* (1828), 15–16; American Tract Society, *Fifth Annual Report* (1830), 64. For a twenty-five-year statistical summary, see American Tract Society, *Twenty-Fifth Annual Report* (1850), 30–32.

37. Chandler, *Visible Hand*, 39, 71, 109–11; H. Thomas Johnson and Robert S. Kaplan, *Relevance Lost: The Rise and Fall of Management Accounting* (Boston: Harvard Business School Press, 1987), 21–24. The society's system for figuring costs is explained in *Report of the Special Committee*, 17–18.

38. Chandler, *Visible Hand*, 3.

39. American Tract Society, *Twenty-Ninth Annual Report* (1854), 64–65; American Tract Society, *Thirty-First Annual Report* (1856), 42–43. Salaries are reported in *Report of the Special Committee*, 23–24.

40. Patricia Cline Cohen, *A Calculating People: The Spread of Numeracy in Early America* (Chicago, Ill.: University of Chicago Press, 1982), 205–7. See also Theodore M. Porter, *Trust in Numbers: The Pursuit of Objectivity in Science and Public Life* (Princeton, N.J.: Princeton University Press, 1995).

41. All the annual reports have detailed statistical tables. For example, see the American Tract Society, *Twenty-Fifth Annual Report* (1850), 30–31, 42–52, 68–71 (quotation, p. 69). See also *American Messenger*, January 1850, 2.

42. American Tract Society, *Twentieth Annual Report* (1845), 73; American Tract Society, *Twenty-Second Annual Report* (1847), 39; American Tract Society, *Twenty-Fourth Annual Report* (1849), 52–55; *American Messenger*, January 1846, 3; October 1848, 38; December 1847, 47; September 1851, 34. For examples of the moral census approach and the use of statistics in the reports of individual colporteurs, see *Colporteur Reports to the American Tract Society, 1841–1846* (Newark, N.J.: Historical Records Survey Project, Work Projects Administration, 1940). This is a mimeographed report, part of the larger project Transcriptions of Early Church Records of New Jersey. The manuscript reports from which this transcription was made are located in the Presbyterian Historical Society, Philadelphia, Pa.

43. American Tract Society, *Twentieth Annual Report* (1845), 73; [Cook], *Home Evangelization*, 92.

44. *Instructions of the Executive Committee of the American Tract Society, to Colporteurs and Agents, with Statements of the History, Character, and Object of the Society* (New York: American Tract Society, 1868), 19–20, 26–28, reprinted in facsimile in *American Tract Society Documents*. Editions of this book were published from the early 1840s into the late nineteenth century. I looked at two editions from the 1850s at the American Antiquarian Society, Worcester, Mass., and they are nearly identical to the one cited here. See also [Cook], *Home Evangelization*, 76–77.

45. *Instructions of the Executive Committee*, 20–21, 28–45 (quotation, p. 33); *American Colporteur System*, 21–23; [Cook], *Home Evangelization*, 79.

46. [Cook], *Home Evangelization*, 82; American Tract Society, *Twenty-First Annual Report* (1846), 22–23; American Tract Society, *Twenty-Sixth Annual Report* (1851), 59–63; *American Messenger*, October 1848, 38; February 1853, 6.

47. American Tract Society, *Twenty-Sixth Annual Report* (1851), 60; *Meetings of Colporteurs and Agents of the American Tract Society at Syracuse, Detroit, Cincinnati, Pittsburgh, and New-York* (New York: American Tract Society, 1845), 9, 19–20.

48. American Tract Society, *Twenty-Sixth Annual Report* (1851), 63.

49. See, for example, "Instructions for Christian Efforts, in Connection with the Monthly Tract Distribution," "Hints for Christian Effort, Connected with Tract Distri-

bution," "Directions to Tract Visitors," and "Personal Christian Effort; or, Way-Marks for Tract Visitors," all reprinted in American Tract Society, *Ninth Annual Report* (1834), 126–28; American Tract Society, *Twelfth Annual Report* (1837), 183–84; and American Tract Society, *Thirteenth Annual Report* (1838), 33–39.

50. *Instructions of the Executive Committee*, 29; [Cook], *Home Evangelization*, 83. Some of the other societies engaged in colportage also published instruction booklets. See, for example, *Instructions for Colporteurs of the Presbyterian Board of Publication;* and *Principles and Purposes of the American Baptist Publication Society* (Philadelphia, Pa.: American Baptist Publication Society, n.d.).

51. *Colporteur Reports to the American Tract Society*, 14–15, 38, 42, 92, 113. These young men were students at the Princeton Theological Seminary and were devoting their summers to colportage for the American Tract Society. See n. 42 above. The *American Messenger* and the annual reports have hundreds of excerpts from colporteur reports, but the manuscript reports themselves have not been saved by the society. The archive at the American Tract Society headquarters in Garland, Texas, has only published materials from this era. The papers of the Presbyterian Board of Publication in the Presbyterian Historical Society, Philadelphia, have some manuscript letters, reports, and forms from colporteurs.

52. *Instructions of the Executive Committee*, 90.

53. Ibid., 47–61; *Meetings of Colporteurs and Agents*, 20.

54. *Instructions of the Executive Committee*, 46–56 (quotation, pp. 46–47). Samples of forms are reprinted on 70–75.

55. Ibid., 40–41; American Tract Society, *Twenty-Fifth Annual Report* (1850), 51, 69.

56. *Colporteur Reports to the American Tract Society*, 18; American Tract Society, *Twenty-Seventh Annual Report* (1852), 53; [Cook], *Home Evangelization*, 86–87.

57. American Tract Society, *Twenty-Fifth Annual Report* (1850), 51.

58. American Tract Society, *Twenty-Sixth Annual Report* (1851), 49; *American Messenger*, January 1848, 2; October 1850, 38; January 1853, 2.

59. *American Messenger*, January 1843, 1; December 1846, 45; October 1848, 38; May 1849, 18. See also *Instructions of the Executive Committee*, 29. The link between American colportage and the larger and grander history of religious publishing, going back to Luther, was a steady theme in American Tract Society publications.

60. American Tract Society, *Twenty-First Annual Report* (1846), 22; American Tract Society, *Twenty-Sixth Annual Report* (1851), 67.

61. *Instructions of the Executive Committee*, 38–41. See also [Cook], *Home Evangelization*, 86–87. On the use of Baxter's *Call* by colporteurs, see *Colporteur Reports to the American Tract Society*. See also chapters 6 and 7 of this book.

62. See essays in Hackenberg, *Getting the Books Out;* and Walter Sutton, *The Western Book Trade: Cincinnati as a Nineteenth-Century Publishing and Book-Trade Center* (Columbus: Ohio State University Press, 1961). See also Ronald J. Zboray, *A Fictive People: Antebellum Economic Development and the American Reading Public* (New York: Oxford University Press, 1993), chap. 3; and Ronald J. Zboray, "Book Distribution and American Culture: A 150-Year Perspective," *Book Research Quarterly* 3 (Fall 1987): 37–59.

63. The manuscript papers of booksellers at the American Antiquarian Society,

Worcester, Mass., contain a good deal of correspondence between publishers and agents. See, for example, the Edward Livermore Letterbooks, several letters from April 1851; and the James Munroe and Co. Correspondence, several letters from the mid–1840s. See also Zboray, "Book Distribution and American Culture," 53–57. Desultory correspondence with agents was typical of premodern manufacturing firms, too. See Yates, *Control through Communication*, 3.

64. Michael Winship, *American Literary Publishing in the Mid–Nineteenth Century: The Business of Ticknor and Fields* (Cambridge: Cambridge University Press, 1995), chap. 6. See also James Gilreath, "American Book Distribution," in *Needs and Opportunities in the History of the Book: America, 1639–1876*, ed. David D. Hall and John B. Hench (Worcester, Mass.: American Antiquarian Society, 1987).

65. American Tract Society, *Twenty-Ninth Annual Report* (1854), 59; American Tract Society, *Eleventh Annual Report* (1836), 41; American Tract Society, *Thirteenth Annual Report* (1838), 18; *Report of the Special Committee*, 16.

66. [Herman Hooker], *An Appeal to the Christian Public, on the Evil and Impolicy of the Church Engaging in Merchandise; Setting Forth the Wrong Done to Booksellers, and the Extravagance, Inutility, and Evil-Working, of Charity Publication Societies* (Philadelphia, Pa.: King and Baird, 1849), 3–4.

67. Chandler, *Visible Hand*, 8; Yates, *Control through Communication*, chaps. 1–2. See also Johnson and Kaplan, *Relevance Lost*, chaps. 2–3.

68. Nathan O. Hatch, *The Democratization of American Christianity* (New Haven, Conn.: Yale University Press, 1989), 11, 142–44, 202–4; Wigger, *Taking Heaven by Storm*, 191–92. See also Mark A. Noll, *America's God: From Jonathan Edwards to Abraham Lincoln* (New York: Oxford University Press, 2002), 195–202; and Nathan O. Hatch and John H. Wigger, introduction to *Methodism and the Shaping of American Culture*, ed. Hatch and Wigger (Nashville, Tenn.: Abingdon, 2001), 40. For examples of the publishing societies' administrative procedures, see John Leyburn, *Presbyterian Board of Publication: Its Present Operations and Plans* (Philadelphia, Pa.: Presbyterian Board of Publication, [1848]); *Instructions for Colporteurs of the Presbyterian Board of Publication;* "General Circular," in American Baptist Publication Society, *Fourth Annual Report* (1843), 16–19, and *Sixth Annual Report* (1845), 38–39; *Instructions to Colporteurs* (New York: Tract Society of the Methodist Episcopal Church, n.d.); and *Documents of the Tract Society of the Methodist Episcopal Church.*

69. *Bible Agent's Manual* (New York: American Bible Society, 1856), 3–8; Wosh, *Spreading the Word*, 10, 175–76.

70. Creighton Lacy, *The Word-Carrying Giant: The Growth of the American Bible Society* (South Pasadena, Calif.: Carey Library, 1977), 96–100; Henry Otis Dwight, *The Centennial History of the American Bible Society* (New York: Macmillan, 1916), 180.

71. American Bible Society, *Forty-Fourth Annual Report* (1860), 21–22.

72. See the annual reports of the American Home Missionary Society (first report, 1827). The papers of the AHMS are located in the Amistad Research Center, Tulane University. The standard history of the AHMS is Colin B. Goodykoontz, *Home Missions on the American Frontier: with Particular Reference to the American Home Missionary Society* (Caldwell, Idaho: Caxton, 1939). See also Michael H. Harris, " 'Spiritual Cakes upon the Waters': The Church as a Disseminator of the Printed Word on

the Ohio Valley Frontier to 1850," in Hackenberg, *Getting the Books Out*. On reform society publishing, see David Paul Nord, "Benevolent Books: Printing, Religion, and Reform," in *An Extensive Republic: Print, Culture, and Society in the New Nation*, ed. Robert A. Gross and Mary Kelley, vol. 2 of *A History of the Book in America* (Cambridge: Cambridge University Press, forthcoming).

73. Peter Dobkin Hall makes a similar argument in "Religion and the Organizational Revolution in the United States," in *Sacred Companies: Organizational Aspects of Religion and Religious Aspects of Organizations*, ed. N. J. Demerath III et al. (New York: Oxford University Press, 1998), 101–2.

74. *Address of the Managers of the American Bible Society, to Its Auxiliaries, Members, and Friends, in Regard to a General Supply of the United States with the Sacred Scriptures* (New York: American Bible Society, 1856), 8; American Bible Society, *Forty-Fourth Annual Report* (1860), 34–35.

CHAPTER 6

1. *American Messenger*, September 1851, 34. The *American Messenger*, the popular monthly newspaper published by the American Tract Society, routinely published accounts of colporteur conventions.

2. *American Messenger*, May 1849, 18. On the spectacular growth of popular publishing in this era, see Isabelle Lehuu, *Carnival on the Page: Popular Print Media in Antebellum America* (Chapel Hill: University of North Carolina Press, 2000).

3. *American Messenger*, November 1853, 43; January 1852, 4; May 1851, 18. See also Michael H. Harris, " 'Spiritual Cakes upon the Waters': The Church as a Disseminator of the Printed Word on the Ohio Valley Frontier to 1850," in *Getting the Books Out: Papers of the Chicago Conference on the Book in Nineteenth-Century America*, ed. Michael Hackenberg (Washington, D.C.: Library of Congress, 1987), 98–99.

4. *American Messenger*, January 1843, 2; February 1847, 6. See also the appendix to this book. In the United States, this was an era of high alcohol consumption and a strong evangelical temperance movement. Many leaders of the ATS were also leaders of the American Temperance Society. See Jack S. Blocker, Jr., *American Temperance Movements: Cycles of Reform* (Boston: Twayne, 1989), chap. 1; and Ian Tyrrell, *Sobering Up: From Temperance to Prohibition in Antebellum America, 1800–1860* (Westport, Conn.: Greenwood, 1979).

5. *Facts Illustrating the Necessity, Method, and Results of Colportage* (New York: American Tract Society, [1846]), 3–4; *American Messenger*, September 1846, 34; January 1847, 2–3.

6. *American Messenger*, February 1843, 6; May 1843, 19; July 1843, 29; January 1844, 1; April 1846, 15; February 1847, 6; [R. S. Cook], *Home Evangelization: View of the Wants and Prospects of Our Country, Based on the Facts and Relations of Colportage* (New York: American Tract Society, [1849]), 41. For general discussions of the opposition to novel reading in America, see Cathy N. Davidson, *Revolution and the Word: The Rise of the Novel in America* (New York: Oxford University Press, 1986), chap. 3; Ronald J. Zboray, *A Fictive People: Antebellum Economic Development and the American Reading Public* (New York: Oxford University Press, 1993), chaps. 6–7, 9; Scott E. Cas-

per, "Antebellum Reading Prescribed and Described," in *Perspectives on American Book History*, ed. Scott E. Casper, Joanne D. Chaison, and Jeffrey D. Groves (Amherst: University of Massachusetts Press, 2002); Candy Gunther Brown, "Salt to the World: A Cultural History of Evangelical Reading, Writing, and Publishing Practices in Mid–Nineteenth-Century America" (Ph.D. diss., Harvard University, 2000), 110–14; and Karl Eric Valois, "To Revolutionize the World: The American Tract Society and the Regeneration of the Republic, 1825–1877" (Ph.D. diss., University of Connecticut, 1994), chap. 6.

7. *American Messenger*, July 1850, 26; October 1851, 37.

8. *American Messenger*, May 1851, 18; October 1851, 37; July 1850, 26.

9. *American Messenger*, February 1843, 7; November 1847, 42; July 1843, 29.

10. Tract Society of the Methodist Episcopal Church, *Third Annual Report* (1856), 12; Tract Society of the Methodist Episcopal Church, *First Annual Report* (1854), 7.

11. American Baptist Publication Society, *Thirty-First Annual Report* (1855), 58. See also Daniel Gurden Stevens, *The First Hundred Years of the American Baptist Publication Society* (Philadelphia, Pa.: American Baptist Publication Society, [1924]).

12. Presbyterian Board of Publication, *Eleventh Annual Report* (1849), 7; Presbyterian Board of Publication, *Twelfth Annual Report* (1850), 38–39; Presbyterian Board of Publication, *Seventeenth Annual Report* (1855), 6; *Home and Foreign Record*, April 1852, 63; June 1850, 183; July 1852, 111; August 1852, 126. See also Willard M. Rice, *History of the Presbyterian Board of Publication and Sabbath School Work* (Philadelphia, Pa.: Presbyterian Board of Publication and Sabbath School Work, [1889]).

13. *American Messenger*, February 1848, 6; November 1847, 42.

14. See, for example, R. S. Cook, "The Power of the Press," in *Proceedings of a Public Deliberative Meeting of the Board and Friends of the American Tract Society, Held in Broadway Tabernacle, New-York, October 25, 26, and 27, 1842* (New York: American Tract Society, 1843), 42–43.

15. *American Messenger*, February 1853, 6; May 1845, 18; American Tract Society, *Twentieth Annual Report* (1845), 91; American Tract Society, *Eighteenth Annual Report* (1843), 25–26. See also Robert Baird, "The Voluntary Principle in America: Its Action and Influence," in *Religion in America; or, An Account of the Origin, Progress, Relation to the State, and Present Condition of the Evangelical Churches in the United States* (New York: Harper and Brothers, 1844), book 4.

16. *American Messenger*, September 1846, 33; July 1849, 26.

17. *American Messenger*, July 1843, 26. The ATS assumed that proper reading could even subdue the "spirit of rebellion" that was manifested in the recent mob attacks on the Mormon settlement at Nauvoo, Illinois, in 1844: "By some means and all means the Gospel must be *carried down to the masses*. . . . Besides its being the only way, it is the cheapest way to suppress a spirit of insubordination. Books are cheaper than cannon-balls; Tracts than bullets; ministers of the Gospel than military officers; Sabbath-school teachers than soldiers; colporteurs than cavalry troops." See *American Messenger*, August 1844, 35.

18. American Tract Society, *Third Annual Report* (1828), 21; American Tract Society, *Tenth Annual Report* (1835), 19.

19. "An Address to Christians Recommending the Distribution of Religious

Tracts," in *Proceedings of the First Ten Years of the American Tract Society, Instituted at Boston, 1814* (Andover, Mass.: Flagg and Gould, 1824). This address was first printed in the United States in 1802 by Samuel Etheridge of Charlestown, Mass.

20. Legh Richmond, *The Dairyman's Daughter: Extracted from an Authentic and Interesting Narrative Communicated by a Clergyman of the Church of England*, 2d ed. (Andover, Mass.: Flagg and Gould, 1815), 1, 6, 13, 19. This is a New England Tract Society version. *The Dairyman's Daughter* went through scores of editions put out by virtually every English and American tract society, and it remains in print today. On the paternalism and pastoralism of Hannah More's Cheap Repository tracts, see Anne Stott, *Hannah More: The First Victorian* (Oxford: Oxford University Press, 2003), 180–81; and Charles Howard Ford, *Hannah More: A Critical Biography* (New York: Lang, 1996), chap. 4.

21. American Tract Society, *Twenty-Sixth Annual Report* (1851), 98–100; *American Messenger*, July 1846, 26. On colportage projects sponsored by the various societies, see chapter 5 of this book.

22. On religious newspapers, see Nathan O. Hatch, *The Democratization of American Christianity* (New Haven, Conn.: Yale University Press, 1989), chap. 5; Brown, "Salt to the World," chap. 3; and Gaylord P. Albaugh, *History and Annotated Bibliography of American Religious Periodicals and Newspapers Established from 1730 through 1830* (Worcester, Mass.: American Antiquarian Society, 1994). The Methodists' *Christian Advocate* (begun in New York in 1826 and later published in several other locations as well) was a widely circulated paper put out by a denominational publishing house. The *American Messenger* was begun in 1843 and was published simultaneously in New York, Boston, Philadelphia, and Baltimore, and later in Cincinnati and New Orleans as well. It achieved a circulation of 200,000 by the early 1850s. The ATS was eager to be part of the rise of the mass newspaper in the United States. For example, see *American Messenger*, October 1847, 36; March 1852, 10; July 1849, 26. In 1852, the ATS launched an illustrated newspaper for children called the *Child's Paper*. The first issue's press run of 70,000 sold out immediately. See *Child's Paper*, January 1852, 1; April 1852, 16. The Presbyterians were similarly fascinated by the power of newspapers, and in 1850 were debating the creation of a cheap, popular national weekly to be operated by the Board of Publication. See "Cheap Presbyterian Newspaper," *Princeton Review* 22 (January 1850): 122–43.

23. *American Messenger*, October 1852, 38. Hymnals and song books were another very popular genre of religious publication in antebellum America, though the ATS was less involved with hymnal publication than were the denominational publishers. See Brown, "Salt to the World," 209–10; and Hatch, *Democratization*, 146–61.

24. *American Messenger*, October 1850, 38; December 1854, 46.

25. *Proceedings of a Public Deliberative Meeting*, 63; *American Messenger*, November 1843, 45; January 1851, 2; July 1851, 26; November 1851, 41.

26. American Tract Society, *Eighth Annual Report* (1833), 5; *American Messenger*, March 1843, 11. Several literary historians have written about the similarity between ATS tracts and sentimental fiction. See, for example, Jane Tompkins, *Sensational Designs: The Cultural Work of American Fiction, 1790–1860* (New York: Oxford University Press, 1985), chap. 6; Brown, "Salt to the World," chap. 2; Cathleen McDonnell

Schultz, "Holy Lives and Happy Deaths: Popular Religious Reading in the Early Republic" (Ph.D. diss., New York University, 1996), chap. 2.

27. *American Messenger*, February 1843, 1. The chair still resides in the offices of the American Tract Society in Garland, Texas, though they now ask Doubting Thomases to look but not sit.

28. *Principles and Plans of the Board of Publication of the Presbyterian Church in the United States of America* (Philadelphia, Pa.: Presbyterian Board of Publication, [1854]), 19–20; *American Messenger*, July 1844, 30; [Cook], *Home Evangelization*, 10–11. As sinners, children also would naturally resist religious instruction, even in popular formats. See American Sunday School Union, *Eleventh Annual Report* (1835), 17–18.

29. *American Messenger*, January 1845, 2. From the beginning of the tract movement, there were always those who feared that popularization would go too far. The founders of the Religious Tract Society (London, 1799) believed that in her Cheap Repository tracts, Hannah More had "sugared her pill too thoroughly," in the words of literary historian Anne Stott. See Stott, *Hannah More*, 209.

30. *American Messenger*, January 1843, 1. See also the appendix to this volume; and Brown, "Salt to the World," 115–21.

31. *American Messenger*, February 1848, 6; *Home and Foreign Record*, April 1852, 63.

32. T. Charlton Henry, *Letters to an Anxious Inquirer* (Philadelphia, Pa.: Presbyterian Board of Publication, 1840), 203–4, 207–9.

33. Ibid., 212–14. See also *American Messenger*, September 1853, 34.

34. John Angell James, *The Anxious Inquirer after Salvation, Directed and Encouraged* (Philadelphia, Pa.: Presbyterian Board of Publication, n.d.), 5–11. This book was also published by the ATS.

35. *American Messenger*, February 1848, 6; *Home and Foreign Record*, August 1851, 127.

36. *Proposed Circulation of the Standard Evangelical Volumes of the American Tract Society to the Southern Atlantic States* (New York: American Tract Society, 1834); "The Volume Enterprise," *American Tract Magazine* 10 (August 1835): 133–46; Lemuel C. Barnes, Mary C. Barnes, and Edward M. Stephenson, *Pioneers of Light: The First Century of the American Baptist Publication Society* (Philadelphia, Pa.: American Baptist Publication Society, [1924]), 36–39; "General Circular," in American Baptist Publication Society, *Fourth Annual Report* (1843), 16; *Documents of the Tract Society of the Methodist Episcopal Church*, ed. Abel Stevens (New York: Carlton and Phillips, 1853), 7–8, 13.

37. *Proposed Circulation of the Standard Evangelical Volumes*, 5; Archibald Alexander, *Practical Truths: Consisting of His Various Writings for the American Tract Society, and Correspondence from the Society's Formation in 1825, to His Death in 1851* (New York: American Tract Society, n.d.), 359–64.

38. The ATS catalog appeared regularly in annual reports and the *American Messenger*. See, for example, *American Messenger*, October 1844.

39. *American Messenger*, February 1843, 4; August 1850, 30; [Jonathan Cross], *Five Years in the Alleghanies* (New York: American Tract Society, 1863), 67. See also William E. Schenck, *The Board of Publication and Its Colportage Work: A Few Earnest*

Words to Ministers, Sessions, and Churches (Philadelphia, Pa.: Presbyterian Board of Publication, n.d.), 4; S. J. P. Anderson, *The Power of Christian Literature: A Sermon on Behalf of the Assembly's Board of Publication* (Philadelphia, Pa.: Presbyterian Board of Publication, 1858), 12. The ATS liked to quote from John Milton's famous tribute to books: "A good book is the precious life-blood of a master spirit, embalmed and treasured up on purpose to a life beyond life." See, for example, *American Messenger*, August 1850, 30.

40. *American Messenger*, May 1843, 17; April 1843, 13, 15; May 1845, 23.

41. *American Messenger*, August 1850, 30.

42. *American Messenger*, October 1843, 42. The ATS continued to reduce prices in the 1840s and 1850s, and colporteurs often gave away these books for free. The Presbyterian Board of Publication boasted in 1848 that it had Baxter's *Call* for 8 cents. See John Leyburn, *The Presbyterian Board of Publication: Its Present Operations and Plans* (Philadelphia, Pa.: Presbyterian Board of Publication, [1848]), 3. Baptist colporteurs also carried Baxter, Alleine, and the others. See American Baptist Publication Society, *Twenty-Ninth Annual Report* (1853), 30. The Methodists also published Baxter, Doddridge, and the rest. See W. F. Whitlock, *The Story of the Book Concerns* (New York: Eaton and Mains, 1903), 31; and James Richard Joy, *The Making of the Book Concern, 1789–1916* (New York: Methodist Book Concern, 1916), i–ii. Even the real-life dairyman's daughter, Elizabeth Wallbridge, read Bunyan, Baxter, and Doddridge.

43. Philip Doddridge, *Rise and Progress of Religion in the Soul* (New York: American Tract Society, n.d.), 175–76; Richard Baxter, *A Call to the Unconverted* (New York: American Tract Society, n.d.), 65, 74, 95. See also Geoffrey F. Nuttall, *Richard Baxter and Philip Doddridge: A Study in Tradition* (Oxford: Oxford University Press, 1951), 3–4, 13; N. H. Keeble, *Richard Baxter: Puritan Man of Letters* (Oxford: Clarendon, 1982), 71–72; and Roger Thomas, "Philip Doddridge and Liberalism in Religion," in *Philip Doddridge, 1702–51: His Contribution to English Religion*, ed. Geoffrey F. Nuttall (London: Independent Press, 1951).

44. *American Messenger*, May 1853, 18; Anderson, *Power of Christian Literature*, 20–21; *Christian Almanac, 1836* (New York: American Tract Society, [1835]), 39. Baxter gave reading advice in the *Call*. He urged people to reread important passages and to mark the pages. See Baxter, *Call to the Unconverted*, 45. See also Geoffrey F. Nuttall, *Richard Baxter* (London: Nelson and Sons, 1965), chap. 6.

45. David D. Hall, "The Uses of Literacy in New England, 1600–1850," in *Cultures of Print: Essays in the History of the Book* (Amherst: University of Massachusetts Press, 1996). See also Lehuu, *Carnival on the Page*, 18–20; and William J. Gilmore, *Reading Becomes a Necessity of Life: Material and Cultural Life in Rural New England, 1780–1835* (Knoxville: University of Tennessee Press, 1989), 354–59.

46. [Cook], *Home Evangelization*, 66–67.

CHAPTER 7

1. *Colporteur Reports to the American Tract Society, 1841–1846* (Newark, N.J.: Historical Records Survey Project, Work Projects Administration, 1940). This 118–

page mimeographed transcript, a part of the larger project Transcriptions of Early Church Records of New Jersey, includes about two dozen reports. See n. 11 below.

2. *A Brief Account of the Present State of the Society for Propagating the Gospel among the Indians and Others in North-America,—with a Sketch of the Manner in Which They Mean to Pursue the Objects of Their Institution* ([Boston: Adams, 1791]), 2. See also *An Account of the Massachusetts Society for Promoting Christian Knowledge* (Cambridge, Mass.: Hilliard, 1806), 21–29.

3. American Tract Society, *Eleventh Annual Report* (1836), 99–100.

4. Michael H. Harris, " 'Spiritual Cakes upon the Waters': The Church as a Disseminator of the Printed Word on the Ohio Valley Frontier to 1850," in *Getting the Books Out: Papers of the Chicago Conference on the Book in Nineteenth-Century America*, ed. Michael Hackenberg (Washington, D.C.: Library of Congress, 1987), 99–101. In the early twentieth century, the bullet or hypodermic needle theory of media effects was a popular notion of how propaganda worked on a mass audience, but no serious communication researcher ever promoted such a simple model. It was always a caricature of other people's views. See Wilbur Schramm, *The Beginnings of Communication Study in America: A Personal Memoir* (Thousand Oaks, Calif.: Sage, 1997), 111–12; and James W. Carey, "The Chicago School and Mass Communication Research," in *American Communication Research: The Remembered History*, ed. Everette E. Dennis and Ellen Wartella (Mahwah, N.J.: Erlbaum, 1996), 11.

5. Norman N. Holland, *The Critical I* (New York: Columbia University Press, 1992), 38; David Morley, "Active Audience Theory: Pendulums and Pitfalls," *Journal of Communication* 43 (Autumn 1993): 13–19. See also Jane Tompkins, ed., *Reader-Response Criticism: From Formalism to Post-Structuralism* (Baltimore, Md.: Johns Hopkins University Press, 1980); and Frank A. Biocca, "Opposing Conceptions of the Audience: The Active and Passive Hemispheres of Mass Communication Theory," in *Communication Yearbook* No. 11, ed. James Anderson (Newbury Park, Calif.: Sage, 1988).

6. Stanley E. Fish, "Interpreting the *Variorum*," in Tompkins, *Reader-Response Criticism*, 182–83; Stanley E. Fish, *Is There a Text in This Class? The Authority of Interpretive Communities* (Cambridge, Mass.: Harvard University Press, 1980), 317–18.

7. Robert Darnton, "First Steps toward a History of Reading," in *The Kiss of Lamourette: Reflections in Cultural History* (New York: Norton, 1990), 155. See also Jonathan Rose, *The Intellectual Life of the British Working Classes* (New Haven, Conn.: Yale University Press, 2001); Roger Chartier, *The Order of Books: Readers, Authors, and Libraries in Europe between the Fourteenth and Eighteenth Centuries* (Stanford, Calif.: Stanford University Press, 1994), chap. 1; and Carl F. Kaestle et al., *Literacy in the United States: Readers and Reading since 1880* (New Haven, Conn.: Yale University Press, 1991), chap. 2.

8. See, for example, the studies collected in Barbara Ryan and Amy M. Thomas, eds., *Reading Acts: U.S. Readers' Interactions with Literature, 1800–1950* (Knoxville: University of Tennessee Press, 2002); James L. Machor, ed., *Readers in History: Nineteenth-Century American Literature and the Contexts of Response* (Baltimore, Md.: Johns Hopkins University Press, 1993); and Cathy N. Davidson, ed., *Reading in America: Literature and Social History* (Baltimore, Md.: Johns Hopkins University Press, 1989). See

also the work of Ronald J. Zboray and Mary Saracino Zboray, including "Reading and Everyday Life in Antebellum Boston: The Diary of Daniel F. and Mary D. Child," *Libraries and Culture* 32 (Summer 1997): 285–323, and " 'Have You Read . . . ?': Real Readers and Their Responses in Antebellum Boston and Its Region," *Nineteenth-Century Literature* 52 (September 1997): 139–70.

9. I have used public documents and institutional records to try to trace the reading of journalism, which is an especially ephemeral genre. See David Paul Nord, *Communities of Journalism: A History of American Newspapers and Their Readers* (Urbana: University of Illinois Press, 2001), chaps. 8–11. For other examples, see Christine Pawley, *Reading on the Middle Border: The Culture of Print in Late Nineteenth-Century Osage, Iowa* (Amherst: University of Massachusetts Press, 2001); William J. Gilmore, *Reading Becomes a Necessity of Life: Material and Cultural Life in Rural New England* (Knoxville: University of Tennessee Press, 1989); and Ronald J. Zboray, *A Fictive People: Antebellum Economic Development and the American Reading Public* (New York: Oxford University Press, 1993).

10. American Tract Society, *Twenty-Sixth Annual Report* (1851), 104. The colportage projects operated by the ATS and other publishing societies are described in chapter 5 of this book.

11. The archive at the present American Tract Society headquarters in Garland, Texas, has no manuscript colporteur reports from this era. Perhaps the best collection of ATS manuscript reports is the set of letters filed by students from Princeton Theological Seminary who worked as ATS colporteurs for several summers in the 1840s. Some of these survive in the manuscript collections of the Presbyterian Historical Society, Philadelphia. They were published in mimeograph form as *Colporteur Reports to the American Tract Society, 1841–1846*. See n. 1 above. The Presbyterian Historical Society also has letters from colporteurs who worked for the Presbyterian Board of Publication, though these deal less with readers than ATS reports do. A few other manuscript colporteur reports and letters are scattered in libraries around the country, including a long letter from Micah S. Croswell to his ATS supervisor, January 1855, in Special Collections, Duke University, Durham, N.C. This report is used by Amy M. Thomas in "Reading the Silences: Documenting the History of American Tract Society Readers in the Antebellum South," in Ryan and Thomas, *Reading Acts*.

12. Solomon B. Smith to Joseph P. Engles, Nov. 26, 1852, in Presbyterian Church of the USA, Board of Publication, Correspondence, 1841–1860, Presbyterian Historical Society, Philadelphia, Pa.

13. American Tract Society, *Twentieth Annual Report* (1845), 173; *Instructions of the Executive Committee of the American Tract Society, to Colporteurs and Agents, with Statements of the History, Character, and Object of the Society* (New York: American Tract Society, 1868), 52–53. Editions of this book were published from the early 1840s into the late nineteenth century. See also Thomas, "Reading the Silences," 110–11.

14. Thomas, "Reading the Silences," 105–36.

15. *The American Colporteur System* (New York: American Tract Society, [1843]), 9. On the rise of colportage, see chapter 5 in this book.

16. These themes appear routinely. See, for example, [R. S. Cook], *Home Evangelization: View of the Wants and Prospects of Our Country, Based on the Facts and Rela-*

tions of Colportage (New York: American Tract Society, [1849]), 71; *American Colporteur System*, 11; American Tract Society, *Twentieth Annual Report* (1845), 73; American Tract Society, *Twenty-Sixth Annual Report* (1851), 46; *American Messenger*, November 1843, 45; February 1848, 6; March 1851, 10–11; February 1853, 7; Presbyterian Board of Publication, *Twelfth Annual Report* (1850), 18–19; American Baptist Publication Society, *Thirty-Second Annual Report* (1856), 22; Tract Society of the Methodist Episcopal Church, *Fifth Annual Report* (1858), 39.

17. American Tract Society, *Thirty-Sixth Annual Report* (1861), 47; American Tract Society, *Twenty-Sixth Annual Report* (1851), 64–65, 92.

18. American Tract Society, *Twentieth Annual Report* (1845), 10; *American Messenger*, October 1848, 38; *Instructions of the Executive Committee*, 50, 70.

19. *American Messenger*, February 1848, 6; March 1848, 10; February 1851, 7; January 1851, 2; November 1852, 43; October 1853, 38; American Tract Society, *Thirty-First Annual Report* (1856), 43. See also American Tract Society, *Nineteenth Annual Report* (1844), 49; Presbyterian Board of Publication, *Thirteenth Annual Report* (1851), 33; American Baptist Publication Society, *Thirty-Second Annual Report* (1856), 38–39.

20. *American Messenger*, November 1843, 45–46; April 1851, 14; June 1851, 23; *Colporteur Reports to the American Tract Society*, 63–64.

21. *American Messenger*, November 1843, 46; July 1844, 31; April 1851, 15; *Colporteur Reports to the American Tract Society*, 83–84.

22. *Colporteur Reports to the American Tract Society*, 5; [Jonathan Cross], *Five Years in the Alleghanies* (New York: American Tract Society, 1863), 94; American Baptist Publication Society, *Thirtieth Annual Report* (1854), 38.

23. *American Messenger*, November 1850, 41; *Colporteur Reports to the American Tract Society*, 39, 45–46, 83.

24. *American Messenger*, March 1850, 10; August 1854, 31.

25. American Tract Society, *Nineteenth Annual Report* (1844), 61; American Tract Society, *Twentieth Annual Report* (1845), 77; American Tract Society, *Twenty-Third Annual Report* (1848), 87; *American Messenger*, September 1844, 37; [Cross], *Five Years in the Alleghanies*, 68.

26. *American Messenger*, October 1843, 43; November 1853, 43; July 1843, 31.

27. *American Messenger*, May 1843, 19; September 1846, 35; December 1851, 47; December 1854, 46; *Facts Illustrating the Necessity, Method, and Results of Colportage* (New York: American Tract Society, [1846]), 14; American Tract Society, *Twenty-Sixth Annual Report* (1851), 100; *Home and Foreign Record*, April 1850, 100.

28. American Tract Society, *Nineteenth Annual Report* (1844), 28; *American Messenger*, December 1850, 47; January 1851, 3; March 1853, 10; [Cross], *Five Years in the Alleghanies*, 104–5, 186.

29. [Cross], *Five Years in the Alleghanies*, 202–3.

30. Ibid., 44–45.

31. American Tract Society, *Twenty-Sixth Annual Report* (1851), 99; *Facts Illustrating the Necessity, Method, and Results of Colportage*, 8; American Baptist Publication Society, *Thirtieth Annual Report* (1854), 37–38; American Baptist Publication Society, *Thirty-First Annual Report* (1855), 43; Presbyterian Board of Publication, *Twelfth Annual*

Report (1850), 29; *American Messenger*, November 1852, 42; [Cross], *Five Years in the Alleghanies*, 141.

32. American Tract Society, *Twenty-Sixth Annual Report* (1851), 100; American Tract Society, *Twenty-First Annual Report* (1846), 91; *American Messenger*, November 1846, 42; May 1853, 18; *Colporteur Reports to the American Tract Society*, 19, 39, 46; American Baptist Publication Society, *Thirty-Second Annual Report* (1856), 39; *Home and Foreign Record*, July 1854, 220; [Cross], *Five Years in the Alleghanies*, 74, 108. On reading in an age of counterfeiting, forgery, and fraud, see David M. Henkin, *City Reading: Written Words and Public Spaces in Antebellum New York* (New York: Columbia University Press, 1998), chap. 6.

33. American Tract Society, *Twenty-First Annual Report* (1846), 91; *Colporteur Reports to the American Tract Society*, 40, 78–80; *American Messenger*, July 1850, 26; [Cross], *Five Years in the Alleghanies*, 73–74.

34. Presbyterian Board of Publication, *Thirteenth Annual Report* (1851), 30; *Colporteur Reports to the American Tract Society*, 10.

35. [Cross], *Five Years in the Alleghanies*, 203; William E. Schenck, *The Board of Publication and Its Colportage Work: A Few Earnest Words to Ministers, Sessions, and Churches* (Philadelphia, Pa.: Presbyterian Board of Publication, n.d.), 3; American Tract Society, *Twentieth Annual Report* (1845), 93; *American Messenger*, February 1850, 7.

36. [Cross], *Five Years in the Alleghanies*, 69; [Cook], *Home Evangelization*, 110–11.

37. American Baptist Publication Society, *Thirty-First Annual Report* (1855), 47; American Baptist Publication Society, *Thirty-Second Annual Report* (1856), 39; *Home and Foreign Record*, December 1852, 191; Presbyterian Board of Publication, *Thirteenth Annual Report* (1851), 30. The manuscript letters in the Presbyterian Board of Publication, Correspondence, Presbyterian Historical Society, Philadelphia, frequently carry laments from colporteurs about hard times for selling books and, therefore, for paying their bills.

38. *American Messenger*, April 1844, 14; August 1851, 30; October 1846, 35; American Tract Society, *Twentieth Annual Report* (1845), 93; Presbyterian Board of Publication, *Fifteenth Annual Report* (1853), 21; Presbyterian Board of Publication, *Twelfth Annual Report* (1850), 25; [Cross], *Five Years in the Alleghanies*, 29–30.

39. *American Messenger*, June 1843, 26; May 1844, 19; American Tract Society, *Twenty-First Annual Report* (1846), 89; [Cross], *Five Years in the Alleghanies*, 47–48, 118.

40. [John McMillan Stevenson] *Toils and Triumphs of Union Missionary Colportage for Twenty-Five Years, by One of the Secretaries of the American Tract Society* (New York: American Tract Society, [1866]), 129; *Facts Illustrating the Necessity, Method, and Results of Colportage*, 16.

41. *Colporteur Reports to the American Tract Society*, 64; [Cross], *Five Years in the Alleghanies*, 54–55.

42. American Tract Society, *Twentieth Annual Report* (1845), 93; *American Messenger*, March 1843, 11; June 1843, 25; June 1844, 26; May 1845, 22; March 1853, 11; July 1854, 26; *Facts Illustrating the Necessity, Method, and Results of Colportage*, 14–15; [Cross], *Five Years in the Alleghanies*, 167; American Baptist Publication Society, *Thirty-Fifth Annual Report* (1859), 39.

43. American Tract Society, *Twenty-Sixth Annual Report* (1851), 102; *American Messenger*, June 1843, 26; July 1850, 26; April 1851, 15.

44. American Tract Society, *Nineteenth Annual Report* (1844), 62; American Tract Society, *Twenty-Sixth Annual Report* (1851), 102; *American Messenger*, April 1851, 14; July 1854, 27; American Baptist Publication Society, *Thirty-Second Annual Report* (1856), 38.

45. *American Messenger*, June 1843, 26; October 1843, 43; April 1844, 15; May 1845, 21; April 1850, 14; September 1851, 35; November 1851, 42–43; April 1853, 15; American Tract Society, *Twentieth Annual Report* (1845), 93.

46. *American Messenger*, June 1843, 46; [Cross], *Five Years in the Alleghanies*, 168.

47. American Tract Society, *Twenty-Third Annual Report* (1848), 78; *American Messenger*, December 1853, 46; September 1853, 35; [Cross], *Five Years in the Alleghanies*, 72–73. The *Tract Primer* was a little schoolbook published by the American Tract Society precisely for this purpose.

48. American Tract Society, *Twenty-First Annual Report* (1846), 90; *American Messenger*, May 1843, 19; December 1844, 49; February 1851, 7; September 1851, 35; May 1854, 18; American Baptist Publication Society, *Thirty-Sixth Annual Report* (1860), 30.

49. *Colporteur Reports to the American Tract Society*, 57, 67, 83.

50. Ibid., 67.

51. Stephen Greenblatt, *Renaissance Self-Fashioning: From More to Shakespeare* (Chicago, Ill.: University of Chicago Press, 1980), 98.

EPILOGUE

1. American Tract Society, *Twenty-Sixth Annual Report* (1851o), 74, 92; Anne M. Boylan, *Sunday School: The Formation of an American Institution, 1790–1880* (New Haven, Conn.: Yale University Press, 1988), 84–85; Peter J. Wosh, *Spreading the Word: The Bible Business in Nineteenth-Century America* (Ithaca, N.Y.: Cornell University Press, 1994), 9, 18–19; *Address of the Managers of the American Bible Society, to Its Auxiliaries, Members, and Friends, in Regard to a General Supply of the United States with the Sacred Scriptures* (New York: American Bible Society, 1856), 10. From its founding in 1816 to 1860, the ABS published more than 14 million Bibles and New Testaments. From its founding in 1825 to 1860, the ATS published 211 million tracts and 16 million books, for a total of 6 billion pages. See American Bible Society, *Forty-Fourth Annual Report* (1860), 25–26; and American Tract Society, *Thirty-Fifth Annual Report* (1860), 25.

2. William Jay, *Letters Respecting the American Board of Commissioners for Foreign Missions and the American Tract Society* (New York: Bates, 1853), 1–2. See also William Jay, *Miscellaneous Writings on Slavery* (Boston: Jewett, 1853).

3. American Bible Society, Minutes of the Board of Managers, June 5, 1834, in American Bible Society Archives, New York; Eric M. North, "Distribution of Scriptures in the United States, 1831–1840," Historical Essay No. 14, part 3 (New York: American Bible Society, 1964), 3; Eric M. North and Dorothy U. Compagno, "Distribution of Scriptures in the United States, 1841–1850," Historical Essay No. 14, part 4 (New York: American Bible Society, 1964), 74–79; *Addresses at the Celebration of the*

Forty-Sixth Anniversary of the American Bible Society (New York: American Bible Society, 1862), 7. See also Wosh, *Spreading the Word*, chap. 8.

4. For the broader story on slavery and Bible interpretation, see Mark A. Noll, *America's God: From Jonathan Edwards to Abraham Lincoln* (New York: Oxford University Press, 2002), chap. 19; John R. McKivigan, *The War against Proslavery Religion: Abolitionism and the Northern Churches, 1830–1865* (Ithaca, N.Y.: Cornell University Press, 1984); Eugene Genovese, *A Consuming Fire: The Fall of the Confederacy in the Mind of the Christian South* (Athens: University of Georgia Press, 1998); and John Patrick Daly, *When Slavery Was Called Freedom: Evangelicalism, Proslavery, and the Causes of the Civil War* (Lexington: University of Kentucky Press, 2002).

5. For overviews of the slavery struggles in the ATS and the ASSU, see Karl Eric Valois, "To Revolutionize the World: The American Tract Society and the Regeneration of the Republic, 1825–1877" (Ph.D. diss., University of Connecticut, 1994), 322–36; and Boylan, *Sunday School*, 80–84.

6. American Tract Society, *Thirty-Second Annual Report* (1857), 226–27.

7. Wm. A. Hallock, O. Eastman, and J. M. Stevenson, *To Our Endeared Fellow-Workers* (New York: American Tract Society, 1857), 10, 16; *To Evangelical Christians, and Especially to the Society's Colporteurs, Superintendents, and General Agents, and to Editors of the Religious Press in the Northern, Middle, Western, and North-Western States* (New York: [American Tract Society], 1857). See also Kenneth M. Stampp, *America in 1857: A Nation on the Brink* (New York: Oxford University Press, 1990).

8. Hallock, Eastman, and Stevenson, *To Our Endeared Fellow-Workers*, 11; *Minute[s]—Adopted on the 18th March, 1858, by the Publishing Committee of the American Tract Society Explanatory of Their Position in Relation to the Report and Resolutions of the Committee of Fifteen* (New York: American Tract Society, [1858]), 17. See also *Responsibilities of the Publishing Committee under the Constitution* (New York: American Tract Society, 1858).

9. [Seth Bliss], *Letters to the Members, Patrons and Friends of the Branch American Tract Society in Boston, Instituted 1814; and to Those of the National Society in New York, Instituted 1825* (Boston: Crocker and Brewster, 1858), 48.

10. *The American Tract Society, Boston* (Boston: Massachusetts Anti-Slavery Society, 1859); *The American Tract Society, New York, to Its Patrons and Friends, Especially in New England* ([Boston]: n.p., 1859).

11. Wosh, *Spreading the Word*, 212–13; Boylan, *Sunday School*, 84.

12. James D. Bratt, "The Reorientation of American Protestantism, 1835–1845," *Church History* 67 (March 1998): 63, 66–67; C. C. Goen, *Broken Churches, Broken Nation: Denominational Schisms and the Coming of the American Civil War* (Macon, Ga.: Mercer University Press, 1985), 66–67. See also Richard J. Carwardine, *Evangelicals and Politics in Antebellum America* (New Haven, Conn.: Yale University Press, 1993); and Mitchell Snay, *Gospel of Disunion: Religion and Separatism in the Antebellum South* (Cambridge: Cambridge University Press, 1993).

13. McKivigan, *War against Proslavery Religion*, 82; Goen, *Broken Churches*, 66–67. See also George M. Marsden, *The Evangelical Mind and the New School Presbyterian Experience: A Case Study of Thought and Theology in Nineteenth-Century America* (New Haven, Conn.: Yale University Press, 1970).

14. Willard M. Rice, *History of the Presbyterian Board of Publication and Sabbath-School Work* (Philadelphia, Pa.: Presbyterian Board of Publication and Sabbath-School Work, [1889]), 7–15, 20–24; *Presbyterian Board of Publication: Its Present Operations and Plans* (Philadelphia, Pa.: Presbyterian Board of Publication, [1848]), 5; Presbyterian Board of Publication, *Twentieth Annual Report* (1858), 19.

15. *A Denominational Press: Shall the Presbyterian Church Use the Press? A Plea for the Presbyterian Publication Committee* (Philadelphia, Pa.: Presbyterian Publication Committee, [1852]), 16–22, 32–33.

16. Goen, *Broken Churches*, 90–98; McKivigan, *War against Proslavery Religion*, 87–90. See also E. Luther Copeland, *The Southern Baptist Convention and the Judgment of History: The Taint of Original Sin*, rev. ed. (Lanham, Md.: University Press of America, 2002).

17. *The Principles and Purposes of the American Baptist Publication Society* (Philadelphia, Pa.: American Baptist Publication Society, [1858]), 7–12; American Baptist Publication Society, *Thirty-Second Annual Report* (1856), 35; *American Baptist Publication Society* (Philadelphia, Pa.: American Baptist Publication Society, [1867]; J. Newton Brown, *History of the American Baptist Publication Society, from Its Origin in 1824, to Its Thirty-Second Anniversary in 1856* (Philadelphia, Pa.: American Baptist Publication Society, [1856]).

18. Richard Carwardine, "Trauma in Methodism: Property, Church Schism, and Sectional Polarization in Antebellum America," in *God and Mammon: Protestants, Money, and the Market, 1790–1860*, ed. Mark A. Noll (New York: Oxford University Press, 2002), 197–205; Goen, *Broken Churches*, 78–90; McKivigan, *War against Proslavery Religion*, 84–87.

19. James Penn Pilkington, *The Methodist Publishing House: A History*, vol. 1: *Beginnings to 1870* (Nashville, Tenn.: Abingdon, 1968), chap. 6; Tract Society of the Methodist Episcopal Church, *First Annual Report* (1854), 6; Abel Stevens, *Life and Times of Nathan Bangs* (New York: Carlton and Porter, 1863), 240. See also Nathan Bangs, *A History of the Methodist Episcopal Church*, vol. 4 (New York: Carlton and Porter, 1857).

20. Doctrinal Tract and Book Society, *Twenty-Fourth Annual Report* (1853), 6–7, 18–19; Congregational Board of Publication, *Twenty-Fifth Annual Report* (1854), 5–6; Congregational Board of Publication, *Twenty-Sixth Annual Report* (1855), 8.

21. *Constitution of the Unitarian Book and Pamphlet Society, Formed August, 1827* (Boston: Dutton and Wentworth, 1829); Henry Ware, Jr., *The Duty of Promoting Christianity by the Circulation of Books: A Discourse, Delivered before the Unitarian Book and Pamphlet Society, at the Annual Meeting, May 31, 1838* (Boston: Unitarian Book and Pamphlet Society, 1838), 9–10.

22. Wosh, *Spreading the Word*, 228, 261; Paul C. Gutjahr, *An American Bible: A History of the Good Book in the United States, 1777–1880* (Stanford, Calif.: Stanford University Press, 1999), 175–78.

23. American Tract Society, *Sixty-Second Annual Report* (1887), 7–8; American Tract Society, *Seventy-Fifth Annual Report* (1900), 11. See also Stephen Elmer Slocum, Jr., "The American Tract Society, 1825–1975: An Evangelical Effort to Influence the Religious and Moral Life of the United States" (Ph.D. diss., New York University, 1975), chaps. 6 and 9.

24. Boylan, *Sunday School*, 98–100.

25. On the changing environment of popular American religion in the late nineteenth and early twentieth centuries, see John M. Giggie and Diane Winston, eds., *Faith in the Market: Religion and the Rise of Urban Commercial Culture* (New Brunswick, N.J.: Rutgers University Press, 2002).

26. Lee K. Iseley, "The AMF Movement," photocopied report (Villanova, Pa.: American Missionary Fellowship, July 2002); American Missionary Fellowship Website, http://americanmissionary.org.

27. *Scripture Resources Catalog, 2002–2003: Tools for Home, Church, School, and Ministry* (New York: American Bible Society, [2002]). See also American Bible Society Website, http://www.americanbible.org.

28. *One Hundred Fifty Years* (Oradell, N.J.: American Tract Society, [1975]); *OnTract*, Fall 2002; "Overview of ATS," American Tract Society Website, http://www. atstracts.org/information/general.php; "Reaching over 3 Million Kids on Halloween," press release, American Tract Society, Sept. 15, 2002. See also Slocum, "American Tract Society," chaps. 6–8. *OnTract* is a magazine/catalog published by the American Tract Society.

29. *Scripture Resources Catalog*, 10–11; Chris Thyberg, "Living Biblically in the Virtual World," *American Bible Society Record* (September–October 2002): 24; "About ForMinistry," ForMinistry Website, http://www.forministry.com/about/forministry.dsp; Bible Technologies Group Website, http://www.bibletechnologies.net. See also Len Wilson, *The Wired Church: Making Media Ministry* (Nashville, Tenn.: Abingdon, 1999); and Andrew Careaga, *eMinistry: Connecting with the Net Generation* (Grand Rapids, Mich.: Kregel, 2001).

30. "Internet Evangelism," American Tract Society Website, http://www.atstracts. org/internet; *OnTract*, Summer 2002, 4; DigiTracts Website, http://www.digitracts. com/about_us.asp.

31. *OnTract*, Fall 2002, 6–7; *Scripture Resources Catalog*, 31, 58.

32. Thomas D. Sullivan, "Read All about It! American Bible Society Reaches the Soul of America with Scripture-Based Literacy Program," *American Bible Society Record* (September–October 2002): 10–11.

33. *Principles and Plans of the Board of Publication of the Presbyterian Church in the United States of America* (Philadelphia, Pa.: Presbyterian Board of Publication, [1854]), 19–20.

34. Paul Gutjahr, "The Perseverance of Print-Bound Saints: Protestant Book Publishing in the United States, 1945–2000," in *A History of the Book in America*, vol. 5: *The Enduring Book*, ed. David Paul Nord, Joan Shelley Rubin, and Michael Schudson (Cambridge: Cambridge University Press, forthcoming).

APPENDIX

1. *American Messenger*, August 1843, 33.

2. *American Messenger*, October 1845, 43.

Index

Breinigsville, PA USA
20 October 2010
247760BV00003B/1/A